The series „Neue Studien zur Politischen Ökonomie"
is edited by

Volume 13

Sebastian Thomasius

Political decision makers and their relevance for public finances

Nomos

Die Deutsche Nationalbibliothek lists this publication in the Deutsche Nationalbibliografie; detailed bibliographic data is available in the Internet at http://dnb.d-nb.de .

Zugl.: Berlin, Freie Univ., Diss., 2013

ISBN 978-3-8487-0814-7

D188

1. Edition 2013

Acknowledgements

This doctoral thesis was submitted to the Department of Economics at the Freie Universität Berlin in November 2012. During its writing, I have received much support from my supervisors and colleagues, my family and friends. First and foremost, I express my sincere gratitude to *Giacomo Corneo* and *Beate Jochimsen* for being my supervisors and providing constant encouragement and support. I have benefited immensely from discussing my work with *Giacomo Corneo*, whose thoughtful suggestions and helpful advice always guided me toward my goal. I am likewise highly indebted to *Beate Jochimsen* for her support, inspiring feedback, and motivation during the past several years. In particular, I am grateful that she accompanied me as I took the first steps toward this doctoral thesis.

Two chapters result from joint work and I would like to thank my co-authors *Ronny Freier* (chapter 3) and *Beate Jochimsen* (chapter 4) for the fruitful and enjoyable collaboration. I have benefited extraordinarily from working with them.

In 2011 and 2012, I had the opportunity to visit the Public Economics department at the German Institute for Economic Research (DIW Berlin). I would like to thank *Ronny Freier* and *Peter Haan* for their invitation and kind hospitality. My research has profited greatly from these visits. Thanks also go to *Viktor Steiner* and *Frank Fossen*, who gave me several opportunities to present my research in their seminar on economic policy at the Freie Universität Berlin. I also want to thank *Florian Ade*, *Charlotte Bartels*, *Timm Bönke*, *Tanja Fendel*, *Robert Jacob*, and *Kai-Uwe Müller* for numerous discussions on and off the topic.

Moreover, I am indebted to my parents for their support during every stage of this dissertation. Special thanks go to *Heike Schirmer*, *Theda Jürjens*, *David Lerch*, *Beate Schürmann*, and *Carina Pirra* for sharing ups and downs in the course of this dissertation project.

I would like thank *Charles B. Blankart* and his co-editors for publishing my thesis in their series 'Neue Studien zur politischen Ökonomie'. Last but not least, I gratefully acknowledge the financial support of the Friedrich-Ebert-Stiftung.

Berlin, September 2013

Contents

List of figures

List of tables

List of abbreviations

ADF	Augmented Dickey-Fuller (unit root) test
AT	Austria
ATE	average treatment effect
BA	*Bundesagentur für Arbeit*, Germany's Federal Employment Agency
BE	Belgium
CEO	chief executive officer
cf.	compare
ch.	chapter
DE	Germany
DIW	*Deutsches Institut für Wirtschaftsforschung*, German Institute for Economic Research
DK	Denmark
DPI	Database on Political Institutions provided by Beck et al. (2001, version December 2010)
DV	dummy variable that takes the value 1 …
e.g.	for example
EBRD	European Bank for Reconstruction and Development
EMU	Economic and Monetary Union of the European Union
ES	Spain
EU	European Union
EU-15	the group of 15 member countries of the European Union before the 2004 enlargement
FI	Finland
fn.	footnote
FR	France
FT	Financial Times
GDP	gross domestic product
GMM	generalized method of moments
GR	Greece
i.e.	that is
IE	Ireland
IMF	International Monetary Fund
ISCED	International Standard Classification of Education
IT	Italy
IV	instrumental variable
KldB	*Klassifikation der Berufe*, German classification system of occupations
LATE	local average treatment effect
LDV	lagged dependent variable

LSDV	least squares dummy variable
LSDVc	bias corrected least squares dummy variable
LU	Luxembourg
MINT	*Mathematik, Informatik, Naturwissenschaft und Technik*, see STEM
NL	Netherlands
OECD	Organisation for Economic Co-operation and Development
OLS	ordinary least squares
p.	page
PP	Phillips-Perron (unit root) test
pp.	pages
PT	Portugal
RDD	regression discontinuity design
RR	Reinhart and Rogoff (2011)
SE	Sweden
STEM	Science, Technology, Engineering, and Mathematics
U.S.	United States (of America)
UK	United Kingdom
UNESCO	United Nations Educational, Scientific and Cultural Organization

Chapter 1: Introduction

> *"[M]odern political economy has tended to focus only on the incentives faced by politicians for good or bad behavior, while neglecting the importance of selection. But no society can run effective public institutions while ignoring the quality of who is recruited to public office and what they stand for."*
>
> Timothy Besley (2005, p. 58)

1.1 Motivation

Political successes and failures are usually attributed to individual political decision makers. They are predominately linked to the competence of the decision makers when political events or policy outcomes are discussed in public. The importance of individual decision makers is also reflected in the electoral systems of several modern democracies that feature either the direct election of political leaders or different types of open party-list systems.[1] During the public debt crisis in Europe, the high value which is put on political decision makers and their individual background became apparent when the technocratic governments led by Lucas Papademos in Greece and Mario Monti in Italy were installed in November 2011. Both countries experienced a severe loss of confidence in their fiscal stability. In particular, the appointment of technocratic governments formed by politically independent experts was considered to be a device to overcome fiscal challenges.[2]

Contrary to the high value that is put on individual decision makers in the public debate, economic theory instead emphasizes the role of institutions – and the incentives they set – for economic outcomes. Political decision makers themselves and their competence or characteristics have received much less attention in the economic and the political economy literature as the above quotation by Besley (2005, p. 58) points out. If any political decision makers are included in theoretical models they are usually

1 For instance, mayors at the local level in Germany, governors at the state level in the United States or the presidents of Brazil, Finland, and France are directly elected. Open party-list systems allow the voters to choose their preferred candidates from the list of their preferred party. Different types of open party-list systems are used, for example, in Brazil, Finland, Ireland, the Netherlands, and Sweden. At the state and federal level in Germany, elections predominately rely on closed party-lists. However, the election system is personalized to some extent as voters have two votes: One for the preferred party (and the respective party list) and one for a local candidate that can either belong to any party or be an independent candidate.

2 See, for example, the discussion of the European debt crisis by the German Council of Economic Experts (Sachverständigenrat zur Begutachtung der gesamtwirtschaftlichen Entwicklung, 2012, paragraph 108 and the following ones).

assumed to be of two ability types and to have either a high or a low level of ability. A common feature of these models is an information asymmetry with respect to the ability level that is unknown to the public and exploited by the politicians in order to enhance their (re-)election chances.[3] However, the economic and political economy theory says little about specific features that characterize competent or incompetent politicians.

Looking at fiscal policy and public finances in particular, the finance minister is typically perceived as the decisive member of the cabinet. For instance, the Financial Times (London edition) has published an annual ranking of the European finance ministers since 2006 and attributes the fiscal performance of the European countries to the respective national minister of finance.[4] Contrary to this perception, the political economy literature usually ascribes fiscal performance to institutional and political factors rather than to the finance minister herself. Even though Hagen and Harden (1995) demonstrate that a 'strong' finance minister is pivotal for fiscal performance, they trace her 'strength' to features of the budget process, but do not consider her competence or other individual characteristics. Interestingly, several proposals for independent fiscal councils reflect the relevance of the competent decision makers for fiscal policy as they recommend the appointment of experts to watch over fiscal policy.[5] To date, existing expert councils predominantly have an advisory role and the political decision makers themselves are still in charge of the budget (cf. Debrun, Hauner, and Kumar, 2009). Nevertheless, the relevance of the politicians' individual characteristics for fiscal policy has not yet been well explored. And to date, it is not evident which of their characteristics – if any – matter for fiscal policy.

Unlike for the field of fiscal policy, there is a growing literature that evaluates other policy areas and takes the individual characteristics of politicial decision makers into account. For instance, the seminal contribution of Jones and Olken (2005) investigates the relevance of individual political leaders for economic growth, while Göhlmann and Vaubel (2007) examine how the education and the work experience of members of central bank councils affect inflation rates.

This thesis takes up this innovation and extends the well-established political economy approach by including the individual characteristics of political decision makers in the analysis of public finances in three empirical studies. Accordingly, the overarching objective of this thesis is to examine whether fiscal performance is affected by the individual characteristics of the political decision makers in fiscal policy. This objective

3 Rogoff and Sibert (1988), for example, explain political business cycles based on such a model.

4 For the latest ranking see Atkins and Whiffin (November 22, 2011).

5 For instance, Calmfors (2003), Wyplosz (2005) and also the Council of Scientific Advisors of the Federal Ministry of Finance Germany (Wissenschaftlicher Beirat beim Bundesministerium der Finanzen, 2005) recommend so-called independent fiscal authorities or fiscal councils with members that are politically independent practioners and scientists. Thomasius (2012) provides a brief overview and discusses different types of these institutions.

is pursued in three empirical studies that employ new data sets and advanced empirical methods.

All three empirical studies assess the relevance of individual characteristics of political decision makers for fiscal performance, i.e., the evolution of public deficits and debt. While fiscal performance can be considered as an indicator of the quality of government and political decisions with respect to fiscal sustainability, it surely does not capture the quality of life in a country, a region or a municipality (for a discussion of quality-of-life or well-being indicators see, e.g., Jochimsen, 2012). Moreover, public deficits do not necessarily imply sub-optimal political decisions with respect to welfare maximization. There are several occasions in which deficits should be used to smoothen taxation or to finance specific expenditures in order to maximize the social welfare (for a discussion on tax policy and expenditures see Corneo, 2009b,a). However, the European debt crisis demonstrates the importance of sound budgeting and fiscal sustainability for preserving the government's general capacity to act and to promote the well-being of the population in the long run. Nevertheless, it is difficult to determine the optimal, i.e., welfare-maximizing, level of public deficits in real life. Therefore, in this thesis an empirical analysis has to rely on the realized public deficits when the relevance of political decision makers for fiscal policy is examined.

The focus of the analysis presented here lies on the position of the finance minister. Two empirical studies investigate whether specific individual characteristics of this central decision maker in fiscal policy affect the evolution of public deficits or the growth of public debt. In particular, the studies examine characteristics which matter for her ability to ensure sound budgeting and characteristics which matter for her budgetary preferences. The former include the political experience of the finance minister and her standing as well as her education and previous work experience, while the latter refer to her ideological leaning, her age, her gender, and parental status. The relevance of these characteristics is assessed based on panel data both for the West German states and for the central governments of 15 European countries.

In addition to the finance ministers at the sub-national and national level, this thesis is also concerned with the mayors as the key decision makers at the local level. In particular, one empirical study is dedicated to the question of whether their background matters for municipal public finances in Germany. The local level is of particular interest as local politics are closer to the people. The municipalities in Germany, *inter alia*, are responsible for investments in the local infrastructure, for local public transportation as well as for child care provision. Hence, local politics affects the everyday life in a more direct fashion than politics at the sub-national or national level. The direct election of the mayor in German municipalities accounts for this. Consequently, this feature of local politics allows us to assess the characteristics of the mayor as the key decision maker in local politics not only with respect to local public finances but also election outcomes.

The thesis is structured as follows. The remainder of the first chapter highlights the contribution and the main findings of this thesis. Chapter 2 reviews the existing literature on the relevance of the politicians' individual characteristics for electoral and policy outcomes. Furthermore, the second chapter highlights the pivotal role of the finance minister as the central decision maker in fiscal policy. Chapters 3, 4, and 5 compose the main part of this thesis as they present three empirical studies on the relevance of individual characteristics for fiscal policy. Chapter 3 is a joint work with Ronny Freier and commences with an analysis of German municipalities. The role of the individual characteristics of the mayor is examined with respect to her electoral success and to local public finances in Bavarian municipalities.[6] The following two chapters are concerned with the finance minister and her relevance for fiscal performance in the West German states (Chapter 4) and in the EU-15 countries (Chapter 5). The study on German states is co-authored by Beate Jochimsen.[7] Finally, Chapter 6 draws a conclusion. It summarizes the results and discusses the differences of the empirical studies, provides policy implications, and identifies directions for further research.

1.2 Contribution and main findings

This thesis includes the individual characteristics of political decision makers in the empirical analysis of public finances across different levels of government, i.e., mayors in Bavarian municipalities and finance ministers in German state governments and European central governments. Thereby, the thesis contributes to the literature in several ways. Generally, it goes beyond the well-established focus on the political orientation of a politician and includes further characteristics which affect her ability or competence, such as her educational and professional background or her political experience. Furthermore, the analyses for the finance ministers include additional characteristics which are relevant for her budgetary preferences, such as her age, gender, or parental status. Throughout the thesis, the empirical analysis employs new and unique data sets which capture the individual characteristics of the respective politicians. The contribution and main findings of the three empirical studies are briefly summarized in the remainder of this section.

In Chapter 3, the first study evaluates the relevance of the mayor's qualification – in terms of experience in office and expected education – for electoral success and local public finances. This study uses real election data for a large panel of 2,031 municipalities in Germany's federal state of Bavaria between 1950 and 2009 and respective budget data starting in 1984. The first part investigates how the candidate's qualifications affect her result in mayoral elections. Using a regression control design, the study

6 An abridged version has appeared as Freier and Thomasius (2012).

7 This study has been accepted for publication in the *European Journal of Political Economy* (Jochimsen and Thomasius, 2014). An earlier version has appeared as Jochimsen and Thomasius (2012).

shows that voters prefer more qualified candidates. In particular, candidates receive a higher vote share if their profession indicated on the ballot sheet signals a university education. There is also strong evidence that mayors enjoy an incumbency advantage when they run for reelection. The second part of this study goes beyond related work and relies on close elections to identify the causal effects of the mayor's qualification on fiscal policy outcomes. According to the author's knowledge, this is the first empirical study that employs this regression discontinuity methodology for local public finances in Germany. Contrary to the strong effects on election outcomes, the analysis demonstrates that the mayor's qualification only has significant effects on some fiscal indicators. In particular, the study finds that the education has no significant effect on local debt, spending, tax rates or specific spending and revenue categories. On the other hand, the results suggest that incumbents lower local public debt and expenditures as well as local tax rates when they are reelected. Furthermore, the examination of particular professions does not identify significant effects on public finances. The only exception are former farmers who are shown to raise local tax rates, including the tax on agricultural property.

The second empirical study in Chapter 4 focuses on finance ministers in the West German states. It examines whether their personal characteristics matter for public deficits. The analysis employs various dynamic panel estimations and uses data on public deficits and the individual characteristics of all 110 finance ministers in the 10 West German states between 1960 and 2009. In particular, the characteristics evaluated are those that matter for the finance minister's ability to ensure sound public finances and those that affect her budgetary preferences. With respect to her ability, the study identifies three characteristics that matter for fiscal performance. Deficits decrease significantly when the finance minister has previous work experience in the field of finance or when she has the political backing of the prime minister as both belong to the same party in a coalition government. Higher-tenured finance ministers achieve lower deficits, too. To the contrary, no significant results are found for the finance minister's education. Regarding the budgetary preferences, the study cannot identify significant effects for her age, gender or parental status, either.

In Chapter 5, the third empirical study considers the national finance ministers of 15 European countries between 1970 and 2010. The study employs dynamic panel estimations to analyze how the growth of the debt-to-GDP ratio is affected by the individual characteristics of the 167 respective central government finance ministers. Regarding the characteristics that matter for the finance minister's ability, this study suggests that the backing of the prime minister matters for fiscal performance as debt growth is lower when she belongs to the party of the prime minister in a coalition government. By and large, there is no evidence that other characteristics related to her ability, such as her education, previous work or political experience, affect fiscal performance. The studies here do not find any significant effects for characteristics related to the budgetary preferences, either. Apparently, neither the ideological orientation, the age, nor the parental status of the finance minister significantly influence the growth of central-government debt relative to the GDP.

Finally, the three studies detect a considerable underrepresentation of women in politics across all three levels of government considered here. The low number of women even precludes an econometric analysis for the Bavarian mayors (ch. 3) and the European finance ministers (ch. 5). A slightly higher female representation barely allows the analysis for the finance ministers in German states. The result shows that the gender of the finance minister does not affect state deficits in Germany in any way.

Taking the results together, this thesis demonstrates how much voters care about the qualification of (local) politicians in terms of (expected) education and experience in office. The qualification of political decision makers, however, affects public finances only to some extent. In general, all three studies demonstrate that the education of political decision makers does not influence fiscal outcomes. On the other hand, the two studies for mayors in Bavaria and finance ministers in German states find some evidence for the relevance of previous work or political experience for public finances. The study for the European finance ministers, however, cannot confirm these results. That the political backing of the head of government, i.e., the same party affiliation, strengthens the finance minister in a coalition government is shown for both the German states and the EU-15 countries. In addition, both studies demonstrate that characteristics related to the budgetary preferences, such as age, parental status, or political leaning, do not matter for fiscal performance. In a nutshell, statistically significant effects on public finances are only found for specific characteristics related to the previous work and political experience or the political standing of the political decision makers.

Chapter 2: Relevance of decision makers and their characteristics in politics

Theoretical models in political economy frequently build on two types of politicians that have either a high or a low level of ability or competence which is unknown to the public. In these models, politicians usually exploit the asymmetric information to their advantage depending on their competence and the institutional incentives they face. Such models are used, for example, to explain political business cycles or other strategies employed to increase the probability of (re-)election (e.g., Rogoff and Sibert, 1988; Besley and Case, 1995; Persson, Roland, and Tabellini, 1997). But what actually makes a politician competent is rarely discussed in these information-asymmetry models. Thus, the general question remains whether there are specific and competence related observable characteristics of political decision makers that affect policy results. Before examining this question empirically in the sphere of public finances in chapters 3, 4, and 5, this chapter highlights the scant but growing literature on the relation between the individual background of decision makers and election or policy outcomes. The first section discusses the relevance for the electoral success of politicians and presents results of recent empirical studies. The following section highlights the empirical evidence for an effect on (policy) outcomes. The third section focuses on the pivotal role of the finance minister in fiscal policy.

2.1 Candidate characteristics and election outcomes

When the costs of information are high, it is a rational behavior for citizens to base political decisions on incomplete information. Voters do not always know what politicians have done in the past, are doing or should be doing (Downs, 1957). Psychological research shows that in such low-information situations, people base their decisions on simple heuristics and information shortcuts (cf., Tversky and Kahneman, 1974). In the context of elections, scholars have identified several types of informational shortcuts based on candidate characteristics, such as party affiliation, incumbency status, ethnicity, and gender (cf., Bartels, 1996; McDermott, 1998). Some authors have investigated the effect of the candidates' appearance on electoral outcomes. Berggren, Jordahl, and Poutvaara (2010), for example, ask survey participants to rate photographs of candidates on different traits such as beauty, trustworthiness and competence. Their results demonstrate, in particular, that the aggregated rating for the trait beauty was a significant predictor of the electoral success of the candidates in the 2003 parliamentary or 2004 municipal elections in Finland. Whereas the competence trait is insignificant when included additionally. For the sake of brevity, I will focus on recent studies

Table 2.1: Overview empirical literature: Education, occupation, and election outcomes

Study	Method* and data	Dependent variable	Results for main explanatory variables
McDermott (2005)	Experimental, random sample survey among registered voters of California (1994)	Vote share	Evidence for use of candidates' occupation as informational cues to infer her/his competence.
Mechtel (2011)	Results of open-list local council elections (2009) in 27 cities with more than 40,000 inhabitants each in the German state of Baden-Württemberg	Position on party list based on votes	Evidence for indicated occupation to affect electoral success (positively for, e.g., bakers, butchers, and police officers, but negatively for salespersons, financial sector employees, or business consultants)
Sajons (2011, ch. 3)	Experimental exit poll of 372 voters at Spanish local elections (2011) in Barcelona with random assignment of occupation infomation	Vote share	Evidence that candidates with high-skilled occupations or with occupations similar to the voters' occupation receive more votes
Galasso and Nannicini (2011)	Quasi-experimental (regression discontinuity) design with data on parliament elections in Italy (1994, 1996, and 2001)	Competence level of candidates (measured by years of schooling, previous market income, and local government experience)	Evidence for higher competence levels in more contested districts
Paola and Scoppa (2011)	OLS and IV regressions with data on mayors and municipal council in Italy (1985 to 2008)	Competence levels of mayors and council members (measured by education level and high-skilled occupations such as professionals, entrepreneurs, and public employees with managerial tasks)	Evidence for higher competence levels in highly competitive municipalities (instrumented by the early termination of the municipal council)

* Method mentioned only if not OLS. *Source*: Own compilation.

which examine the effect of the candidates' education or occupation in the remainder of this section. Table 2.1 gives an overview.

McDermott (2005) uses experimental survey data related to the run-off elections for state-wide government positions in California 1994. She demonstrates that voters use the indicated occupation as an information shortcut to infer the candidates' competence. In particular, her results show a significant electoral advantage for candidates if the indicated occupation is related to the aspired position. For instance, the candidate running for the state treasurer office receives significantly more votes when the occupation 'businessman, financial manager' is indicated. An unpublished working paper by Mechtel (2011) reports similar results based on real outcomes of local council elections in 2009 in the German state of Baden-Württemberg. Analyzing the results of more than 4,400 candidates running in 27 cities with more than 40,000 inhabitants, he finds the indicated occupation on the ballot paper to significantly affect the success of a candidate. Candidates are less successful when an occupation as a salesperson, a secretary, an employee in the financial sector, or as a business consultant is indicated. While candidates working as a baker, a butcher, a farmer, a gardener, or a police officer perform best. Sajons (2011, ch. 3 of his doctoral thesis) provides an experimental study based on an exit poll with more than 350 voters at the Spanish local elections of 2011 in Barcelona. His results demonstrate that, first, candidates with high-skilled occupations receive significantly more votes and, second, voters are more likely to vote for candidates with occupations similar to their own. These findings suggests that voters use the indicated (and randomly assigned) occupation to identify either more competent candidates or candidates with a background similar to themselves.

Two other empirical studies find supporting evidence that the competence levels of politicians significantly depends on the competitiveness of the political environment. Paola and Scoppa (2011) use data on mayors and municipal councils in Italy between 1985 and 2008 and demonstrate that the competence of mayors and council members (measured by education level and high-skilled occupations) is higher in more competitive municipalities.[1] Using a regression discontinuity design, Galasso and Nannicini (2011) obtain similar results for parliament elections in Italy between 1994 to 2001. They show that politicians with higher competence levels, measured by years of schooling, previous market income, and local government experience, are more likely to run in contested districts, i.e., when the margins of victory in past elections was low. Moreover, they find candidates of opposing political coalitions to converge to high-competence levels in close electoral races despite differences in average competence levels for both coalitions. The results of both studies suggest that political parties adjust candidate selection to match those of voters valuing the qualification level of the politicians.

The first part of Chapter 3 in the present thesis follows Mechtel (2011) in using real election data from local elections in Germany to examine how the indicated occupation on the ballot paper affects the election outcome (see results in Section 3.4.1). The second part of Chapter 3, however, goes beyond Mechtel (2011) and matches election data with fiscal data.

---

1 They use the early termination of the municipal council as an instrument for competitiveness.

2.2 Decision maker characteristics and (policy) outcomes

There is a scant but growing literature dealing with the effect that characteristics of political decision makers have on policy outcomes. The related studies are briefly discussed in the following subsections.[2] Table 2.2 provides an overview.

2.2.1 Economic policy and economic growth

Dreher et al. (2009) investigate the influence of the educational and professional background of the head of government on the implementation of market-liberalizing reforms. Their study provides empirical evidence for the relevance of the professional background. In particular, they find reforms to be more likely when former entrepreneurs are in office. Congleton and Zhang (2009) use a similar approach and analyze the influence of U.S. presidents on economic growth. Their results indicate that a higher level of education and the specific professional experiences of a president substantially increase economic growth. The results of Dreher et al. and Congleton and Zhang are more robust for the professional experience than for the educational background.

In another related study, Jones and Olken (2005) examine how the death of a political leader affects economic growth based on a data set comprising 130 countries. They find a statistically significant effect of exogenous leadership transitions on growth – especially in autocratic countries. Likewise, Jong-A-Pin and Mierau (2011) analyze – both theoretically and empirically – how the age of a dictator influences economic growth. Based on data for 372 political leaders in 116 countries, they find supporting evidence for the result of their theoretical model that economic growth decreases the older the dictator becomes. However, neither study considers the educational or occupational background of the political leaders.

Besley, Montalvo, and Reynal-Querol (2011) study whether higher educated political leaders promote economic growth and employ data for 1,654 political leaders in 197 countries. Following Jones and Olken (2005), they focus on 183 random leadership transitions due to natural death or terminal illness. The results indicate higher economic growth when leaders are more highly educated.

2.2.2 Monetary policy

In the field of monetary policy, scholars had already started to discuss individual characteristics of decision makers in the early 1990s. Of particular interest was how the voting behavior in the Federal Open Market Committee and the resulting U.S. inflation rate is affected by the educational and professional background of the committee's

2 Parts of this section have been used in Jochimsen and Thomasius (2012).

Table 2.2: Overview empirical literature: Education, occupation, and (policy) outcomes

Study	Method* and data	Dependent variable	Results for main explanatory variables
Economic policy and economic growth			
Dreher et al. (2009)	Panel data estimations using a data for more than 500 political leaders from 72 countries (1970–2002)	Change of economic freedom index (Fraser Institute)	Evidence that market-liberalizing reforms are more likely under former entrepreneurs. No robust results for education
Congleton and Zhang (2009)	Time series estimations for 41 presidents of the United States of America (1789–2000)	Average change in real GDP over the entire term in office	(Weak) evidence for higher growth rates during the term of presidents with higher education and specific career paths, but results depend on specification
Besley, Montalvo, and Reynal-Querol (2011)	Panel data estimations focusing on random leadership transitions, data for 1,654 political leaders in 197 countries incl. 183 random transitions (1875–2004)	Real economic growth (Maddision data set)	Evidence that leadership transitions affect growth in general and growth is higher when an higher educated leader is in office
Monetary policy			
Göhlmann and Vaubel (2007)	Panel data estimations using data for 391 members of central bank councils in the Euro area and 11 other countries (1973–2003)	Inflation rate (with a lag of 2 years)	Evidence that former members of the central bank staff realize lower inflation rates. Against this, former union leaders and politicians are associated with higher inflation. Results for education are less robust.
Farvaque, Hammadou, and Stanek (2009, 2011)	(Dynamic) panel data estimations using data for 175 members of central bank councils in the Euro area and 8 other (OECD) countries (1999–2008)	Inflation rate	Evidence that former private sector members, academics and central bank staff achieve lower inflation. Likewise, women realize lower inflation rates
Corporate performance			
Hau and Thum (2009)	Data on 592 supervisory board members of Germany's 30 largest banks (2007–2008)	Losses relative to total assets	Evidence for higher losses when the competence levels of supervisory board members are low. Competence is measured by educational attainments (insignificant) and professional experience in business or finance (significant effect)
Bertrand and Schoar (2003)	Panel data estimations using data on about 600 U.S. companies and 500 executives (1969–1999)	Market value (Tobin's Q), investments, debt leverage and others	Evidence for effects of the educational background, age and tenure of the CEO on several corporate decisions and corporate performance

* Method mentioned only if not OLS. *Source*: Own compilation.

members (cf. Chappell, Havrilesky, and McGregor, 1995). In the first international study in this field, Göhlmann and Vaubel (2007) find strong evidence that the inflation preferences of members of the central bank council depend on their education and professional experience. According to them, more law graduates in the council lead to higher inflation rates compared to having economists on the council, while former members of the central bank staff result in significantly lower inflation rates than when former politicians are members. Related studies by Farvaque, Hammadou, and Stanek (2009, 2011) support these results for professional experience. Additionally, they find evidence that more women in the council reduce the inflation rate. Again, and similar to economic policy, the results for education are less robust than for professional experience.

2.2.3 Spending priorities and public good provision

To the best of my knowledge, there are no studies to date that examine whether the educational or professional background of political decision makers affect spending priorities or the provision of public goods. However, some studies investigate the effect of other characteristics of politicians or leadership changes. For instance, Brender and Drazen (2009) demonstrate that the replacement of the central government leader has no significant effect on the composition of government expenditures in the short run. But four years after the leadership transition, the composition changes significantly compared to a counterfactual situation. Persson and Zhuravskaya (2011) analyze the influence of the regional parentage of provincial leaders in China. They find that politicians, who built up their career within the region they govern, provide more local public goods.

Other researchers examine the impact of gender. Chattopadhyay and Duflo (2004), for example, analyze the influence of female representation in local councils in India on public good provision. They show that female council members invest more in infrastructure that is directly related to the needs of women. Similar results can be found in Svaleryd (2009). She studies the effect of female representation in Swedish local councils on local public expenditures and finds higher spendings on childcare and education relative to elderly care when the share of women in the council increases. However, more recent studies using a regression discontinuity design cannot confirm that female representation matters for policy outcomes at the local level. Ferreira and Gyourko (2011), for instance, do not find an effect of the gender of the mayor on the size of local government or the composition of municipal spending in the United States. Likewise, Campa (2011) shows that the introduction of gender quotas in Spanish municipalities does not affect size and composition of public expenditures.

Using data from the German *Länder*, Hayo and Neumeier (2012) identify prime ministers from a poor socioeconomic background as spending significantly more on social security, education, health, infrastructure, and public safety. Nevertheless, none of the studies mentioned above considers the education or profession of political decision makers and therefore no conclusions can be drawn with respect to the effect of these characteristics on spending priorities or public good provision.

2.2.4 Changes in the form of government

Another strand in the literature explores the relation between political decision makers and institutional and constitutional changes in the form of government. Jones and Olken (2009), for instance, investigate the effects of 59 assassinations and assassination attempts against political leaders on the institutional setup within 45 countries between 1875 and 2004. They find that a successful assassination of an autocrat will significantly increase the likelihood of a transition to democracy thereafter. A related study by Hayo and Voigt (2013) yields similar results. While both studies trace changes in the form of government to the circumstances under which the reign of political leaders is terminated, they do not examine whether individual characteristics such as education or occupation are relevant here.

2.2.5 Corporate performance

In the field of corporate performance, several scholars have examined the effect of the characteristics of decision makers. Hau and Thum (2009), for example, trace the underperformance of Germany's state-owned banks in the financial crisis to less competent supervisory board members. They measure competence based on educational attainments and professional experience in business or finance and find the latter to be relevant, but not the former. Other studies emphasize the role of the CEO. Bertrand and Schoar (2003) find that the CEO's educational background, age, and tenure matter substantially for corporate decisions on investments, cash holdings or the debt leverage.

Other studies focus on the gender of corporate decision makers. However, results are rather mixed. Dezsö and Ross (2008) show a higher share of women in the top management is associated with a higher market value of the company (measured by Tobin's Q), although they could not find a significant effect of the gender of the CEO herself. Against this, Adams and Ferreira (2009) find a negative relation between the fraction of female directors and both the market value (Tobin's Q) and return on assets.[3]

2.3 Strength of the finance minister and fiscal policy

The previous sections of this chapter highlight the empirical literature on the relevance of the individual characteristics of politicians. In particular, their educational

3 Both, Dezsö and Ross (2008) and Adams and Ferreira (2009), provide extensive literature reviews.

and professional background has proven to be relevant for election outcomes and several policy outcomes. The following section takes up this discussion and focuses on the specific role of the finance minister in fiscal policy. The theoretical considerations are followed by an overview of the existing empirical literature.

2.3.1 Theoretical considerations

The traditional political economy theories trace the persistent public deficits in most OECD countries to partisan politics, political opportunism, and weak governments. In the run-up to the Economic and Monetary Union of the European Union (EMU), the focus shifted to the government budget process and the involved actors that determine the key public finance indicators expenditures, (tax) revenues, and the deficit (e.g., Hagen and Harden, 1994). The starting point of this discussion is the incongruence of the groups of general taxpayers and the beneficiaries of specific government activities or expenditures. As a results, the net benefits of an increase in government activity are higher for the beneficiaries than for the general taxpayer. Following Hagen and Harden (1995), the same incongruence applies when the government prepares the budget. In particular, each spending minister will assume higher net benefits from her projects which are financed out of the general budget, than other ministers would. If the budget is set up decentralized by the spending ministers, this common pool problem (Buchanan and Tullock, 1962, ch. 11) leads to a suboptimally large budget.

Hagen and Harden (1995) emphasize the pivotal role of the finance minister[4] to solve or at least reduce the described spending bias since she is the only cabinet member – beside the prime minister – not promoting the particular interest of a spending ministry. Instead, her political success depends on sound public finances. In order to raise her prestige and, thereby, her renomination or reelection chances, the finance minister can be assumed to be more in line with the average taxpayer regarding public expenditures and deficits. Hagen and Harden (1995) develop a straightforward theoretical model of the budget process and demonstrate that a finance minister with a strong position in the budget process reduces the common pool problem by disciplining the spending ministers.

2.3.2 Empirical evidence

While the theoretical argument of Hagen and Harden (1995) is well established, there is no common understanding of what makes a finance minister strong. Hagen and

4 Note that Hagen and Harden (1995) use the term 'finance minister' to describe the minister in charge of budgeting. While in most countries this responsibility is carried out by the 'finance minister', the title might be different in some countries such as the United Kingdom or there might be an independent 'budget minister' beside the 'finance minister' in countries such as Belgium, France, Denmark, or Italy (see data description in ch. 5).

Harden (1995) themselves and related research (e.g., Hallerberg and Hagen, 1999; Hallerberg, Strauch, and Hagen, 2007) focus on the procedural rules of the budget process that determine the strategical power of the finance minister. More recent research also considers individual characteristics that enhance the finance minister's ability.

Before I pick up this approach and examine the effect of the educational and occupational background of mayors in Bavarian municipalities (ch. 3), in German *Länder* (ch. 4), and of finance ministers in Europe (ch. 5), this subsection surveys studies which focus on individual decision makers in fiscal policy[5]. Table 2.3 presents the main features.

Feld and Schaltegger (2010) employ a time-series analysis for 32 federal finance ministers in Switzerland from the creation of the Confederation in 1849 until 2007. They show that finance ministers serving for a long period are associated with higher budget surplus and lower expenditures at the federal level, while revenues and debt are largely unaffected. However, the authors regard the tenure of the finance minister more as an indicator for general government stability, than a specific individual feature or strength of the minister herself. Jochimsen and Nuscheler (2011) take a different perspective and are first to consider the relation of the finance minister toward the prime minister as a potential factor strengthening the finance minister's position. They hypothesize that the finance minister in a coalition government is stronger and, therefore, can keep debt growth lower if she belongs to the party of the prime minister. Employing a panel data set for 10 West German *Länder* between 1960 and 2005, they find debt growth indeed to be lower when the finance minister has strong ties with the prime minister due to the same party affiliation in coalition governments.

The two studies discussed above are, to the best of my knowledge, the only articles that analyze the individual characteristics of the finance minister while the relevance of her educational and professional background for fiscal performance is so far unexplored. The only exception is a working paper by Moessinger (2012). He uses data on finance ministers in European central governments between 1981 and 2009 and analyzes how debt growth is affected by the finance ministers' field of studies, their ideological leaning, their tenure, and their experience as national ministers prior to their appointment as finance ministers. He shows that neither the educational background nor the ideological leaning matter for debt growth. However, his results indicate that finance ministers with more previous experience as a spending minister and finance ministers with a high tenure realize lower deficits. Nevertheless, his analysis refers to the cabinet members holding the title 'finance minister' even though there are 'budget ministers' with full cabinet rank besides the 'finance ministers' in some of the countries considered.[6]

5 The focus of this subsection is on effect on public debt or deficits, while Section 2.2.3 presents related research on spending priorities and the provision of public goods.

6 Examples are Belgium, France, Denmark, or Italy (see fn. 4, p. 28, and the description in ch. 5).

Table 2.3: Overview empirical literature: Characteristics of finance (and prime) ministers and fiscal performance

Study	Method* and data	Dependent variable	Results for main explanatory variables
Studies focusing on characteristics of the finance minister			
Feld and Schaltegger (2010)	Time series estimations using data for 32 finance ministers of the Swiss federal government (1849–2007)	Federal surplus, debt, expenditure and revenues (all normalized by GDP)	Evidence that expenditures are lower and the surplus is higher when a finance minister stays in office for a long time. No robust effects for revenues and debt
Jochimsen and Nuscheler (2011)	Dynamic panel data estimation using data for all 10 West German *Länder* (1960–2005)	Growth rate of real debt (state level)	Evidence that finance ministers in a coalition government who belong to the party of the prime minister keep the deficit as low as in a single party government
Moessinger (2012)	Panel data estimations using data for 111 finance ministers in 15 European countries (1981–2009), budget ministers beside the finance minister not considered	Change in debt (central government level, normalized by GDP)	Evidence that debt is the lower the longer the finance minister has previously served as spending minister or the higher her tenure, no effects for ideology and educational background
Related studies focusing on characteristics of the prime minister			
Hayo and Neumeier (2011)	Dynamic panel data estimations using data for prime ministers of 13 German non-city *Länder* (West: 1985–2009, East: 1992–2009)	Expenditures and net borrowing (state level, normalized by GDP)	Evidence that expenditures and borrowing are higher when prime ministers from a poorer socio-economic background are in office
Mikosch (2012, ch. 5)	Dynamic panel data analysis using data for the presidents or prime ministers of 25 OECD countries (central government level, 1975–2010)	Deficit (general government, i.e., all government levels together, normalized by GDP)	Evidence for lower deficits when the government is lead by a politician without working experience outside of politics. No effects for other professions or education variables (if not interacted). Lower deficits in times of weak majority of the government in the parliament or of highly fragmented parliaments when a trained economist heads the government, same for former entrepreneurs or managers and fragemented parliaments

* Method mentioned only if not OLS.*Source*: Own compilation.

Two related studies consider the prime minister herself and her characteristics when analyzing fiscal performance. The first study by Hayo and Neumeier (2011) traces fiscal performance in German *Länder* to the socio-economic status of the prime minister. Employing panel data for 13 non-city *Länder* between 1985 and 2009, they demonstrate that tenures of prime ministers from a poorer socioeconomic background are associated with higher levels of public spending and debt financing. The second study by Mikosch (2012, ch. 5 of his doctoral thesis) focuses on the educational and professional background of the heads of the central government to examine the fiscal performance of the general government, i.e., the central government and all other government levels, in 25 OECD countries between 1975 and 2010. He uses a dynamic panel data model to show that the education of the head of government is itself not relevant. However, his results indicate that deficits are lower as long as a trained economist leads the government when the parliament is highly fragmented or the majority is weak. The same holds for former entrepreneurs and managers when the parliament is fragmented. An unexpected, further result is that deficits are lower when the government leader is a career politician without any experience outside politics. However, he finds no effect for other occupations such as lawyers, scientists or workers and unionists.

The discussion above shows that individual characteristics of decision makers matter for fiscal performance. However, there is, again to the best of my knowledge, no study that examines the relation between fiscal performance and the both the finance ministers' educational and professional background.[7] Therefore, the present dissertation takes a first step in this direction.

7 While Moessinger (2012) analyzes the relevance of previous experience as a spending minister, the effect of professional experience outside politics is as yet unexplored.

Chapter 3: Mayors in Bavarian municipalities

3.1 Introduction[1]

Politics is made by politicians and both political successes and failures are often attributed to individual political decision makers. The importance of individual politicians is also reflected in the electoral system of most modern democracies as they lead to direct elections of political leaders (e.g., mayors of municipalities in Germany, governors at the state level in the United States, or the president in France). In this setting, we would naturally presume that, first, voters take the personal characteristics of politicians into account and that, second, those attributes matter for policy outcomes once a politician gets into office. In fact, a large body of the theoretical literature in political economy has taken these presumptions as the main ingredients of their models of political accountability and political agency (see, for example, Rogoff and Sibert, 1988; Besley and Case, 1995; Persson, Roland, and Tabellini, 1997).

This paper studies the empirical relevance of politicians' characteristics for electoral success and for fiscal policy outcomes in Germany. In particular, we look at direct mayoral elections in German municipalities and we evaluate the effects of a candidate's level of qualification, i.e., education and experience as indicated on the ballot sheet. In the first part of this study, the focus is on the importance of a candidate's qualification for her electoral success and whether better qualified candidates enjoy an electoral advantage. In the second part, we are then concerned with estimating the causal effect of having a competent politician in power on policy outcomes.

A number of papers in the political economy literature has confirmed that information on the ballot sheet about the specific professions of politicians indeed matter for the voter's decision.[2] Mechtel (2011) investigates how the indicated profession of candidates for German municipal town councils affects their electoral success. He shows that candidates working in specific highly respected occupations are more likely to win elections. McDermott (2005) and Sajons (2011, ch. 3 of his doctoral thesis) highlight the informational value of statements on the ballot sheets in an experimental setting.

1 This chapter is joint work with Ronny Freier. An abridged version has appeared as Freier and Thomasius (2012). The authors would like to thank Florian Ade, Giacomo Corneo, Peter Haan, Beate Jochimsen, Henrik Jordahl, and Christian Odendahl. Comments of seminar participants at the Annual Meeting 2012 of the Verein für Socialpolitik, at the IIPF Conference 2013 and of colleagues at DIW Berlin, Stockholm School of Economics as well as Freie Universität Berlin are also gratefully acknowledged. Ronny Freier gratefully acknowledges financial support from the Fritz Thyssen Foundation (Project: 10.12.2.092). Sebastian Thomasius is grateful to his coauthor and Peter Haan for their kind hospitality during research visits at the DIW Berlin in 2011 and 2012. The usual disclaimer applies.

2 Section 2.1 of this dissertation provides a literature review.

They show that voters use the information about the candidate's professional background to update their belief about the competence or experience of the candidate and vote accordingly.[3]

Taking the impact on the electoral success as a first insight, it is an interesting empirical question whether the individual characteristics of political decision makers actually affect their political choices and policy outcomes.[4] Besley, Montalvo, and Reynal-Querol (2011) as well as Congleton and Zhang (2009) show that more educated political leaders can stimulate economic growth. Dreher et al. (2009) provide evidence that the professional background of the head of government matters for the implementation of market-liberalizing reforms. Such reforms are more likely under political leaders who were entrepreneurs before coming into office. Similarly, Göhlmann and Vaubel (2007) as well as Farvaque, Hammadou, and Stanek (2009, 2011) demonstrate that the educational and professional background as well as the gender of decision makers in monetary policy councils is relevant for inflation.

Other studies document similar results with respect to spending priorities and public finances. Based on data for Chinese provinces, Persson and Zhuravskaya (2011) find evidence that more public goods are provided by "inside" provincial leaders, i.e., leaders governing the province where they started and stayed during their career. On the other hand, "outside" provincial leaders, i.e., leaders originally from another province, tend to undertake more infrastructure investments. Jochimsen and Thomasius (2014, see also ch. 4) consider the role of the finance minister and investigate how her educational and professional background affects public deficits in German states. They demonstrate that the education of the finance minister does not matter for the size of the deficit. It is the professional background that matters rather than the education. Finance ministers with professional expertise gained in the financial sector prior to their appointment incur lower deficits.

Our analysis is based on a large panel for all 2,031 municipalities in the state of Bavaria, Germany. For these municipalities, we have collected three types of data. These are, first, outcomes of mayoral elections from 1950 through 2009; second, information on the qualification level of the candidates based on the occupation indicated on the ballot sheet; and third, information on municipality budgets from 1984 through 2009. In the first part of the paper, we use a regression control framework to estimate the effect of a candidate's qualification on electoral success. We expect that voters give an electoral premium to candidates that signal higher formal qualifications on the ballot sheet. For the second part, we rely on regression discontinuity design (RDD) methodology focusing on the outcomes of close elections in order to estimate the causal effects of

3 Note that there is also evidence that the qualification level of politicians increases in a highly competitive political environment, which is further evidence that voters indeed put value on the qualification level of politicians (see Galasso and Nannicini, 2011; Gagliarducci and Nannicini, 2013; Paola and Scoppa, 2011).

4 See Chapters 2.2 and 2.3 for a literature review.

the education and experience of elected mayors on fiscal outcomes such as debt, total expenditures as well as local tax rates. Here, we hypothesize that elected mayors with a higher level of formal qualification will work toward a lower level of debt and a higher efficiency in the provision of public goods that will lead to lower expenditures and lower taxes.

The results of our paper are twofold. First, we indeed find a strong and significant electoral advantage for better educated candidates as well as the well-known incumbency advantage for mayors that run again for reelection. Incumbents receive a bonus of 15–18 percent in vote share or 34–41 percent in the probability of winning. Similarly, if the stated profession on the ballot sheet signals a university education, the candidate receives an additional 1.7–2.2 percent in vote share or 2.4–3.6 percent in the probability of winning.

Our second result is that the qualification of the mayor only has significant effects on some policy outcomes. We can show that mayors who have held the mayoral position before have a tendency to reduce local public debt, lower the level of total expenditures and decrease local taxes. While those results are only sometimes significant, they show a clear trend toward the anticipated direction. When we test for the fiscal effects of education on our main outcomes, we cannot report any significant and stable effects. Overall, these results remain partly surprising and raise the question of why voters indeed seem to care about getting a highly qualified mayor into office if it does not matter much for fiscal policy. Besides general education and experience, we also test for the effects of having a member of a particular profession getting into the mayor's office. Here, we can run regression discontinuity designs for the following groups: (1) entrepreneurs, (2) farmers, (3) professionals from the finance sector, (4) lawyers, and (5) public employees. We find no causal effect of those groups on our main outcome variable: local public debt. For the group of farmers, however, we report an intriguing result in which we can show that they increase all local tax rates. This is of particular interest as one of the local tax instruments is directly targeted at property in agricultural use.

Finally, the paper shows a strong and statistically significant electoral disadvantage for female politicians that goes along with an underrepresentation of women among mayors in Bavaria and is unexpected in size. The representation of women in Bavarian mayoral elections is indeed so low that we completely refrain from analyzing potential gender effects on public finances using the regression discontinuity design.

This chapter proceeds as follows. Section 2 describes the institutional background of local politics in Germany and our data set. In section 3, we discuss the empirical model and the methodologies we apply. Our main results for electoral success, the effects on fiscal outcomes, and the validity of the research design are presented in section 4. Section 5 concludes.

3.2 Institutional setting and data

3.2.1 Politics and public finances at the local level in Germany

In Germany, government activity is divided across three governmental tiers. Besides the federal level, Germany is organized into 16 states, and approximately 12,500 municipalities. The municipal level is responsible for a number of tasks within this structure. Municipalities are directly responsible for the provision of child care, expenditures for culture and recreation as well as investments in local infrastructure. Moreover, they oversee local firms in the public service sector and they administrate mandated spending allocated by higher tiers. In total, German municipalities run a yearly budget of about 1,400 Euro per capita, which amounts to almost a third of all government spending.[5]

Principally, municipalities receive revenues from three sources: (i) taxes and fees in their own authority; (ii) a proportion of federal taxes; and (iii) conditional transfer payments from both the state and, to some extent, the federal level. The local taxes, such as trade tax, property taxes on farmland or real estate, account for a substantial part of municipal revenues (about 20 %, see Ade and Freier, 2011b). The municipalities are free to decide these tax rates themselves. A share of federal tax revenues, like income and value-added taxes, is allocated to municipalities based on fixed rules and, therefore, this source of income cannot be directly influenced by the municipalities. Conditional transfers cover specific expenditures such as infrastructure investments and administrative tasks on behalf of the federal and state level authorities.

All affairs of a municipality are part of the joint responsibility of the municipal council and the mayor. Together they are free (within limits) to decide on important infrastructure investments, actively lobby for transfers, issue public debt and/or levy local taxes. The state constitution in Bavaria grants mayors an unusually strong and independent position within local politics. The mayor is put in charge of the entire administration as well as all operative decisions. She holds active voting rights in the council and presides over all council committees. In practice, she is often the only full-time working politician and acts as the agenda setter.[6]

The independent role of the mayor is also highlighted by the fact that the mayor is directly elected. Bavaria had already introduced direct mayoral elections after World War II.[7] Generally, mayoral elections are held every six years, simultaneously with

5 See Deutsche Bundesbank (2007).

6 Note that, under the current law, a full-time mayor is required if a municipality exceeds 10,000 inhabitants. Municipalities can have a full-time mayor if they have between 5,000 and 10,000 inhabitants. However, they may deviate and employ a part-time mayor instead. With fewer than 5,000 residents, a municipality shall have a part-time mayor but can also opt to employ a full-time mayor, see Ade and Freier (2011b).

7 Other German states (except Baden-Württemberg) introduced direct elections for the mayor only after reunification, see Ade (2013).

local council elections (see Ade and Freier, 2011a).[8] The elections of local mayors follow a majoritarian electoral system with a run-off election if needed. Candidates must receive more than 50 % of the votes to become mayor. If no candidate wins 50 % in the first ballot, a run-off election among the two leading candidates is held.

One peculiarity of local elections in general is that political parties are less important than for elections to state or federal parliament. This is reflected in the fact that, first, candidates are often supported by several parties and, second, that both the largest group of mayoral candidates and most winning candidates are either independent or belong to a local party. In the late 1970s, several local parties merged and formed the *Freie Wähler* (FW) party. However, Bavaria's most important party is the politically center-right *Christlich Soziale Union* (CSU)[9], followed by the center-left *Sozialdemokratische Partei Deuschlands* (SPD). Candidates from smaller parties, such as *Die Grünen* (Green Party) or the liberal *Freie Demokratische Partei* (FDP), rarely win mayoral elections.

Given the large number of independent candidates and political parties that are only locally active, it is the individual candidate's profile rather than the affiliation with a political party that matters. Thus, the starting point of our investigation is the information about the candidates' professional background that is usually provided on the ballot sheet next to the names and the supporting party or parties of each candidate.

3.2.2 Description of our data set

In the remainder of this article, we investigate two different aspects of mayoral elections. First, we focus solely on the election outcomes and the influence of the candidates' characteristics on their vote share and their probability of winning. Then, we look at the effect of the characteristics of the *elected* mayor on fiscal outcomes using a regression discontinuity design in which we rely on close elections. While the empirical methodology is discussed in detail later on, we introduce our unique data set in the following paragraphs.

Our data set comprises both the information from the ballot sheet and the results of mayoral elections in all 2,031 municipalities in Germany's federal state Bavaria from 1950 through 2009.[10] Figure 3.1 in the appendix depicts a sample ballot sheet from one

8 Note, that a municipality may deviate from the usual election dates if its mayor passed away or was removed from office.

9 The CSU exists only in the federal state of Bavaria. At the federal level, the party is closely connected with the *Christlich Demokratische Union* (CDU) and forms one group within the federal parliament.

10 Together with 25 independent cities, there are a total of 2,056 authorities at the lowest tier in Bavaria. Out of the 12.5 million inhabitants in Bavaria in 2007, roughly 9 million live in those 2,031 municipalities and the remaining 3.5 million in the independent cities.

Table 3.1: Number of elections and candidates by election outcome (1950–2009)

	Elections			Candidates		
	All	10 % window	5 % window	All	10 % window	5 % window
Successful elections						
Clear election result	21,233	1,595	796	33,623	3,221	1,594
Run-off election	1,892	874	454	3,783	1,748	908
Coin toss (same votes)	4	4	4	8	8	8
Total	23,129	2,473	1,254	37,414	4,977	2,510
No mayor elected						
Run-off election needed	1,901	–	–	5,916	–	–
Invalid election	21	–	–	41	–	–
Total	1,922	–	–	5,957	–	–
Total	25,051	2,473	1,254	43,371	4,977	2,510

Notes: Our sample includes the mayoral elections in 2,031 municipalities between 1950 and 2009 in the German state of Bavaria. *Source*: Own calculations, based on the data provided by the state statistical office of Bavaria.

mayoral election in our data set. In total, we observe the results of 25,051 elections[11] with 43,371 candidates (see Table 3.1); thereof 2,473 are close elections with a margin of victory of no more than 10 % for the winner and out of those 1,254 with no more than 5 %. In 21,233 elections, one candidate received a clear majority of votes, while a run-off election was needed after 1,901 elections. In 1,892 cases, a mayor was elected in a run-off election.[12] Further descriptive statistics on the election data are presented in Table 3.10 in the appendix.

Party cooperation and joint nominations are common for mayoral elections in Bavaria; we observe 8,745 candidates nominated by at least two parties. However, the CSU clearly dominates the political arena in Bavaria and is the party with the largest number of candidates, some 9,483. The SPD follows with 6,173 candidates. The minor parties and independent election groups had a total of 16,948 candidates, while 2,022 candidates indicated no party affiliation at all.

There are 3,997 different professions indicated on the ballot sheet for all candidates running for the mayor's office since 1950. Based on this information, we assess the education level of each candidate and generate the variable *university* representing the probability that a candidate is a university graduate (including both universities and universities of applied sciences). The first step in our assessment is to classify all those candidates as university graduates who either explicitly indicate that they hold

11 Initially, our data set included 25,085 elections since 1950. However, we excluded 34 elections due to missing information about the total number of voters or incomplete election results. Among them are 22 elections with only one candidate.

12 The difference between 1,901 elections without a result and causing a run-off election and only 1,892 run-off elections held in our sample is largely due to the elections that were excluded due to incomplete data. Recall, there was only one candidate for the majority of excluded elections, see footnote 11.

a university degree or work in a profession legally requiring a university degree in Germany (e.g., teachers, physician or lawyers). Consequently, the variable *university* takes the value of one for those candidates. Then, we draw on the average share of university graduates within a specific occupation category for the remaining candidates as a second step. For that purpose, we group all candidates into 105 specific professional clusters matching Germany's official job-classification system and use the average share of university graduates within the respective professional group.[13] Table 3.11 in the appendix illustrates the wide range of qualification levels along different industry clusters.

More than 16,000 candidates indicate the occupation 'mayor' on the ballot sheet. In these cases we use the occupation that was indicated in the election when the candidate was elected into the mayor's office for the first time in order to obtain the probability that the candidate holds a university degree. Furthermore, we use this information to identify more experienced candidates that have already served as a mayor and gained on-the-job experience.

It is striking how underrepresented women are among local politicians in Bavaria. There are only 1,442 female candidates, representing 3.3 % of all candidates in our full sample of 43,371 candidates since 1950. Female candidates are elected mayor in only 314 out of 23,129 elections; with 41 close elections where the margin of victory did not exceed 5 %.[14] Given these low numbers, we are not able to draw upon any statistical interference using the regression discontinuity design and, therefore, we cannot investigate whether female mayors act differently and realize different fiscal outcomes. Nevertheless, we can analyze how the gender of candidates affects their vote share and the likelihood to win an election.

After the analysis of the effect of the candidates' education and profession on their electoral success, we investigate their impact on the fiscal outcomes of the municipality. Our analysis is based on a unique data set comprising fiscal information of the 2,031 municipalities in Bavaria between 1984 and 2009. The data includes the municipal debt level, total expenditures as well as three local tax rates (trade tax, property taxes A on land, and property tax B on real estate). Descriptive statistics for those fiscal outcome variables are contained in Table 3.2.

13 We rely on the national, so-called 'Classification System of Occupations 1988' (*Klassifikation der Berufe* or *KldB 1988*) used by Germany's Federal Employment Agency (BA), who provided us with the data. The data covers all employees subject to social insurance contributions in Bavaria. Due to limited data availability, we assigned the share of university graduates in 1999 to all candidates running for election before December 31, 2000, and the share of graduates in 2009 to all candidates running for election thereafter. In both cases we assign the gender-specific shares of graduates, i.e., a female candidate working as a farmer is assigned the average share of university graduates among women working in agriculture and a male candidate, respectively, the share of graduates among men.

14 On the federal level and the level of the regional states, female representation is much higher with more than 30 % female members of parliament (Bundestag) and about 30 % female members of state parliaments. Given that approximately 50 % of the population is female, these shares are still well below the population mean (McKay, 2004).

Table 3.2: Descriptive statistics of fiscal data (1984–2009)

Variable	Observations	Mean	Std. dev	Min	Max
Debt per capita	7,984	55.968	361.587	−4,031	4,144
Expenditures per capita	8,333	183.976	695.662	−6,435	21,741
Property tax A (multiplier)	8,333	6.111	22.247	−220	500
Property tax B (multiplier)	8,333	7.321	21.982	−170	500
Trade tax (multiplier)	8,333	2.771	12.234	−150	140

Notes: The table shows the descriptive statistics for the fiscal data used in the analysis, i.e., the change over five years following a mayoral election in the respective variable. Data on debt, expenditures are per capita in Euro and tax rate multipliers for the tax rates. *Source*: Own calculations, based on the data provided by the state statistical office of Bavaria.

Table 3.3: Samples used in the regression discontinuity analyses

	Experience		Education		Farmers	
	Elections	Municipalities	Elections	Municipalities	Elections	Municipalities
Full sample	3,093	1,529	3,544	1,673	836	544
10 % window	487	416	615	527	158	148
5 % window	264	241	291	271	68	68

Notes: The table shows the samples (1984–2009) used in the regression discontinuity design (RDD). The sample sizes differ because only those elections in which the winning mayor and the best opponent differ in terms of education and previous experience as a mayor or a farmer are included. *Source*: Own calculations, based on the data provided by the state statistical office of Bavaria.

We assess the impact on public finances from three different angles. First, we investigate the effect of on-the-job experience when an incumbent runs for reelection. Second, we look at the effect of the mayor's education level. The third angle focuses on specific professions of the mayor. This analysis considers the following five professions: entrepreneurs, farmers, professionals with financial expertise, lawyers and public employees. Table 3.3 summarizes the different samples used in these three analyses. For the third analysis, only the sample characteristics for professionals with financial expertise are presented.

3.3 Empirical model and methodology

In this section, we introduce the main methodological approach used in this study, the regression discontinuity design (RDD). This empirical strategy was first developed by Thistlethwaite and Campbell (1960) to evaluate the effect on students of receiving a merit-based commendation. They analyze whether the commendation and the public recognition for this achievement affect the likelihood of receiving a scholarship, the student's attitude and their career plans. The main idea of their study is to exploit the mechanism of the decision which students are awarded the commendation. The decision rule is a deterministic function of the student's test score. Those students with test scores above a specific threshold receive the award, those below the threshold do not. Based on this *sharp* discontinuity, Thistlethwaite and Campbell investigate the effect of the commendation by comparing students with test scores just above and those just below the threshold, i.e., students merely receiving or not receiving the commendation.

The RDD methodology has frequently been applied in different areas of economic research since the late 1990s (see the literature review in Lee and Lemieux, 2010). Researchers in political economy started using the RDD idea after the turn of the millennium (e.g., Lee, Moretti, and Butler, 2004; Lee, 2008; Pettersson-Lidbom, 2008; Ade and Freier, 2011a).

In the following two subsections, we will lay out the general types applied in this study: the *sharp* and the *fuzzy* RDD. We use the sharp design in the analysis of the effects of the mayor's incumbency experience and specific professional expertise, while we implement a fuzzy RDD to identify the effect of mayor education on fiscal outcome variables. For a discussion on how both RDD approaches are implemented using parametric or non-parametric methods, we refer the reader to the appendix.

3.3.1 Sharp regression discontinuity design

We are interested in evaluating the effect of specific characteristics of the mayor on fiscal outcomes using the following model.[15]

$$y_{i,t} = \beta_0^k + d_{i,t}^k \beta_1^k + x_{i,t}' \gamma^k + f(\cdot) + \varepsilon_{i,t}^k \tag{3.1}$$

where $y_{i,t}$ represents the fiscal outcome of municipality i in year t, and $d_{i,t}^k$ is the treatment variable for whether the elected mayor has the specific attribute k. The vector $x_{i,t}$ comprises a set of control variables like the linear and squared terms of the local size of population as well as year fixed effects. The different choices for the implementation of the function $f(\cdot)$ is discussed in the appendix.

The main characteristic of RDD models is the definition of the treatment variable $d_{i,t}^k$. For the sharp RDD, $d_{i,t}^k$ is defined as a deterministic function of the assignment variable $\text{margin}_{i,t}^k$:

$$d_{i,t}^k = \begin{cases} 0 & \text{if } \text{margin}_{i,t}^k < 0 \\ 1 & \text{if } \text{margin}_{i,t}^k \geq 0 \end{cases}$$

15 For the exposition here, we closely follow Pettersson-Lidbom (2008).

The assignment variable[16] $\text{margin}_{i,t}^{k}$ is defined as the margin of victory (or loss) of a candidate with the specific attribute k in an election in municipality i in year t. It is calculated as the difference in vote shares between this candidate and the best opponent. At the threshold $\text{margin}_{i,t}^{k} = 0$, we will thus have a sharp discontinuity in the binary treatment variable $d_{i,t}^{k}$, where the word sharp here indicates that the treatment changes deterministically from 0 to 1 at the threshold.

Note that the absolute value of the assignment variables $\text{margin}_{i,t}^{k}$ of one election in municipality i at time t is the same for any attribute k under investigation, but its sign depends on the specific attribute k. The assignment variable is greater than zero if the candidate with the considered attribute k wins the election and is negative if this candidate loses the election.

To illustrate this, consider an election in which the incumbent mayor is reelected with a vote share of 51 %, the best opponent achieves 47 % while 2 % of the votes are distributed among other candidates. If we investigate the effect of a reelected incumbent versus a non-reelected incumbent here the assignment variable $\text{margin}_{i,t}^{\text{incumbent}}$ would take the value $+0.04$ since the candidate with the attribute 'incumbent' won the election with a margin of 4 %. Now, for the same data point, let the best opponent be a graduate from a university, while the winner of the election does not hold a university degree. Here, the assignment variable $\text{margin}_{i,t}^{\text{education}}$ would take the value -0.04 for this election if the effect of having a university graduate as a mayor or, more generally, the effect of electing the candidate with the highest education is under consideration. For simplicity, however, we will omit the superscript for the specific attribute k and the subscript for the time t in the following discussion.

The main idea of the regression discontinuity design is to focus on the observations close to the threshold. The argument then follows that in a very close election the final result, and whether a candidate (with a specific attribute) wins the election, can be as random as the result of a coin toss. If local randomization indeed works we can use those observations slightly below the threshold as a counterfactual for those observations slightly above the threshold as they differ only in the treatment status. All observable as well as unobservable characteristics should be similar (on average) on either side of the threshold.

Hahn, Todd, and Klaauw (2001) developed the econometric theory to underpin this intuitive idea. They make the case that the fundamental assumption needed for identification in an RDD is the continuity assumption. This condition implies that all characteristics (except treatment) are distributed continuously around the threshold. Lee

16 Different names are used for this variable in the literature. Referring to the seminal work of Thistlethwaite and Campbell (1960) and its focus on the test scores of students, Lee (2008) and Freier (2011) use the term 'score variable'. The term 'assignment variable' is used by Pettersson-Lidbom (2008), Klaauw (2008) and Lee and Lemieux (2010). Imbens and Lemieux (2008) call it 'forcing variable' and use the term 'assignment variable' for the treatment variable instead.

(2008) points out that this continuity assumption is in itself neither disputable nor empirically testable in any direct way. Though Lee introduces a relatively weak and testable condition under which this assumption is fulfilled, he only requires that the assignment variable which determines whether the treatment is received is comprised of a random element that cannot be precisely controlled by the individuals. This implies a continuous density function of the assignment variable and leads to a randomized variation in the treatment allowing inferences of causal effects. This even holds if the individuals (the candidates in our study) are able to influence their assignment variable (the margin of victory or loss, $margin_i$) as long as the assignment variable (the margin resulting from the candidates' final vote shares) contains a random element. Thus, all that is needed is that a *precise* selection or sorting just around the threshold is not possible. Lee (2008) proposes testing whether the (predetermined) baseline characteristics are similar in the two groups just below and just above the threshold. In addition to this, McCrary (2008) suggests examining the continuity of the assignment variable to identify potential manipulations around the threshold under which the RDD would be invalid.

Given our specific assignment variable $margin_i$, the margin of victory or loss in the mayoral elections, we consider it likely that the continuity assumption is fulfilled. It is very plausible that there is a sufficient random component to the vote share and the resulting margin of victory or loss.[17] Thus, we argue that we are able to identify causal effects using the RDD in this setting. To further show the validity of the design, we implement the tests proposed by Lee (2008) and McCrary (2008) in the discussion of results in subsection 3.4.4.

We should point out the local nature of the estimate. The local average treatment effect (LATE) that we estimate will draw inference only from observations for which two candidates with different incumbency status saw one candidate just winning the election. Our results will be internally valid because observations just right and just left of the threshold have similar characteristics. But what can we say about external validity? One may ask if an incumbent that just won or lost has the same characteristics as just any incumbent. We emphasize that this is only a constraint to external validity while internal validity is given if election outcomes at the margin are subject to some randomness.

17 Lee (2008) discusses this point in the context of U.S. House elections and argues, for example, that the weather on Election Day constitutes a random component that influences turnout among voters. Similarly, one can plausibly argue that shocks to party popularity due to certain media coverage or such can affect the election results. Note that the credibility of RDD designs using close elections is under scrutiny. Caughey and Sekhon (2011) challenge the initial David Lee results and argue that U.S. House elections are rarely close enough to argue for sufficient randomness. They are able to show that running incumbents are still more likely to win close elections and so are candidates with more financial resources. While we take their criticism seriously and present several tests to show that our design indeed works, we also think the case is fundamentally different in German local elections. Mayoral elections in Germany are generally low-information and low-budget elections (the information of expected closeness is very low (there are few polls taken) and the financial resources are very limited).

We will implement the sharp RDD in our analysis with respect to the effect of a mayor's experience. Additionally, we will also use it to evaluate the effect of having a mayor with a specific former occupation getting into office. The data allows us to implement such analyses for farmers, public employees, professionals, and entrepreneurs.

3.3.2 Fuzzy regression discontinuity design

The sharp RDD developed above is applied to the analysis of the effect of mayoral on-the-job experience and specific professions on fiscal outcomes. When we analyze how a mayor's education affects fiscal outcomes, we instead use a *fuzzy* RDD that relies on a similar idea. The RDD discussed above is characterized by a sharp change in the treatment variable d_i^k from 0 to 1 as soon as the assignment variable margin_i^k passes a specific threshold. In the fuzzy RDD, the treatment variable does not necessarily change from 0 to 1 at the threshold. The term fuzzy goes back to William M.K. Trochim who described this extension of the RDD in 1984 (see Lee and Lemieux, 2010).[18]

To analyze the effect of the mayor's education, we focus on those elections won by the better educated candidate.[19] Our treatment variable $d_i^{\text{education, fuzzy}} = \text{education}_{i,\text{winner}}$ represents the probability that the winner of the mayoral election holds a university degree (as before, we omit the time index t). It can take the value 0 (no university degree), 1 (sure university degree), or a value in between (for details see the discussion of the data set in Section 3.2.2). The definition of the assignment variable $\text{margin}_i^{\text{education}}$ follows exactly the sharp RDD introduced above and it is defined as the margin of victory (or loss) of the better qualified candidate. In contrast to the sharp RDD, however, passing the threshold of zero in the margin of victory implies only a discontinuous shift in the education level of the actual mayor, $d_i^{\text{education, fuzzy}}$, but not a deterministic change from 0 to 1.

We follow Lee and Lemieux (2010) and implement the fuzzy RDD as an instrumental variable (IV) estimator to evaluate the effect of treatment $d_i^{\text{education}}$ on a fiscal outcome outcome_i. For that, define a variable $z_i^{\text{education}}$ as

$$z_i^{\text{education}} = \begin{cases} 0 & \text{if } \text{margin}_i^{\text{education}} < 0 \\ 1 & \text{if } \text{margin}_i^{\text{education}} \geq 0 \end{cases}$$

This indicator variable $z_i^{\text{education}}$ is 1 if the better qualified candidate won the election. Like the treatment in the sharp RDD this variable changes deterministically at the threshold. We can now use this indicator variable $z_i^{\text{education}}$ as an instrument for

18 This section largely borrows from Lee and Lemieux (2010, pp. 299) who discuss the fuzzy RDD.

19 This implies that we cannot include those elections where the winner and the best opponent do not differ in their education levels.

the treatment variable $d_i^{\text{education, fuzzy}}$. This implies that we use only that variation in $d_i^{\text{education, fuzzy}}$ that is induced by the discontinuous shift in the treatment when one passes the vote threshold. As a result, all the same arguments for the validity of the design based on close elections still apply.

The second-stage equation of the IV estimator is the same as defined for the sharp RDD in equation 3.3 on page 60. Note again that the crucial difference now is that $d_i^{\text{education, fuzzy}}$ is no longer a binary variable. Omitting the superscript education, the first stage of the IV estimator then reads as follows:

$$d_i = \delta_0 + z_i\delta_1 + x_i'\gamma + f(\cdot) + \varepsilon_i \quad (3.2)$$

We follow the discussion in Lee and Lemieux (2010) and assume the same function $f(\cdot)$ and the same set of control variables x_i for the first- and the second-stage equation above. The specific purpose of the function $f(\cdot)$ and different implementations are discussed in the appendix.

Again, we want to draw attention to the local characteristics of our estimator (LATE). Inference is drawn from observation in which a candidate with a high level of education just won or lost against a less educated opponent. While the results are internally valid, one might object to the potential external validity. Observations in which a highly educated candidate won with a large vote margin might be very different from the observations considered here, so the results should be generalized with care.

3.4 Estimation results

The discussion of our results consists of four parts. The first part presents our findings regarding the effects of a candidate's education and experience on her electoral success (Section 3.4.1). Then we discuss the causal effects on the fiscal outcomes of the major's experience in office and his education (3.4.2) and mayors with specific professions and characteristics (3.4.3). Finally, we highlight the validity of our RDD approach (3.4.4).

3.4.1 Education and incumbency experience on electoral success

The first part of our analysis clearly indicates that individual characteristics of mayoral candidates and their background matter for electoral success. Table 3.4 presents the results from a regression control framework for the vote share achieved by the running candidates. We find clear evidence for the well-known incumbency advantage effect in our first panel, i.e., incumbent candidates enjoy a highly significant electoral advantage of 18.1 percentage points in vote share compared to other candidates.

Turning to the individual characteristics of the candidates in column 2, we include a dummy variable for all candidates either directly indicating a university degree on the

Table 3.4: Electoral success and characteristics of mayoral candidates: Vote share

	OLS				
	(1)	(2)	(3)	(4)	(5)
Incumbent	0.176***	0.181***	0.158***	0.158***	0.151***
	(0.002)	(0.002)	(0.003)	(0.003)	(0.003)
Interaction			0.090***	0.087***	0.085***
(# of voters * incumbent)			(0.006)	(0.006)	(0.006)
Dummy university		0.022***			
		(0.002)			
University			0.017***	0.017***	0.018***
			(0.003)	(0.003)	(0.004)
Interaction			0.029***	0.028***	0.027***
(# of voters * university)			(0.006)	(0.006)	(0.006)
Female candidate				−0.051***	−0.050***
				(0.004)	(0.004)
Set of Dummies for Jobs (F-Stat)					21.91
(p-value in parentheses)					(0.00)
Observations	43,371	43,128	42,349	42,349	42,349
R2	0.74	0.74	0.74	0.74	0.74

Notes: Significance levels: * $p < 0.10$, ** $p < 0.05$, *** $p < 0.01$. Standard errors in parentheses are robust and clustered on the level of each individual municipality election. All results presented are derived from OLS regressions and always include year and county fixed effects that are not shown here. Furthermore, the regressions include a set of dummy variables for the party of the candidate and for the respective total number of candidates in elections with more than one candidate which are not presented either. The dependent variable is the vote share of the individual candidate. The regression in column 1 highlights the effect of a candidate being the incumbent in an election. In columns 2 and 3, we add variables on the education level of the candidate. First, we add a dummy indicating whether a candidate holds a university degree with certainty (university and university of applied sciences). Second, we include our constructed measure of the expected education level as well as its interaction with the number of voters (in 10 tsd). In column 4 we include dummy variables for whether the candidate is female. Finally, in column 5 we add a set of dummies for the 14 job categories described in table 3.11 in the appendix (the table here highlights the F-test statistic for joined significance and the p-value of that test statistic is given in parentheses). *Source*: Own calculations.

ballot sheet (including graduates from universities of applied science) or those candidates working in any occupation requiring a university degree. We find that candidates with a university degree receive a vote share that is a significant 2.2 percentage points higher compared to other candidates.

In our models 3 to 5 we include the variable *university* capturing the share of university graduates in the candidate's occupation instead of the dummy variable and thereby include the publicly available information about the candidate's background which is indicated on the ballot sheet. Again, our estimations 3–5 show that candidates with a university degree or, to be more precise, candidates in occupations with a higher share of graduates enjoy an electoral advantage of 1.7–1.8 percentage points in vote share that is statistically significant at the 1 % level.

Furthermore, we include two interaction terms which test for the heterogeneity in the qualification effects with regard to the size of the constituency. We interact both the experience on the job (incumbency status) as well as our measure for education (university) with the number of voters. Both interaction terms (columns 3–5) have positive signs and are statistically significant. Thus, the electoral advantage of candidates with a higher qualification increases with the size of the electorate. An incumbent in an election with an additional 10,000 voters enjoys an additional advantage of 9 percentage points in vote share. Similarly, a candidate with an occupation requiring a university degree, e.g., a lawyer or physician, will receive an additional vote share of 2.9 percentage points with every 10,000 additional voters.

There are two arguments that may explain the positive results on the two interaction terms. Firstly, the electoral premium for qualification increases in towns with larger populations as the mayoral position requires a larger skill set. Voters may put more focus on the ballot sheet information about the qualification of the candidate when it matters more. Secondly, we may also assume that the informational value of the ballot sheet is larger in big towns than in smaller villages. Voters in small municipalities may personally know the candidates and rely less on ballot sheet information, while the electorate in larger cities receives a more informative signal from the ballot.

In column 4 we also include the gender of the candidate, which does not change our previous findings. However, we show that female candidates suffer from an electoral disadvantage and receive 5.4 percentage points less votes than male candidates. This effect is statistically significant at the 1 % level.

In model 5 we also include dummies for specific occupational groups and find strong support for our hypothesis that the information on the ballot sheet affects the electoral success of candidates. While these specific dummy variables are jointly statistically significant, the coefficients of the other variables do not really change and remain highly significant. Our result confirms the study of Mechtel (2011) who uses data from local council elections in the German state Baden-Württemberg and shows that the occupation indicated on the ballot sheet matters for the electoral success of the candidates.

Looking at the probability of winning, we confirm that the above effects are also of equal importance for the actual chance to win an election (see Table 3.12 in the appendix). As expected, all coefficients go into the same direction and are larger than in our first panel for the vote share. Notably, the results are well in line with the evidence presented by Freier (2011). Freier applies a causal inference approach and shows a party incumbency effect of about 38–40 percentage points in the probability of winning.[20]

20 Note, that the estimate here refers to the individual (legislature) incumbency advantage instead of the party incumbency advantage. The difference is that here we consider the advantage for the single candidate and not for her party. Freier (2011) relies on an RDD approach to have exogenous variation in the party identity of the previous mayor and estimates the advantage to any candidate of that party in the next election.

Our results show that the candidate's occupation given on the ballot sheet and her implied education significantly affect her electoral success both in vote shares and in the probability of winning. Incumbents and candidates with a higher education receive a significantly higher vote share and are more likely to win the mayoral elections. Both effects are reinforced as the population of a municipality becomes larger. Specific job groups also positively affect the electoral success. Female candidates, however, suffer from an electoral disadvantage of more than 5 % in vote share and 10 % in probability of winning. This electoral disadvantage might explain the surprisingly low overall number of female candidates as well and is well in line with the finding of McKay (2004) that women are significantly underrepresented in top-level positions at the state and federal level in German politics.[21]

3.4.2 Education and incumbency experience on fiscal outcomes

In this subsection, we highlight our evidence on the effect of mayor qualification, i.e., education and experience, on fiscal outcomes of the municipalities. We will mainly show two sets of results: (1) for the most aggregate fiscal outcomes debt and expenditures and (2) for local taxes as the main revenue sources under the discretion of the municipality.

Table 3.5 shows the results for our main outcome variables, debt and expenditures. We look at changes in debt and expenditures from just prior to the start to the very end of the election period. Panel 1 indicates the results for our measure of experience (incumbency status), while panel 2 holds the findings for the education variable. Columns 1 and 2 present estimates of simple OLS and Fixed Effects (FE) models respectively. In columns 3 to 7, we show the results of different RDD specifications. Here, columns 3 and 4 use a global parametric estimation procedure in which we use the entire sample and specify a linear or fourth order control function. Columns 5–7 use specifications in which we limit the sample around the threshold. The bandwidth is 10 % in the margin of victory in column 5, 5 % in column 6 and an optimal bandwidth (based on the algorithm proposed by Imbens and Kalyanaraman, 2012) in column 7.

For the analysis of the effect of experience (panel 1), we find a tendency for more experienced mayors, i.e., mayors that have been in office before, to lower the local public debt and decrease total expenditures. The sign of the effect thus goes in the expected direction. For the five-year change in public debt, we find that the estimates in all RDD specifications are negative and in two cases also marginally significant. For the outcome of total municipal expenditures all estimates (also in the OLS and FE specifications) show a negative sign. Overall, we must note that despite the clear negative

21 The results discussed above are based on OLS regression using data for all elections between 1950 and 2009 in 2,031 German municipalities. Using a restricted sample with elections between 1984 and 2009 only (as for the following analyses), we obtain almost exactly similar results. Results are not shown here, but are available upon request.

Table 3.5: Qualification and key public finance indicators

	OLS	FE	Global parametric RDD		Discontinuity-sample RDD		
	(1)	(2)	(3)	(4)	(5)	(6)	(7)
				Panel 1: Experience			
Debt	7.51	10.62	−22.59	−65.42	−134.15*	−165.74*	−28.58
	(21.81)	(26.05)	(36.70)	(68.16)	(75.55)	(95.69)	(43.06)
	[2.928]	[2.928]	[2.928]	[2.928]	[457]	[248]	–
Expenditures	−41.98	−28.39	−51.29	−136.05	−81.49	−245.69	−127.69
	(34.17)	(43.15)	(65.69)	(145.02)	(133.10)	(219.27)	(94.54)
	[3.019]	[3.019]	[3.019]	[3.019]	[471]	[258]	–
				Panel 2: Education			
Debt	23.80	52.23*	5.99	−17.06	88.18	−151.73	61.68
	(15.47)	(27.52)	(49.04)	(119.64)	(145.44)	(220.46)	(94.34)
	[3.312]	[3.312]	[3.312]	[3.312]	[570]	[274]	–
Expenditures	0.23	43.86	162.95	169.81	144.01	19.63	123.32
	(27.41)	(56.25)	(104.68)	(191.36)	(217.00)	(324.24)	(120.47)
	[3.440]	[3.440]	[3.440]	[3.440]	[587]	[282]	–
Control function	none	none	linear	4th order	linear	linear	linear
Sample size	full	full	full	full	$+/-10\%$	$+/-5\%$	optimal

Notes: Significance levels: * $p < 0.10$, ** $p < 0.05$, *** $p < 0.01$. Standard errors in parentheses are robust. The number of observations for each regression is stated in square brackets. Dependent variables are indicated in the left column. They refer to changes in yearly per capita data (the change over five years from the election year to the year before the next election). Results are reported for different estimations for education (fuzzy RDD) and on-the-job experience as a mayor ("sharp" RDD). Note, that results for education in the fuzzy RDD refer to the second-stage IV regression and each coefficient is the estimate on the variable of whether the mayor is highly educated instrumented from a separate first-stage regression. All regressions include linear and squared controls for the number of inhabitants in the municipalities as well as year fixed effects. Column 1 shows the OLS results, column 2 the results for a simple fixed effects estimation (with municipality fixed effects). In columns 3 and 4 we present results of the parametric implementation (global polynomial) with control functions of the first and fourth order. Results from different non-parametric implementations are reported in columns 5 to 7. In the last column, we implemented the optimal bandwidth estimator by Imbens and Kalyanaraman (2012). The optimal bandwidth for experience ranges from $+/-25.2\,\%$ for total expenditures and $+/-30.2\,\%$ for public debt, for education it ranges from $+/-21.6\,\%$ for public debt and $+/-45.2\,\%$ for expenditures. All control functions are specified to be flexible on both sides of the threshold. *Source*: Own calculations.

trend and the substantial economic size of the effect the estimates are imprecisely estimated and remain mostly insignificant. Given this lack of significance, we may not put too much weight on those results.

The results of the effect of education (panel 2) show high sensitivity both in sign and size. For local public debt, we see no clear pattern in direction and estimates are far from significant. For the outcome variable of total expenditures, estimates are positive throughout, however, they vary in size and the standard errors on those estimates are very large. We conclude that this part of the analysis does not support the hypothesis that education matters for economic policy outcomes.

As mentioned above (see Section 3.3), we might be concerned that our RDD estimates pick up a specific local average treatment effect (LATE). While this is of no concern for the internal validity, external validity may be harder to argue. It is possible that our weak findings for experience and our zero findings for education are driven by the specific LATE properties of our estimators.

In the case of the experience measure, for example, we may expect that incumbent mayors who only won reelection in a close race are not as "good" candidates (compared to the average incumbent) or faced a very competent challenger. We would, therefore, expect the LATE to underestimate the more general average treatment effect (ATE). However, if the ATE was even larger, we would expect to pick it up in the OLS and FE estimates. Given that even those estimates are insignificant, we consider it unlikely that our findings are only driven by the LATE properties of our RDD specifications.

In Table 3.6, we turn to the results for the tax rates as outcome variables.[22] Specifically, we test for effects on the three tax rate multipliers that are directly levied at the local level (property tax A and B as well as the local trade tax on businesses). The table is constructed similar to Table 3.5 above.

Again, the results for experience follow a clear pattern. We find that point estimates have a negative sign throughout, a result that is consistent with the negative patterns that we also observed for debt and expenditures. In contrast to the above, we can estimate the effects on local tax rates more precisely. Both the effects on the property taxes A and B are sizable and show significance at the 5 and 10 percent level. Results for the local trade tax are also negative, but they are very small and remain insignificant.[23] For education, again the picture is less clear, as point estimates are jumping in sign and are insignificant throughout. Also, this is consistent with our findings above.

Figure 3.2 in the appendix illustrates the findings for experience graphically. For the four outcomes of debt, expenditures, and the local property taxes A and B, we graph the local fiscal measures and look for a discontinuity at the winning threshold. Similar to the results in the regression tables, we find a tendency for lower debt, expenditures and taxes, however, these trends are not necessarily significant.

Finally, in addition to our main outcome variables debt, expenditures and taxes, we also test for effects in more disaggregated spending and revenue categories. In Table 3.13 in the appendix, we highlight the results for spending on personnel, investment spending, revenues from taxes as well as revenues from fees. The table is again constructed in the

22 Similar to above, we use changes in the three local tax rate multipliers (over five years following the mayoral election) as the dependent variables in the regressions.

23 The fact, that effects cannot be shown for the local trade tax, may in part be explained by local tax competition. While inhabitants that are exposed to property taxes are said to be immobile (especially given the relatively small effect that property taxes have on their entire tax bill), firms that pay the trade tax are more flexible and are more likely to respond to a change in taxation.

Table 3.6: Qualification and local taxation

	OLS	FE	Global parametric RDD		Discontinuity-sample RDD		
	(1)	(2)	(3)	(4)	(5)	(6)	(7)
	Panel 1: Experience						
Property tax A	−1.17	−1.41	−3.62*	−7.19*	−7.82**	−6.60	−5.05**
	(1.14)	(1.43)	(1.90)	(4.23)	(3.84)	(5.95)	(2.32)
Property tax B	−1.10	0.12	−3.60**	−4.54	−5.00	−6.38	−4.29*
	(1.06)	(1.34)	(1.77)	(3.47)	(3.64)	(5.61)	(2.20)
Trade tax	0.78	1.38	0.53	−0.17	−0.06	−3.66	−0.15
	(0.61)	(0.89)	(1.08)	(2.46)	(2.63)	(3.82)	(1.39)
Observations	3,019	3,019	3,019	3,019	471	258	–
	Panel 2: Education						
Property tax A	0.44	1.93	−1.47	1.75	1.67	1.65	−5.34
	(0.84)	(1.44)	(2.69)	(5.84)	(6.38)	(9.35)	(3.86)
Property tax B	0.99	1.37	−3.91	−1.92	−5.13	−1.83	−7.45*
	(0.86)	(1.46)	(2.80)	(5.99)	(6.56)	(9.48)	(3.70)
Trade tax	0.65	2.18**	−0.48	0.99	0.23	7.00	−1.18
	(0.60)	(1.02)	(1.80)	(4.42)	(5.15)	(7.56)	(2.91)
Observations	3,440	3,440	3,440	3,440	587	282	–
Control function	none	none	linear	4th order	linear	linear	linear
Sample size	full	full	full	full	$+/-10\%$	$+/-5\%$	optimal

Notes: Significance levels: * $p < 0.10$, ** $p < 0.05$, *** $p < 0.01$. Standard errors in parentheses are robust. The dependent variables for local taxes are indicated in the left column. They refer to changes in local tax multipliers over five years following the election year. Results are reported for different estimations for on-the-job experience as a mayor (sharp RDD) in panel 1 and education (fuzzy RDD) in panel 2. Note, that results for education in the fuzzy RDD refer to the second-stage IV regression and each coefficient is the estimate on the variable of whether the mayor is highly qualified instrumented from a separate first-stage regression. All regressions include linear and squared controls for the number of inhabitants in the municipalities as well as year fixed effects. Column 1 shows the OLS results, column 2 the results for a simple fixed effects estimation (with municipality fixed effects). In columns 3 and 4 we present the results of the parametric implementation (global polynomial) with control functions of first and fourth order. Results from different non-parametric implementations are reported in columns 5 to 7. In the last column, we implemented the optimal bandwidth estimator by Imbens and Kalyanaraman (2012). The optimal bandwidth for experience ranges from $+/-35.7\%$ for property tax B and $+/-42.9\%$ for property tax A, for education it ranges from $+/-30.6\%$ for trade tax and $+/-43.6\%$ for property tax B. All control functions are specified to be flexible on both sides of the threshold. *Source*: Own calculations.

same way as Table 3.5. Here, we find no significant effects of the mayor's experience or education on the fiscal measures of the municipalities.

We conclude that the mayor's qualification does not have strong effects on the public finances of her municipality. While the results for experience generally fall in line with our hypothesis, they are not always significant. From the analysis on education, we cannot find significant results for debt, total spending, tax rates or more disaggregated revenue and spending categories. Overall, the results are partly surprising given the highly significant electoral advantage of better qualified candidates running for the mayor's office (see Section 3.4.1). This leaves us with an unclear picture and one question remains: Why do voters care so much about the mayor's qualification when it does not affect fiscal outcomes such as debt, expenditures or tax rates?

Recent studies investigated how female representation affects public finances (Svaleryd, 2009; Ferreira and Gyourko, 2011; Campa, 2011). Initially, our intention was to replicate their analyses here as well. However, as already mentioned in Section 3.2.2, women are strikingly underrepresented in Bavaria's local politics. We observe less than 3.3 % female candidates and only 314 of them succeed in 23,129 elections. Given these low numbers, we are not able to draw upon any statistical interference using the regression discontinuity design on fiscal outcomes at all. For this reason, we are not able to investigate whether female and male mayors act differently; though we find strong evidence for a severe political underrepresentation of women in Bavaria.

Up to now, we have looked at general outcome variables. We asked whether more qualified mayors lower the debt burden or decrease local taxes. Implicitly, we have assumed that this is what voters care for. However, one of the reasons that we do not detect strong general effects of mayor qualification could be that researchers cannot observe what good policy for the voters of a municipality really is. A more qualified mayor might indeed make good policy decisions for her local constituency, but this can involve a reduction of local debt in the one case and the financing of a large infrastructure project in the other case. To that extent, there might still be good reasons for voters to vote for the more qualified candidate, however, measuring the quality of the fiscal outcomes is a much harder task. In order to get closer to this type of analysis, we devote the following section to the analysis of the effects of specific occupational groups in the mayoral office.

3.4.3 Specific professions on fiscal outcomes

This part of the analysis is concerned with the policy effects of having a member of a specific professional group become the mayor of a municipality. Specifically, we will study the fiscal effects when the mayor has a background as (1) an entrepreneur, (2) a farmer, (3) a financial professional, (4) a lawyer or (5) a public employee. As outcomes, we will again focus on local public debt. Moreover, we will investigate specific fiscal outcomes for one group in particular. For farmers, we will specifically highlight the results for the property tax rates on farmland.

Table 3.7 shows the main results for the effect of particular professional groups on local public debt. The table is constructed similar to Table 3.5. We present the results

Table 3.7: Specific professional expertise and public debt

	OLS	FE	Global parametric RDD		Discontinuity-sample RDD		
	(1)	(2)	(3)	(4)	(5)	(6)	(7)
Entrepreneurs	−11.01	−62.88	−24.29	−91.54	−124.08	−175.20	−137.76*
	(18.64)	(44.50)	(34.07)	(89.38)	(97.71)	(146.96)	(75.87)
	[1,255]	[1,255]	[1,255]	[1,255]	[222]	[103]	-
Farmers	−44.49*	−93.25	−59.34	−26.62	−85.81	−297.76	−22.54
	(23.99)	(63.87)	(46.37)	(116.91)	(138.44)	(198.45)	(67.80)
	[787]	[787]	[787]	[787]	[149]	[63]	-
Finance professionals	70.22**	26.92	40.09	−23.06	181.97	55.83	−20.91
	(32.01)	(106.22)	(58.78)	(121.67)	(175.59)	(180.34)	(67.15)
	[608]	[608]	[608]	[608]	[110]	[51]	-
Lawyers	−14.35	−15.71	15.59	−254.76	−433.97	−1,066.07	−134.62
	(42.81)	(141.77)	(75.27)	(200.28)	(277.63)	(752.27)	(128.48)
	[280]	[280]	[280]	[280]	[53]	[21]	-
Public employees	19.44	−6.85	24.34	7.69	−71.82	78.27	4.92
	(18.87)	(58.36)	(33.25)	(75.39)	(98.40)	(142.49)	(42.74)
	[1,163]	[1,163]	[1,163]	[1,163]	[188]	[81]	-
Control function	none	none	linear	4th order	linear	linear	linear
Sample size	full	full	full	full	+/− 10%	+/− 5%	optimal

Notes: Significance levels: * $p < 0.10$, ** $p < 0.05$, *** $p < 0.01$. Standard errors in parentheses are robust. The number of observations for each regression is stated in square brackets. The dependent variable in all regressions is change in per-capita public debt over five years from the election year to the year before the next election. All regressions include linear and squared controls for the number of inhabitants in the municipalities as well as year fixed effects. Column 1 shows the OLS results, column 2 the results for a simple fixed effects estimation (with municipality fixed effects). In columns 3 and 4, we present results of the parametric implementation (global polynomial) with control functions of the first and fourth order. Results from different non-parametric implementations are reported in columns 5 to 7. In the last column, we implemented the optimal bandwidth estimator by Imbens and Kalyanaraman (2012). The optimal bandwidth ranges from +/ − 18.0% for entrepreneurs and +/ − 39.7% for public employees. All control functions are specified to be flexible on both sides of the threshold. *Source*: Own calculations.

for the five professional groups in five different rows. Overall, the table does not show significant effects of either professional group on the local level of debt.[24]

24 We have also employed these specific job categories in our analysis of electoral success in Section 3.4.1. Using these five categories instead of the official occupational groups does not yield other results compared to model 5 in tables 3.4 and 3.12. However, farmers enjoy a statistically significant electoral advantage of 2 percentage points in vote share and 4.5 percentage points in the probability of winning. The same holds for public employees who gain additional 4.6 percentage points in vote share and 12.0 percentage points in probability of winning. Lawyers, finance professionals, and entrepreneurs enjoy a significantly higher vote share by 2.5, 1.6, and 0.5 percentage points respectively, but do not benefit from a significant increase in their probability of winning.

Table 3.8: Farmers and local taxation

	OLS	FE	Global parametric RDD		Discontinuity-sample RDD		
	(1)	(2)	(3)	(4)	(5)	(6)	(7)
Property tax A	0.55	−1.40	5.57*	9.93	9.99	15.23*	11.47**
	(1.41)	(3.02)	(3.22)	(6.45)	(6.98)	(7.76)	(4.79)
Property tax B	0.65	−1.51	5.59*	9.68	10.93	14.49*	7.42**
	(1.38)	(3.00)	(3.21)	(6.29)	(6.90)	(7.33)	(3.59)
Trade tax	0.38	−2.50	4.20**	5.99	5.97	8.50*	5.96**
	(0.93)	(2.59)	(1.80)	(3.97)	(4.46)	(4.78)	(2.24)
Control function	none	none	linear	4th order	linear	linear	linear
Sample size	full	full	full	full	$+/-10\%$	$+/-5\%$	optimal
Observations	821	821	821	821	153	66	–

Notes: Significance levels: * $p < 0.10$, ** $p < 0.05$, *** $p < 0.01$. Standard errors in parentheses are robust. Dependent variables are indicated in the left column. They refer to changes in local tax multipliers over five years after the election year. All regressions include linear and squared controls for the number of inhabitants in the municipalities as well as year fixed effects. Column 1 shows the OLS results, column 2 the results for a simple fixed effects estimation (with municipality fixed effects). In columns 3 and 4, we present results of the parametric implementation (global polynomial) with control functions of the first and fourth order. Results from different non-parametric implementations are reported in columns 5 to 7. In the last column, we implemented the optimal bandwidth estimator by Imbens and Kalyanaraman (2012). The optimal bandwidth ranges from $+/-34.6\%$ for the property tax *A* to $+/-70.7\%$ for property tax B. All control functions are specified to be flexible on both sides of the threshold. *Source*: Own calculations.

For former entrepreneurs as well as for farmers, the point estimates of the OLS, FE and RDD specifications all show a negative effect, indicating that members of those groups tend to reduce local debt. However, we do not have statistical significance on those results. For the remaining three professional groups, the results are mixed in signs throughout the different specifications and are mostly insignificant. We should add that this lack of significance for the RDD results can be a result of the fact that we rely on a small number of observations around the threshold (in contrast to the analysis above). Here, identification only comes from cases in which a member of the specific occupational group just made it into office or not. However, this is not true for the OLS and FE estimates which are also insignificant.

In Table 3.8, we investigate how mayors with a background as farmers enact tax policy. This is of particular interest as one of the local tax instruments specifically targets property in agricultural use (the property tax A). We can thus analyze the mayor's policy making with regard to the professional group that she belongs to.

Our results here are indeed interesting. While the OLS and FE estimation again point to a zero effect, the RDD results are much less variable and are often statistically significant (at least at the 10 % level). Throughout all specifications, they point toward a positive effect of having a former farmer in the mayor's office. For the property tax *A*, the results range between 5.6 and 15.2 in the tax rate multiplier. As the multiplier is about 330 points on average, the effects also constitute a sizable impact. That is even more so, when we recognize that those tax rate multipliers rarely change and that the average increase of the property tax multiplier in Bavaria has been around 6–8 points per election period.

From a political economics perspective, the sign and significance of the tax effect of mayors with a background as a farmer is surprising. Considering special issue politics, we might have expected the farmer to decrease tax rates for the constituency that is closest to her. However, we find the opposite is true. The former farmer increases the local property tax on farmland (compared to a mayor of a different former profession). And more, also the general property tax *B* and the tax on local businesses are being increased. These results correspond well with the negative sign on the local debt that we consistently found for former farmers (although not significant).

We also investigated the potentials effects of other professions on specific fiscal outcomes such as the effect of entrepreneurs on the tax rate of trade tax and identified a negative point estimate as expected. However, this effect is not statistically significant in any specification.[25] In the appendix, we further highlight the results of professionals of the finance sector on detailed categories of the municipality budget (see Table 3.14). This analysis directly compares to Jochimsen and Thomasius (2014, see also ch. 4) who find that finance ministers that have a professional background in the financial sector incur lower debt. For the German municipal level, we cannot confirm that experience in finance causally affects the components of the municipal budget.

Our results on the effects of particular professions in the mayoral position provide only little evidence that specific experience affects local public finances. For all five professions that we can look at, we find no significant effects on our main outcome variable: the level of local public debt. For the group of former farmers, however, we can analyze the specific effects on a local tax instrument which is targeted directly at the group of professionals from which the mayor is recruited. Surprisingly, we find that mayors with a background as farmers increase all taxes including the property tax rate on farmland. To that extent, we highlight that mayors do not act as 'professional partisans'.

3.4.4 Validity of the regression discontinuity design

In this section, we evaluate the validity of our RDD. The RDD analyses based on close elections crucially relies on randomized variations just around the threshold. While we cannot directly test this assumption, it is possible, as Lee (2008) points out, to observe necessary (but not sufficient) conditions. In particular, we apply two implicit tests proposed by Lee (2008) and McCrary (2008). We check the histograms of the

25 Results are available upon request.

Table 3.9: McCrary test results

	Experience	Education	Farmers
Discontinuity estimate	−0.113	−0.108	0.329
(log difference in height)	(0.147)	(0.127)	(0.221)
Used bin size	0.008	0.011	0.022
Used bandwidth	0.171	0.208	0.268

Notes: Significance levels: * $p < 0.10$, ** $p < 0.05$, *** $p < 0.01$. Standard errors are shown in parentheses. This table reports the results of the test proposed by McCrary (2008) and its STATA implementation 'DCdensity.ado'. *Source*: Own calculations.

frequency around the thresholds to assess the continuity of the assignment variable margin of victory (or loss). Significant discontinuities in the distribution around the threshold $\text{margin}_i = 0$ would indicate potential manipulations under which randomization would be violated and the RDD invalid. Moreover, we look at variables that were determined before the outcome of the election was decided. For observations around the threshold, we should not observe significant differences in those predetermined characteristics.

In the histograms in figure 3.3 in the appendix, we show that the frequency of observations shows no significant differences around the threshold. We present the histograms for the three samples used in the analyses for the education level, for experienced mayors, and for farmers. In the upper panels, we chose a wide range of the margin of victory. For experience as a mayor, the distribution is considerably skewed to the left, whereas the distributions are more uniform for education and farmers. The skewness to the left reflects the electoral advantage of incumbents. In the lower panels, we focus instead on the range of the margin of victory very close to the threshold. The upper histogram for experience differs from the two histograms for education and farmers from the increasing frequency of observations in the margin of victory for experience. Table 3.9 presents the results of the formal McCrary statistic which tests for the size of the jump at the threshold and its significance level. As indicated, we find no significant differences.

Next, we highlight that also variables that were determined before treatment was decided show no significant differences around the threshold. Table 3.15 in the appendix holds the findings for this particular test. For this analysis, we run the same RDD models as above on outcome variables that are lagged by one period.[26] If randomization indeed works, we should find no effect of treatment on those predetermined variables. Indeed, we find no effects both in the experience analysis (column 1–3) and the education analysis (columns 4–6).

26 To shorten the exposition, we reduced the number of specifications to the main three for both experience and education.

As an additional test, we run two placebo regressions. Table 3.16 in the appendix simulates the effect if treatment was at alternative thresholds. In panel 1, we test the effects on local public debt if a higher qualified candidate obtained the mayor's office with a margin of victory of -0.05. This means that we artificially construct the case as if a high-qualified candidate could win with just above 47.5 percent. In panel 2, we test the opposite case, in which the high-quality candidate artificially needs more than 52.5 percent to carry a win. The results are interesting for two reasons. First, we should not observe a treatment effect at those constructed thresholds (which would otherwise invalidate the research design). And in fact we find no such effects. Secondly, we can compare the point estimates and standard errors to our actual treatment effects. We find that in the placebos, the point estimates and standard errors are small and undetermined in sign. Our actual treatment effects for public debt, in comparison, have a clear direction, are much larger and have larger standard errors. While we still cannot conclude that there is a treatment effect, this highlights that at the actual threshold there is more change.

Finally, we also present graphical evidence that the first stage in our fuzzy RDD in fact induced a significant difference at the threshold. Figure 3.4 in the appendix shows that the treatment of observing a highly educated mayor in office changes discontinuously at the threshold. If the highly educated candidate wins the elections (on the margin), we observe the probability of the mayor holding a university degree by more than 40 %. This is the jump in the education variable that we then use to identify the effects in the education analysis.

Overall, all tests of the validity of the RDD indicate that the research design is valid. Even if our analysis showed few findings of a mayor's qualification on the fiscal outcomes of a municipality, these results are not driven by misspecification on the part of the statistical methodology.

3.5 Conclusion

In this study, we examine the importance of a politician's qualification, i.e., education and experience, for their electoral success and later fiscal outcomes. We apply regression discontinuity methodology and use the outcomes of close elections to identify causal effects. Our analysis is based on a large panel for 2,031 municipalities with roughly 9 million inhabitants in Germany's federal state of Bavaria. We have collected information on election results and qualification levels of mayor candidates as well as municipality budgets for these municipalities from 1950, respectively from 1984, through 2009.

Our results are twofold and puzzling. First of all, we find that the electoral success of a candidate running for the mayor's office is significantly affected by her education based on the occupation indicated on the ballot sheet. Candidates with (expected) higher education receive a higher vote share and are more likely to win the election. The same holds for candidates with on-the-job experience (incumbents). Specific job groups also positively affect electoral success.

Given the strong results for electoral success, our other results are intriguing. We find only little robust evidence that the fiscal performance of the municipality is affected either by the qualification level or the professional background of the mayor. Mayors who have been in office before tend to lower the level of debt and total municipal expenditures as well as decrease local taxes. While those effects are only sometimes significant, they show a clear tendency in the expected direction. For the analysis of education, we cannot detect any statistically significant effect of the mayor's qualification level on local debt level, spending, tax rates or more detailed revenue and spending categories. Moreover, the estimates vary largely in size and signs. While these results might reflect the limited leeway in fiscal decision-making on the local level (cf. Bundesministerium der Finanzen, 2012), they leave us with an unclear picture and raise the question of why voters care so much about the mayor's qualification and, here in particular, the education of the mayoral candidate when it does not matter for fiscal outcomes such as debt, expenditures and tax rates.

In addition to education and experience, we can also highlight the effects of specific professional groups when they get into the mayoral office. Here, the only relevant effect on fiscal outcomes that we find is for the case in which a former farmer becomes the local mayor. We report significant effects that those candidates alter tax policy and increase all three local tax rates. This finding is again surprising, as one of the local tax instruments directly targets agricultural property.

Furthermore, we find strong evidence for a sizeable electoral disadvantage and a resulting political underrepresentation of women in Bavaria. Hence, we cannot even investigate whether female mayors realize different fiscal outcomes. The share of female candidates is simply too low with 3.3 % and the number of females who win the mayor's office is even lower. This keeps us from drawing upon any statistical interference using the regression discontinuity design.

Drawing our results together, many questions remain unanswered. This opens up room for further research on the influence of a politician's characteristics on election outcomes and policy outcomes. Besides the role of their education and professional experience, the effect of a politician's gender requires further analysis.

3.A Appendix: Parametric and non-parametric implementation

There are two different ways to implement a regression discontinuity design irrespective of whether it is a fuzzy or a sharp RDD.[27] These implementations are either clas-

27 This section largely borrows from Lee and Lemieux (2010, pp. 314), who discuss the two approaches.

sified as parametric or non-parametric and generally differ with respect to the identifying assumption that is introduced by the function $f(\cdot)$ in the equation 3.1 and equation 3.2.[28] In both cases, the function $f(\cdot)$ describes the relationship that captures the effect of the assignment variable on the outcome variable and, thereby, controls for any correlation of the treatment with omitted variables in the error term. In their seminal work, Thistlethwaite and Campbell (1960) implement a regression model that is linear in the assignment variable so that the function $f(\cdot)$ in equation 3.1 would comprise the assignment variable itself.

However, when the true model is unknown, it is at least questionable whether this linear functional form is correctly specified for the identifying assumption to hold. A functional form that is incorrectly specified as linear would yield biased estimates for the treatment effect of d_i. To avoid biased estimates, a higher-order polynomial function of the assignment variable is included in the parametric implementation of the RDD. Additionally, all available observations are included in the regression instead of using only the data points around the threshold since the higher-order polynomial functions fully capture the potential impact of the assignment variable on the outcome variable. In practice, the order of the polynomial functional is increased stepwise to explore the robustness of the RDD estimates (Lee and Lemieux, 2010). Given the usage of the entire data set and the functional form of the polynomial series, this approach is also called a global polynomial estimation (e.g., Imbens and Kalyanaraman, 2012). If we use such a global polynomial series estimation in our study, the regression will not only include close elections but also those elections in which the winner has a far higher vote share than the best opponent.

As the identification in the RDD is based on the observations close to the threshold (in any implementation), researchers have also implemented parametric specifications in which they do not include the entire sample. Instead they limit the sample to observations within a certain margin from the threshold (an approach that is sometimes referred to as a "discontinuity-sample approach" Pettersson-Lidbom, 2008). The advantage of such specifications is that within a small margin from the threshold the potential bias from a misspecified control function is less severe. Typically, in the restricted discontinuity-sample it will suffice to specify a linear control function which is a good-enough local approximation of the relationship between the assignment variable and the outcome. The disadvantage of limiting the sample is that estimates are often less precise. Also, the choice of what margin to use to limit the sample is essentially arbitrary. In our application, we use discontinuity-samples of 10 and 5 % margins around the threshold.

In both the global and the discontinuity-sample implementation cases, we follow Lee and Lemieux (2010) and estimate separate polynomial control functions on each side

28 Equation 3.1 is used for the sharp RDD and as a second-stage equation for the fuzzy RDD. Equation 3.2 is the first stage for the fuzzy RDD.

of the threshold in our assignment variable margin_i to allow for different functional forms. Omitting the time index t and the superscript k, the estimated model for the "sharp" RDD then takes the following form:

$$y_i = \beta_0 + d_i\beta_1 + f(\text{margin}_i) + x_i'\gamma + \varepsilon_i \tag{3.3}$$

with

$$\begin{aligned} f(\text{margin}_i, n\text{-th order}) = {} & \text{margin}_i\beta_{21} && + d_i\text{margin}_i\beta_{31} \\ & + \text{margin}_i^2\beta_{22} && + d_i\text{margin}_i^2\beta_{32} \\ & \vdots && \vdots \\ & + \text{margin}_i^n\beta_{2n} && + d_i\text{margin}_i^n\beta_{3n} \end{aligned}$$

In the global parametric specifications, we will consider polynomial specifications of different degrees. While, we will use a linear control function ($n = 1$) only for the discontinuity-sample regressions.

The non-parametric approach – as an alternative implementation of the RDD – does not impose a functional form for the entire continuum of the assignment variable a priori and, therefore, provides flexible estimates of the regression function. Most non-parametric implementations of RDD use a kernel regression to estimate the local effect of the treatment on the outcome. This local effect is computed by weighting the observations differently depending on their distance to the particular point of the assignment variable under consideration. Usually, closer observations receive a higher weighting factor[29] than observations that are further away from this point. Although such kernel regressions are generally suitable for estimations at particular interior points, they perform poorly when estimating boundary points such as the threshold in the assignment variable (Lee and Lemieux, 2010). Instead of kernel estimations, Hahn, Todd, and Klaauw (2001) propose a local linear regression with a restricted sample that comprises observations within a small bandwidth around the threshold in the assignment variable only. In other words, only those observations just above or just below the threshold are used. In practice, the robustness of the non-parametric RD estimates is explored by changing this bandwidth (Lee and Lemieux, 2010). Imbens and Kalyanaraman (2012) derive the asymptotically optimal bandwidth for the local linear regression approach. We implement this optimal bandwidth estimator in our analysis as well.

The sharp and the fuzzy RDD do not differ much regarding their parametric or non-parametric implementation. The characteristics of function $f(\text{margin}_i)$ developed above are the same for both fuzzy and sharp RDD. However, the additional interaction

29 Lee and Lemieux (2010) discuss a rectangular kernel function in which all observations receive the same weighting factor independently of their position, i.e., the simple average of the outcome variables is calculated within each bin of the assignment variable.

terms in the control function relate to the indicator variable z_i in the fuzzy design and not to the treatment variable d_i as in the sharp design if they are included to allow for different functional forms below and above the threshold (Lee and Lemieux, 2010).

3.B Appendix: Figures and tables

Auf dem Stimmzettel darf nur
ein Bewerber angekreuzt werden.

Stimmzettel
zur Wahl des ersten Bürgermeisters
in Berg b.Neumarkt i.d.OPf.
am 02. März 2008

Wahlvorschlag Nr. 01 Kennwort Christlich Soziale Union in Bayern e.V. (CSU)	**Feihl Richard**, Krankenpfleger, Gemeinderatsmitglied, Berg	◯
Wahlvorschlag Nr. 02 Kennwort Sozialdemokratische Partei Deutschlands (SPD)	**Himmler Helmut**, Dipl.Pädagoge, 1.Bürgermeister, Kreisrat, Berg-Unterrohrenstadt	◯
Wahlvorschlag Nr. 04 Kennwort Liste Bürgernahe Gemeindepolitik (LBG)	**Kreuzer Richard**, Dipl.Geograph(Univ.), Wirtschaftsgeograph, Gemeinderatsmitglied, Berg	◯

MUSTER

Figure 3.1: Sample ballot paper

Notes: Sample ballot sheet for the mayoral elections in the municipality *Berg bei Neumarkt in der Oberpfalz* that took place on March 2, 2008 (own illustration based on the bulletin of the municipality, January 2008). The ballot sheet states the names of the three candidates and the respective party affiliation: Richard Feihl (CSU), Helmut Himmler (SPD), and Richard Kreuzer (local independent party list). Additionally, the profession of each candidate is indicated. The first candidate works as a hospital nurse and is a member of the local council. The second candidate is the incumbent and holds a university degree in education. The third candidate holds a university degree in geography and works as an economic geographer.

Table 3.10: Descriptive statistics of election data (1950–2009)

Variable	Observations	Mean	Std. dev	Min	Max
Number of voters	43,371	2,971	3,637	82	38,461
Dummy for mayor status	43,371	0.391	0.488	0	1
Interaction voters and mayor status	43,371	0.093	0.223	0	3.846
Dummy for professions requiring a university degree	43,128	0.168	0.374	0	1
Share of university graduates according to profession	25,391	0.361	0.425	0	1
Interaction voters and share of university graduates	25,391	0.174	0.349	0	3.706
Dummy for female candidates	43,371	0.033	0.179	0	1

Notes: The table shows the descriptive statistics for variables from the electoral data used in the analysis. *Source*: Own calculations, based on the data provided by the state statistical office of Bavaria.

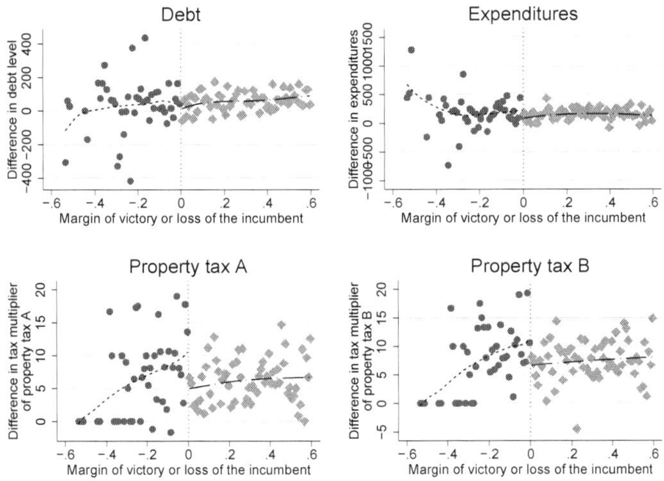

Figure 3.2: Main result – experience and fiscal outcomes

Notes: This figure illustrates the effect of having an experienced (i.e., reelected) mayor in office on fiscal outcome variables: local public debt per capita (upper left panel), total spending per capita (upper right), the multipliers of the local property tax A (lower left) and the local property tax B (lower right). We only include elections in which an incumbent mayor is running. Then, we measure the margin of victory of the incumbent against her best opponent. Just right of the thresholds are thus elections in which the incumbent just about won. The observations just left have the incumbent just losing. For clarity, the data have been grouped in bins, each bin representing an interval of 1 percent in the margin of victory. The outcome variable on the horizontal axis is the difference of the respective variable over five years following the election. The line fitted onto the data is based on a local kernel regression using endogenous Epanechnikov weights. *Source*: Own calculations.

Table 3.11: Education and professional background of candidates

Type of job	IDs included (KldB 1988)	Observations by education information: Total	Manually assigned	Data from BA	Share of graduates
Agriculture, forestry, gardening and mining	01 – 09	4,402	4,262	140	.081
Assembly and manufacturing, contruction and craftmen	10 – 54	3,559	3,425	134	.014
Engineers and technicians	60 – 63	1,520	1,151	369	.459
Professional services	68 – 70	2,403	1,882	521	.131
Logistics, communication, gastronomy and other remaining jobs	71 – 74, 91 – 93	1,370	1,183	187	.138
Entrepreneurs, consultants, tax advisers	75	1,069	992	77	.388
Politicians, senior government officials and association officials	76	596	307	289	.698
Business and public administration	77, 78	4,126	2,276	1,850	.444
Security	79, 80	977	816	161	.260
Judiciary	81	931	82	850	.930
Journalists, artists and other graduates or students	82, 83, 88	1,916	195	1,721	.929
Physicians, pharmacists, social work and body care	84 – 86, 90	483	224	259	.486
School and university education	87	1796	227	1,569	.932
Unspecified employees (average of 60–79 used for university)	60 – 79	332	321	11	.200
Former mayors	–	16,958	–	–	–
No job specified, housemen, pensioners or matching not possible	–	933	–	–	–
Total	–	43,371	17,343	8,321	.360

Notes: Candidates were classified based on the information for each candidate on the ballot. We used the official job-classification system (*Klassifikation der Berufe* or *KldB 1988*) of Germany's Federal Employment Agency (BA, *Bundesagentur für Arbeit*). The information about the education of the candidates stems from two sources: (i) For those professions where a university degree is compulsory in Germany (e.g., teachers, physicians or lawyers) and when a university degree was explicitly indicated, we manually classified the candidates as university graduates and assigned the value of one to the variable *university*; (ii) For the remaining candidates, the variable *university* takes the value of the average share of graduates among employees in Bavaria that are registered in the specific job classification. Data on education covers all employees subject to social insurance contributions in Bavaria on June 30, 1999, and June 30. 2009, and was provided by the Federal Employment Agency.
Source: Federal Employment Agency, own calculations.

Table 3.12: Electoral success and characteristics of mayoral candidates: Probability of winning

	OLS				
	(1)	(2)	(3)	(4)	(5)
Incumbent	0.408***	0.415***	0.354***	0.354***	0.338***
	(0.005)	(0.006)	(0.007)	(0.007)	(0.009)
Interaction			0.257***	0.251***	0.249***
(# of voters * incumbent)			(0.017)	(0.017)	(0.017)
Dummy university		0.036***			
		(0.007)			
University			0.031***	0.031***	0.024*
			(0.010)	(0.010)	(0.013)
Interaction			0.071***	0.069***	0.070***
(# of voters * university)			(0.018)	(0.018)	(0.019)
Female candidate				−0.096***	−0.100***
				(0.014)	(0.014)
Set of Dummies for Jobs					12.81
(F-Stat)					
(p-value in parentheses)					(0.00)
Observations	37,414	37,236	36,591	36,591	36,591
R2	0.40	0.40	0.40	0.40	0.41

Notes: Significance levels: * $p < 0.10$, ** $p < 0.05$, *** $p < 0.01$. Standard errors in parentheses are robust and clustered on the level of each individual municipality election. All results presented are derived from OLS regressions and always include year and county fixed effects that are not shown here. Furthermore, the regressions include a set of dummy variables for the party of the candidate and for the respective total number of candidates in elections with more than one candidate which are not presented either. The dependent variable is an indicator variable of whether the respective person won the mayor's office in this election. The regression in column 1 highlights the effect of a candidate being the incumbent in an election. In columns 2 and 3, we add variables on the education level of the candidate. First, we add a dummy indicating whether a candidate holds a university degree with certainty (university and university of applied sciences). Second, we include our constructed measure of the expected education level as well as its interaction with the number of voters (in 10 tsd). In column 4 we include dummy variables for whether the candidate is female. Finally, in column 5 we add a set of dummies for the 14 job categories described in Table 3.11 in the appendix (the table here highlights the F-test statistic for joined significance and the p-value of that test statistic is given in parentheses). *Source*: Own calculations.

Table 3.13: Qualification and specific expenditure and revenue categories

	OLS	FE	Global parametric RDD		Discontinuity-sample RDD		
	(1)	(2)	(3)	(4)	(5)	(6)	(7)
			Panel 1: Experience				
Spending on personnel	4.34	2.56	6.10	−5.40	−1.43	8.65	−1.14
	(5.51)	(3.44)	(5.90)	(10.45)	(6.84)	(11.93)	(7.00)
Investment spending	−26.14	−25.12	−18.30	−20.06	29.41	−80.74	−12.00
	(20.86)	(26.37)	(35.00)	(67.71)	(74.22)	(94.71)	(49.58)
Revenues from taxes	−16.04***	−2.70	−10.13	2.96	−1.02	6.43	−23.41
	(5.85)	(11.74)	(10.34)	(21.69)	(20.13)	(29.30)	(19.41)
Revenues from fees	11.32	5.37	10.70	−1.80	−3.95	8.08	−5.05
	(12.13)	(5.72)	(12.42)	(19.35)	(11.09)	(17.16)	(10.28)
Observations	3,019	3,019	3,019	3,019	471	258	–
			Panel 2: Education				
Spending on personnel	1.01	−0.89	−0.79	2.11	7.56	4.81	−5.30
	(1.73)	(3.23)	(5.26)	(11.98)	(13.31)	(18.86)	(6.14)
Investment spending	−0.91	−2.88	48.30	46.86	37.86	13.12	98.30
	(16.11)	(31.33)	(52.42)	(127.55)	(154.48)	(225.18)	(82.18)
Revenues from taxes	6.65	5.22	18.97	83.69**	43.96	32.12	38.06
	(6.17)	(12.30)	(17.81)	(36.36)	(36.13)	(55.50)	(31.20)
Revenues from fees	4.36	5.93	10.34	12.13	24.72	42.02	5.71
	(3.45)	(5.83)	(10.24)	(27.19)	(30.54)	(44.99)	(13.84)
Observations	3,440	3,440	3,440	3,440	587	282	–
Control function	none	none	linear	4th order	linear	linear	linear
Sample size	full	full	full	full	+/− 10%	+/− 5%	optimal

Notes: Significance levels: * $p < 0.10$, ** $p < 0.05$, *** $p < 0.01$. Standard errors in parentheses are robust. The dependent variables for specific expenditure and revenue categories are indicated in the left column. Results are reported for different estimations for on-the-job experience as a mayor (sharp RDD) in panel 1 and education (fuzzy RDD) in panel 2. Note that results for education in the fuzzy RDD refer to the second-stage IV regression and each coefficient is the estimate on the variable of whether the mayor is highly qualified instrumented from a separate first-stage regression. All regressions include linear and squared controls for the number of inhabitants in the municipalities as well as year fixed effects. Column 1 shows the OLS results, column 2 the results for a simple fixed effects estimation (with municipality fixed effects). In columns 3 and 4, we present the results of the parametric implementation (global polynomial) with control functions of the first and fourth order. Results from different non-parametric implementations are reported in columns 5 to 7. In the last column, we implemented the optimal bandwidth estimator by Imbens and Kalyanaraman (2012). The optimal bandwidth for experience ranges from +/− 19.3% for spending on personnel and +/− 27.3% for revenues from local taxes, for education it ranges from +/− 32.0% for investment spending and +/− 62.7% for spending on personnel. All control functions are specified to be flexible on both sides of the threshold. *Source*: Own calculations.

Table 3.14: Financial expertise and public finances

	OLS	FE	Global parametric RDD		Discontinuity-sample RDD		
	(1)	(2)	(3)	(4)	(5)	(6)	(7)
Expenditures	44.66	117.43	54.47	−28.93	−19.89	133.16	−34.96
	(53.67)	(160.22)	(90.43)	(216.82)	(217.65)	(361.85)	(130.65)
Spending on personnel	2.23	11.24	−2.15	−18.47	−6.19	−8.27	−14.29
	(2.65)	(8.29)	(4.91)	(13.87)	(17.53)	(34.86)	(8.87)
Investment spending	25.77	50.04	24.51	−15.02	45.55	84.65	−17.08
	(30.87)	(101.99)	(59.00)	(129.33)	(139.04)	(207.10)	(86.96)
Revenues from taxes	4.15	6.57	9.20	38.90	34.99	11.66	31.62
	(9.00)	(27.83)	(14.63)	(34.89)	(33.28)	(55.27)	(30.93)
Revenues from fees	−11.30*	−25.67	−24.10*	−28.77	−12.23	46.91	−23.71
	(6.31)	(21.46)	(12.36)	(31.53)	(30.93)	(49.62)	(24.16)
Control function	none	none	linear	4th order	linear	linear	linear
Sample size	full	full	full	full	+/− 10%	+/− 5%	optimal
Observations	626	626	626	626	112	53	–

Notes: Significance levels: * $p < 0.10$, ** $p < 0.05$, *** $p < 0.01$. Standard errors in parentheses are robust. Dependent variables are indicated in the left column. They refer to changes in yearly per capita data (the change over five years from the election year to the year before the next election). All regressions include linear and squared controls for the number of inhabitants in the municipalities as well as year fixed effects. Column 1 shows the OLS results, column 2 the results for a simple fixed effects estimation (with municipality fixed effects). In columns 3 and 4, we present the results of the parametric implementation (global polynomial) with control functions of the first and fourth order. Results from different non-parametric implementations are reported in columns 5 to 7. In the last column, we implemented the optimal bandwidth estimator by Imbens and Kalyanaraman (2012). The optimal bandwidth for experience ranges from +/− 21.8 % for revenues from fees to +/− 32.7 % for spending on personnel. All control functions are specified to be flexible on both sides of the threshold. *Source*: Own calculations.

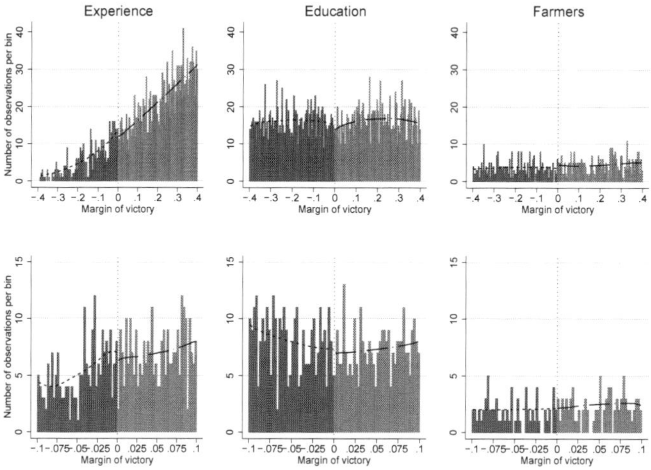

Figure 3.3: Histograms of assignment variables

Notes: This figure presents the frequencies of observations for the analysis of on-the-job experience (left-hand side), of education (center) and of former farmers (right-hand side). The data is ordered by the assignment variable margin of victory (or loss). The upper panel shows the frequencies within a margin of victory of $+/-40$ percentage points and each bin represents an interval of 0.5 percentage point in the margin of victory. In the lower panel, the graphs are zoomed in further and represent the frequencies within bins of 0.25 percentage points in the margin of victory. *Source:* Own calculations.

Table 3.15: RDD validity: Predetermined variables

	Experience			Education		
	Global (1)	Lim. Sample (2)	Opt. Band (3)	Global (4)	Lim. Sample (5)	Opt. Band (6)
Debt per capita in $t-1$	31.34	47.30	8.13	−4.71	46.02	11.84
	(79.57)	(77.25)	(47.12)	(26.94)	(52.18)	(36.10)
Expenditures per capita in $t-1$	−138.89	−162.03*	−117.31*	−34.19	−44.28	−67.00
	(90.85)	(94.03)	(67.22)	(41.57)	(62.02)	(54.72)
Property tax A in $t-1$	12.93	12.47	14.70**	−0.62	6.33	2.32
	(9.31)	(9.71)	(7.35)	(3.55)	(7.66)	(5.76)
Property tax B in $t-1$	7.65	6.51	9.49	−1.49	7.74	5.81
	(8.24)	(8.52)	(6.01)	(2.99)	(6.45)	(4.22)
Trade tax in $t-1$	7.22*	1.73	3.53	0.60	2.11	−1.06
	(4.34)	(4.63)	(3.11)	(1.44)	(2.87)	(2.59)
Control function	4th order	linear	linear	4th order	linear	linear
Sample size	full	+/−10%	optimal	full	+/−10%	optimal

Notes: Significance levels: * $p < 0.10$, ** $p < 0.05$, *** $p < 0.01$. Standard errors in parentheses are robust. The predetermined variable that we use as the outcome variable in the regression is indicated in the left column. Results are reported for different estimations for on-the-job experience as a mayor (sharp RDD) in columns 1–3 and education (fuzzy RDD) in columns 4–6. Note, that results of education in the fuzzy RDD refer to the second-stage IV regression and each coefficient is the estimate on the variable of whether the mayor is highly qualified instrumented from a separate first-stage regression. All regressions include linear and squared controls for the number of inhabitants in the municipalities as well as year fixed effects. Columns 1 and 4 present results of the parametric implementation (global polynomial) with a control function of the fourth order. Results from limited sample regressions (within a 10 % margin) are reported in columns 2 and 5. In columns 3 and 6, we implemented the optimal bandwidth estimator by Imbens and Kalyanaraman (2012). All control functions are specified to be flexible on both sides of the threshold. *Source*: Own calculations.

Table 3.16: RDD validity: Placebo test

	Experience			Education		
	Global (1)	Lim. Sample (2)	Opt. Band (3)	Global (4)	Lim. Sample (5)	Opt. Band (6)
	Panel 1: Placebo - 5 percent					
Debt per capita	14.60 (69.66)	23.00 (66.82)	17.89 (35.29)	7.85 (24.32)	−27.01 (37.55)	−43.26 (34.70)
	Panel 2: Placebo + 5 percent					
Debt per capita	57.02 (103.54)	8.74 (101.35)	−12.32 (56.19)	9.43 (24.35)	42.33 (84.30)	−55.50 (36.78)
Control function	4th order	linear	linear	4th order	linear	linear
Sample size	full	+/ − 10%	optimal	full	+/ − 10%	optimal

Notes: Significance levels: * $p < 0.10$, ** $p < 0.05$, *** $p < 0.01$. Standard errors in parentheses are robust. The table presents two placebo tests in which we artificially change the vote threshold at which a mayor is elected. In panel 1, the thought experiment is that a specific candidate also obtained the mayor office if she lost the election with at most 5 percent. In panel 2 we look at the reverse placebo in which we treat candidates to need more than a 5 percent vote margin to carry the win. The outcome variable is indicated in the left column. Results are reported for different estimations for on-the-job experience as a mayor (sharp RDD) in columns 1–3 and education (fuzzy RDD) in columns 4–6. Note that the results of education in the fuzzy RDD refer to the second-stage IV regression and each coefficient is the estimate on the variable of whether the mayor is highly qualified instrumented from a separate first-stage regression. All regressions include linear and squared controls for the number of inhabitants in the municipalities as well as year fixed effects. Columns 1 and 4 present results of the parametric implementation (global polynomial) with a control function of the fourth order. Results from limited sample regressions (within a 10 % margin) are reported in columns 2 and 5. In columns 3 and 6, we implemented the optimal bandwidth estimator by Imbens and Kalyanaraman (2012). All control functions are specified to be flexible on both sides of the threshold. *Source*: Own calculations.

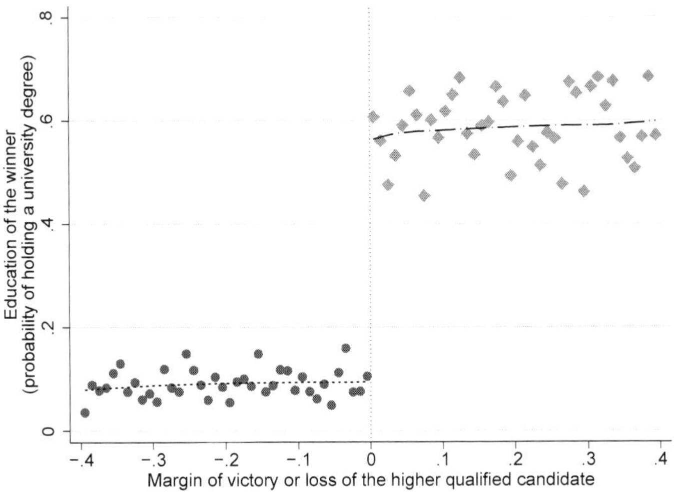

Figure 3.4: First stage of fuzzy regression discontinuity design for education

Notes: This figure graphically illustrates the validity of the instrument (first-stage results) used in the analysis for the effect of education of the mayor. We have organized the data as follows. For every election, we took the two best candidates and compared their education level. Then, we measure the margin of victory of the better qualified candidate over the less qualified. Just right of the 0 thresholds are thus elections in which the high education candidate just won, while the observations just left have those candidates just losing. Given that the first stage indeed works, we should observe a clear jump in the average education level between observations just left and just right of the threshold. We present this graph to show that this is indeed the case. We highlight the jump in the fuzzy design (described above). For clarity, the data have been grouped in bins, each bin representing an interval of 1 percent in the margin of victory. The outcome variable on the horizontal axis is the average education level of the elected mayors in each bin. The line fitted onto the data is based on a local kernel regression using endogenous Epanechnikov weights. *Source:* Own calculations.

Chapter 4: Finance ministers in German states

4.1 Introduction[1]

While a benevolent dictator or a welfare-maximizing government would choose the optimal level of debt to finance public expenditures, in reality politicians face many incentives to leave the path of welfare-maximizing indebtedness. Particularly, as the optimal level of debt is not accurately measurable. The debt crisis in European countries and in the United States has triggered a new debate on the reasons for excessive budget deficits and public debt. Besides general economic circumstances, much of the discussion focuses on the institutional and political factors that cause poor fiscal performance. Theories on political business cycles, partisan behavior, and weak governments try to explain the emergence of excessive deficits (e.g., Alesina, Perotti, and Tavares, 1998; Persson and Tabellini, 1999; Rogoff and Sibert, 1988; Alesina, 1988; Roubini and Sachs, 1989b).

Some researchers include the position of the minister of finance within the cabinet in their analysis. Compared to spending ministers who represent only the interests of their own ministries, the finance minister is the most crucial cabinet member with respect to the deficit. She is the only minister with an overall responsibility for the budget. Therefore, the strength of the finance minister might have an influence on fiscal performance. As factors strengthening the minister of finance, the literature examines her procedural rights (Hagen and Harden, 1995; Hallerberg, Strauch, and Hagen, 2007), her relationship with the prime minister (Jochimsen and Nuscheler, 2011) and the number of spending ministers in opposition to her (Hagen and Harden, 1995; Kontopoulos and Perotti, 1999; Volkerink and Haan, 2001). Somewhat surprisingly, however, the individual characteristics of the finance minister, such as personal career planning, educational background and professional experience as well as gender and parenthood, are as yet unexplored.

However, the relevance of the individual characteristics of political decision makers on economic outcomes has been analyzed in related areas.[2] Persson and Zhuravskaya

---

1 This chapter is joint work with Beate Jochimsen. A revised version has been accepted for publication in the *European Journal of Political Economy* (Jochimsen and Thomasius, 2014). An earlier version was published as Jochimsen and Thomasius (2012). The autors would like to thank Ronny Freier, Benny Geys, and Marcel Thum as well as two anonymous referees for their advice and helpful suggestions. Comments by participants in seminars at the 2nd World Congress of the Public Choice Societies 2012, the IIPF Conference 2012, and in seminars at Technical University of Dresden, University of Siegen, and the 10th Public Finance Workshop at WZB Berlin are also gratefully acknowledged. The usual disclaimer applies.

2 Goemans (2008) uses a different approach and investigates the exit modes of political decision makers. He shows that potential future exit modes affect actual policy decisions.

(2011) analyze the influence of the background of provincial leaders on local public policy in China. They find that politicians who built up their career within the region they govern provide more local public goods. Dreher et al. (2009) investigate the influence of the educational and professional background of the head of government on the implementation of market-liberalizing reforms and find that the professional background matters. Congleton and Zhang (2009) use a similar approach and analyze the influence of U.S. presidents on economic growth. Their results indicate that higher levels of education and the specific professional experiences of a president substantially increase economic growth.

Furthermore, some researchers concentrate on the impact of women on economic policy. Chattopadhyay and Duflo (2004) as well as Svaleryd (2009) analyze the influence of female representation in local councils on local public expenditure structures. Both find that a high representation share of women goes along with higher spending in areas related to women's needs.

In the field of monetary policy, scholars started discussing individual characteristics of decision makers in the early 1990s. Of particular interest is how the voting behavior in the Federal Open Market Committee and the resulting U.S. inflation rate is affected by the educational and professional background of the committee's members (cf. Chappell, Havrilesky, and McGregor, 1995). In the first international study, Göhlmann and Vaubel (2007) find strong evidence that the inflation preferences of members of the central bank council depend on their education and professional experience. Related studies by Farvaque, Hammadou, and Stanek (2009, 2011) support these results on the relevance of professional experience.

Other scholars investigate how the individual characteristics of decision makers affect corporate performance. Hau and Thum (2009), for example, study the influence of supervisory board members on the profitability of Germany's largest banks. They measure competence based on educational attainments and professional experience in business or finance and find the latter to be relevant, but not the former. Bertrand and Schoar (2003) examine the impact of the CEO and show that her educational background, her age, and her tenure are substantially relevant for several corporate decisions on investments, cash holdings, or the debt leverage. In a related study, Benmelech and Frydman (2012) demonstrate that CEOs with military experience differ in their decisions regarding investments, fraudulent activity and corporate performance especially during industry downturns.

Results are rather controversial when the gender of corporate decision makers is taken into account. Carter, Simkins, and Simpson (2003), for example, show that the firm value increases relative to a higher share of female executives in the top management. Others, such as Adams and Ferreira (2009), find a negative relation between the share of female directors and both the firm value and return on assets.[3]

3 Adams and Ferreira (2009) provide an extensive literature review.

This article is a first step to address the personal characteristics of a political decision maker in the field of public finance. With a new data set that includes biographical information on the ministers of finance in German federal states, we test several hypotheses derived from existing theories on the political economy of budget deficits. The new data set comprises information on the educational, the professional, and the political background as well as on gender and parenthood of all ministers of finance in former West German states from 1960 to 2009. We find that the personal characteristics of finance ministers do influence fiscal performance. Our main finding is that the professional experience of the finance minister prior to her nomination affects public deficits. Finance ministers who gained financial expertise, e.g., in the financial business sector, achieve significantly lower deficits than all others. We do not find evidence that her education affects the deficit in any way. Apparently, it does not matter if the finance minister has a university degree or which subject she studied. Furthermore, we find that neither the finance minister's gender nor the existence of children or her age affect public deficits. However, the strength of the finance minister within the cabinet increases with her tenure. The longer she is in office the lower annual deficits are. In coalition governments the finance minister's position is even stronger if she and the prime minister belong to the same party. However, we do not find support for the partisan theory, i.e., politically left finance ministers do not incur higher deficits than politically right ones.

We employ various dynamic panel estimation methods and our main results are robust. Our findings are relevant for the design of democratic institutions, too. Perhaps the nomination process of party candidates has to be reconsidered because, so far, professional experience is not the most important selection criterion. This opens up room for further analyses.

The article consists of five sections. The following section briefly discusses Germany's political and institutional background. In section three, we derive the hypotheses to be tested from a review of the literature focusing on the weak government hypothesis to explain fiscal performance. The fourth section introduces our data set and also presents the estimation models and the results. The final section provides concluding remarks and some fiscal policy suggestions.

4.2 Institutional setting

4.2.1 Germany's federal design and political parties

The 'Federal Republic of Germany' (FRG) is a federal state consisting of three levels of government, namely the federal level (*Bund*), 16 states (*Länder*), and about 11,340 local authorities (*Gemeinden*). Germany has only had 16 states since 1990: 10 former West German states, five former East German states, and Berlin. Note that not all 10 West German states existed when the FRG was founded. Three southwestern states formed Baden-Württemberg after a merger in 1952. The Saarland joined the FRG in 1957, following a period of French administration. As the Saarland budget was only fully integrated into the German system some years later, we start our analysis in 1960. Furthermore, we follow the related literature and do not include Berlin and the five East German states. The time following German reunification in 1990 is too short to provide a sufficient variation in the (political) variables of interest for the five East German states. The city state of Berlin is not included because Berlin was divided prior to reunification. While divided, the Eastern part was the capital of the GDR and the Western part was affiliated with the FRG. Both parts received substantial funding from the respective central government, thus limiting the need to issue debt.

Prior to 1960, the party system was relatively unstable and several small regional parties were in government coalitions for a short period and, subsequently, disappeared or merged with other parties. Modern Germany has five major political parties. The Christian Democratic Union (CDU, i.e., center-right)[4], the Social Democratic Party (SPD, i.e., center-left), the Free Democratic Party (FDP, i.e., liberal), the Green Party (i.e., ecological), and the Left Party (i.e., very left-wing). The first three have participated in elections since 1960. The Green Party was founded in 1980 and was first elected to state parliament in 1982 in Hamburg and Hesse; seats in the federal parliament followed in 1983. The Left Party appeared in 2007 after a merger of the Party of Democratic Socialism (PDS), the former East German communist party, with the Labour and Social Justice – The Electoral Alternative (WASG), a party formed by union members and former Social Democrats.

Since 1960, West German states have been governed either by a single party government, led by the CDU or SPD, or by coalitions typically consisting of two parties. Usually the CDU forms coalitions with the FDP or with the SPD, with the latter called 'grand coalitions'. Starting in 2008, the CDU has formed coalitions with the Green Party (mid-2008 in Hamburg and at the end of 2009 in Saarland). The SPD governs with the CDU ('grand-coalitions'), FDP, Green, and the Left Party. However, the latter coalition between the SPD and the Left Party only exists in East Germany and Berlin and, therefore, does not appear in our analysis.

4.2.2 Fiscal federalism in Germany

The 16 states are endowed with their own powers including an autonomous budget. Although the local authorities have the right to independently administer their own affairs, their fiscal independence is rather limited. Thus, due to the formal independence of the local authorities, state governments cannot be made responsible for narrowly

4 For historical reasons the CDU never runs for elections in Bavaria. Instead, their so-called sister party, the Christian Social Union (CSU), participates in elections. As both parties have similar programs and have always formed a parliamentary group in the federal parliament, we do not distinguish between them and label both the CDU.

limited local deficits. Therefore, it is logically consistent to concentrate on state deficits and neglect local deficits.

The fiscal federalism structure in Germany is dominated by joint taxes and the tax revenue is shared across all three levels of government. While the federal level has no restrictions concerning the design of its own taxes, sub-national governments have little power when it comes to setting taxes. States do not have any tax-setting autonomy.[5] The local level can raise some smaller taxes and can determine the tax rates for real property tax and for trade tax. Still, the federal and the state level negotiate the distribution of tax revenue out of joint taxes. As a consequence, citizens often have no idea which level of government is responsible for their tax burden. That makes it almost impossible for them to control their governments in this policy area and this might give politicians incentives to pursue fiscal policy in a suboptimal way.

Until the end of 2010, there were no restrictions for federal- and state-level debt issue. In the federal as well as in many state constitutions there was a formal requirement that a government's net borrowing should not exceed its planned investment expenditures. However, this requirement was linked to standard economic conditions, which lessened the strictness of the rule. As politicians face incentives to raise debt to a suboptimal level, this golden rule was not successful in limiting indebtedness in Germany. With the European Economic and Monetary Union, Germany faces additional restrictions for indebtedness. Still, the development since the introduction of the Euro shows that the economic sanctions for violating these criteria were not implemented. Since the beginning of 2011, Germany has implemented completely new debt rules, namely a debt brake. It is far too early to evaluate this new setting.

Among the states there is a sophisticated fiscal equalization system in which financially strong states provide equalization payments to financially weak states. It ensures that all states have adequate financial resources to carry out their tasks and maintain their sovereignty. Aligning the revenue of the states is intended to create and maintain equal living conditions for the entire population of Germany.[6] Fiscal equalization is based on a federal law lasting for a long period of time. The present law, for example, was passed in 2001 and is valid from 2005 to 2019. Therefore, it is not possible for a state finance minister to influence the share of joint revenue or equalization transfers for her state in the short or medium term. Between 1994 and 2004 two German states, Bremen and the Saarland, were bailed out by the federal government. This bailout reduced budget deficits in these states, but not to the anticipated degree. Furthermore, this federal bailout might have altered the incentives for all other states to issue debt. We account for these aspects in our analysis.

5 Since 2006 there has been one exemption to this rule: Following stage one of the federalism reforms, the states can set the rate of the real property transfer tax.

6 See Bönke, Jochimsen, and Schröder (2011) for an analysis of the incentives that the states face as the tax collector given this fiscal equalization system.

4.2.3 Budgeting procedures in Germany

State budget are usually passed annually for one calendar year. The budgeting process starts at the beginning of the preceding year with negotiations between the spending ministries and the ministry of finance on the anticipated input costs – such as staff costs and supplies. Before the summer holidays of the preceding year these bilateral negotiations come to an end and the budget for the following year is passed in cabinet. Beginning in autumn, the budget is debated and potentially modified in the state parliaments before being passed by parliament at the end of the year. However, the finance minister has a non-negligible influence on the budget during the entire following budget year. It is based, first, on budget execution and, second, on supplementary budgets. Of course, the finance minster is likely to use this influence extensively if she came into office after the budget had passed parliament. Therefore, we assume in our analysis that the current finance minister is mainly responsible for the actual budget.

As mentioned above, states have no tax-setting autonomy and the fiscal equalization system distributes tax revenue more or less equally per capita among the states. Consequently, state revenue is almost completely given in the short and medium term. Therefore, the finance minister can only influence expenditures in the budgeting process.

4.3 Personality of the finance minister and public deficits in German states

Public finance theories on budget deficits concentrate on partisan politics, political opportunism and weak governments. For the German states there are several empirical studies which try to explain the development of state deficits using these theories (e.g., Seitz, 2000; Galli and Rossi, 2002; Jochimsen and Nuscheler, 2011). Therefore, we take most variables based on these theoretical attempts as controls only.

Instead, we focus on the preferences and abilities of the finance minister. Traditional public finance theory assumes that all cabinet members have control over some part of the budget, but no member is responsible for the entire budget. In those settings, sound public budgets have the same characteristics as public goods. A common pool problem emerges (Buchanan and Tullock, 1962, ch. 11) that could be overcome – or at least softened – by centralizing financial responsibility. If the budget is set up decentralized, spending ministers independently develop their expenditure plans. According to Hagen and Harden (1995), a suboptimally large budget will result. Within the cabinet, the minister of finance is particularly important for fiscal performance because she is the only member of the cabinet – besides the prime minister – not promoting the interests of a spending ministry: She is assumed to be immune to the spending bias of her colleagues. Her political success comes along with a sound fiscal policy and only this policy will raise her prestige and, thereby, her renomination or reelection probability. Consequently, her interests regarding borrowing should be more in line with those of the average taxpayer (cf. Hagen and Harden, 1995; Hallerberg and Hagen, 1999; Feld and Schaltegger, 2010; Jochimsen and Nuscheler, 2011; Wehner, 2010). Therefore, we concentrate on a still unexplored aspect of the theory on weak governments, namely the position of the finance minister within the cabinet.

The common view is that a strong minister of finance may resolve the common pool problem of weak governments by disciplining her minister colleagues. However, there is no common understanding of what makes a finance minister strong. Some contributions focus on the procedural rules of the finance minister in the budget process (e.g., Hagen and Harden, 1995; Hallerberg and Hagen, 1999; Hallerberg, Strauch, and Hagen, 2007). Yet procedural rules are roughly identical in all German states. Other authors focus on tenure (Feld and Schaltegger, 2010) and party affiliation (Jochimsen and Nuscheler, 2011). We pick up those approaches and include them in this study.

Still, the personality of the finance minister and the relevance of her individual characteristics for fiscal performance are unexplored. Besley (2005, p. 58) argues that 'modern political economy has tended to focus only on the incentives faced by politicians for good or bad behavior, while neglecting the importance of selection. But no society can run effective public institutions while ignoring the quality of who is recruited to public office and what they stand for.' This article takes first steps in this direction. We thereby distinguish between the finance minister's preferences and her ability regarding deficit size.

4.3.1 Budgetary preferences of the finance minister

Hibbs (1977) argues that economic policy outcomes are driven by government ideology. Ideologically motivated politicians want to win elections only in order to implement their desired policy. Left-wing politicians are expected to be more concerned with redistribution and the pursuance of more expansionary policies compared to right-wing politicians. As finance ministers in the German states cannot influence their tax revenue, politically left finance ministers have to increase the deficit to finance their preferred spending programs.

Hypothesis 4.1 *Deficits will be higher with politically left finance ministers.*

Following Barro's (1973) discussion on a politician's time horizon and the potential 'lame duck' effect, it is plausible that the time horizon of the finance minister affects fiscal policy and public debt. Tirole (1994) points out that career concerns are probably the main driver for politicians. In the absence of substantial monetary rewards (compared to the business sector), they are concerned with the effect of their current performance on their reputation and future career, i.e., reelection or career prospects in the private and public sector. Besley and Case (1995) expand this idea in their *reputation building model* in which the incentives for reputation building are weakened by shorter time horizons due to term limits. Basically, this describes the well-known last period problem in a repeated game setting. Following Besley and Case (1995), finance ministers with a short time horizon, e.g., ministers close to retirement may not be as effective as younger finance ministers.

Hypothesis 4.2 *The closer finance ministers are to retirement, the greater the deficit will be.*

Moreover, the gender of the finance minister might affect the deficit as well. Several studies in behavioral economics find women to be more risk averse than men.[7] However, other studies focusing on managers and business professionals could not find differences in financial risk preferences between men and women, once the financial and managerial knowledge is taken into account (Johnson and Powell, 1994; Atkinson, Baird, and Frye, 2003). Given the latter results, we do not expect different deficits for female and male finance ministers.[8]

Hypothesis 4.3 *Female and male finance ministers will not differ in deficits.*

Having children can influence her attitude toward debt, too. If the finance minister has children one might assume that intergenerational equity is more important for her than otherwise. Due to an increased awareness of the implication of high public debt for future generations and of the importance of fiscal sustainability finance ministers with children should realize lower deficits (Barro, 1974).

Hypothesis 4.4 *Finance ministers with children will have lower deficits than others.*

4.3.2 Ability of the finance minister

Jochimsen and Nuscheler (2011) are the first to define the 'strengths' of the finance minister in the context of an empirical study. They consider the finance minster to be in a strong position if she belongs to the party of the prime minister. This definition

7 Eckel and Grossman (2008) and Croson and Gneezy (2009) offer two reviews of the economic literature on gender differences in risk preferences.

8 However, an alternative reason is that women and men may differ in their abilities to lead. Sociologists have explained this underrepresentation of women in top-level positions with double standards for women and men (Foschi, 2000) and higher barriers for women to be appointed for a leadership position, like the finance minister in our case (Lyness and Heilman, 2006). Reskin and Bielby (2005) review the literature on the underlying social differentiation process. If a woman must be 'twice as good as a man' in order to be appointed to a leadership position – like the finance minister – then women may be more effective leaders and superior performers compared to their male colleagues (Eagly, Karau, and Makhijani, 1995). Therefore, female ministers of finance may be stronger than their male colleagues.

fits well to Hallerberg and Hagen (1999), who put forward that the finance minster can only set up the budget according to her and the taxpayers' preferences if she is supported by the prime minister. This backing is more likely to come if both the prime minister and the finance minister have the same party affiliation because then they will probably have more political views in common.

Hypothesis 4.5 *If the finance minister and the prime minister belong to the same party in a coalition government the finance minster will be stronger and, therefore, the deficit will be lower than otherwise.*

Feld and Schaltegger (2010) regard finance ministers with a greater tenure as an indicator of government stability and argue that longer-tenured ministers of finance enjoy more authority and a politically powerful position toward the legislative, interest groups, and the other members of the cabinet, namely the spending ministers. Also Lott and Reed (1989) say that political markets sort out poorly performing politicians over time.

Hypothesis 4.6 *The longer the tenure of the finance minister the stronger her position is in the cabinet and the lower the deficit will be.*

It is a difficult task to measure the quality of politicians since there is not a single unquestionable indicator for politician quality. We will follow the related literature (e.g. Dreher et al., 2009; Göhlmann and Vaubel, 2007; Hau and Thum, 2009) and draw upon the human capital of politicians, which they acquired during their education and previous employment, in order to measure their competence. One could expect that trained economists and business people are more successful in convincing their cabinet colleagues of sound budgets with low deficits.

Hypothesis 4.7 *An education in economics or business and professional work experience in the finance sector will strengthen the finance minister and, consequently, lower budget deficits.*

Having deducted hypotheses on the impact of the finance minister's individual characteristics on public deficits, we regard it as necessary to discuss the potential issue of reverse causality. The electorate might choose specific politicians as an instrument to ensure the adoption of a specific policy and in the same way parties might use candidate nomination as a signal for their commitment to specific policies (Besley, 2005).[9] Then, the selection of politicians would be endogenous. And indeed, some studies suggest that the qualification of politicians depends on the intensity of political competition.

9 Besley (2005) discusses that the election of qualified politicians will improve government quality, in general, if *ex post* control through elections is limited.

Paola and Scoppa (2011) show empirically that the qualification of local politicians in Italy increases with political competition. Galasso and Nannicini (2011) find a similar effect for the Italian parliament and furthermore show that politicians from opposing political coalitions – with different qualification levels on average – converge to high levels of qualification in highly contested electoral districts. Besley (2005) discusses the self-selection of politicians as another source of endogeneity when he suggests that high opportunity costs make it unlikely that business people engage in politics in developed societies with a booming private sector. Gehlbach, Sonin, and Zhuravskaya (2010) have an even more pessimistic view. They take 'businessman candidacy' as an indicator for weak institutions and as a means to avoid the cost of lobbying in immature democracies.

Looking at heads of governments Dreher et al. (2009) illustrate that the education and profession of selected politicians do not depend on the state of the economy. Accordingly, we do not regard reverse causality as a major issue here given the usual restrictions in the complex process of cabinet formation in the German states. The appointment of the finance minister and other cabinet members in the German states follows a differentiated pattern. First, the number of potential candidates will usually be limited and will not cover the entire set of educational attainments and professional backgrounds. Second, the prime minister has to present a well-diversified and balanced cabinet to ensure the representation of all relevant groups, for example, varying regions, conflicting party wings, and different genders. Therefore, it is very unlikely that the education or the professional experience of the candidates will be the pivotal point in the selection process.

4.3.3 Traditional theories on budget deficits as control variables

Following Downs (1957), the aim of an incumbent politician is to remain in office. In this case the objectives of all politicians become identical and party ideology does not matter any more. The resulting opportunistic behavior might cause political business cycles. Alesina, Perotti, and Tavares (1998), Persson and Tabellini (1999), Rogoff and Sibert (1988) and Rogoff (1990) discuss such political business cycles for fiscal policy. If there is a political business cycle in the German states, deficits in pre-election or election years should differ significantly from those in all other years.[10]

Furthermore, weak governments might cause high deficits. According to Hagen and Harden (1995), fragmentation of government can be taken as an indicator for weakness. Government fragmentation increases with the number of coalition partners or with the overall number of ministers within a cabinet. Following the seminal contributions of Roubini and Sachs (1989a,b), several empirical studies show that more

10 Freier (2011) finds evidence for electoral advantages of incumbent parties at the local level in Germany.

fragmented governments are associated with higher government expenditures and larger deficits.[11]

4.4 Empirical analysis

4.4.1 Model specification

In our analysis, we consider the deficit of the German states in real terms per capita as the most appropriate indicator of the finance minister's strength. In the empirical public finance literature it is well established that in order to ensure stationary panels, the variable of interest, here the public deficit, must be transformed. Three concepts are principally used: First, growth rates; second, normalizing to a ratio of gdp; or, third, normalizing to per capita values. We follow the latter and deflate the deficit data and normalize it with the state population for mainly three reasons. First, by using the deficit data we avoid comparing apples and oranges given the large differences of indebtedness between German states. Taking the debt level or its growth rate implicitly relates the performance of the finance minister to her predecessors within a state.[12] Second, an interpretation of the deficit to gdp ratio might be misleading for the German states. The regional gdp differs largely between states and over time, but it has only limited impact on regional revenues as the equalization scheme levels out per capita tax revenue differences between the states. Whereas business cycle-related expenditures, like unemployment benefits, are not borne by the states (for a discussion of the expenditure structure of the states see Seitz, 2008). It is not the state level, but the local level that benefits from increases in regional gdp because local tax revenue remains to a far higher degree in the region than that of the state. Third, the equalization scheme allocates revenues to the states on a per capita basis and, therefore, the per

11 For example, the case of coalition governments is considered by Haan, Sturm, and Beekhuis (1999), the case of large cabinets by Wehner (2010) while Volkerink and Haan (2001), Perotti and Kontopoulos (2002) and Schaltegger and Feld (2009) cover both aspects. Ashworth, Geys, and Heyndels (2005) and Wehner (2010) present extensive surveys of the empirical contributions on the common pool problem arising of political fragmentation. Persson and Tabellini (1999, chapter 6) offer an extensive survey of the literature on fragmentation over time and fragmented (coalition) governments as sources of political instability.

12 To illustrate this, compare two states with different levels of debt and assume both finance ministers to be equally strong and to realize the same deficit in absolute terms. Looking at the debt level or its growth rate, the finance minister of the more indebted state faces a lower relative number or growth rate and thereby appears stronger than the minister of the less indebted state. Whereas for two states with the same growth rates of debt, the finance minister of the less indebted state appears to perform better as the absolute deficit is lower.

capita normalization is most appropriate for state finances in Germany. After having examined its stationarity, the real deficit per capita is our variable of interest.[13]

The deficit in one period is not only influenced by current developments, but by past deficits, too. Therefore, we use a dynamic model in which we include the first lag of the dependent variable. Compared with other model specifications like a finite distributed lag or a model with an autoregressive error term, this specification assumes a geometrically declining influence of both the influencing factors and error terms of the past.[14]

Our dynamic model takes the following form:

$$\text{deficit}_{i,t} = \gamma \text{deficit}_{i,t-1} + p'_{i,t}\beta_1 + a'_{i,t}\beta_2 + c'_{i,t}\beta_3 + \text{time}'_t\beta_4 + \mu_i + \varepsilon_{i,t} \qquad (4.1)$$

in which $\text{deficit}_{i,t}$ represents the real per capita public deficit in state $i = 1,\ldots,N$ at time $t = 1,\ldots,T$ and $deficit_{i,t-1}$ its first lag. The vectors $p_{i,t}$ and $a_{i,t}$ comprise all variables referring to the preference and the ability of the finance minister. The economic and political control variables are summarized in vector $c_{i,t}$. The vectors are described in detail later on. We capture nationwide time fixed effects with the vector $time_t$. Finally, μ_i represents time-invariant state fixed effects. With respect to the error term we assume $\varepsilon_{i,t}$ to be normally distributed and

$$E(\varepsilon_{i,t}\varepsilon_{j,s}) = 0 \quad \text{for } i \neq j \text{ or } t \neq s \qquad (4.2)$$

$$E(\mu_i\varepsilon_{j,s}) = 0 \quad \text{for } \forall i, j \text{ and } s \qquad (4.3)$$

$$E((p'_{i,t}a'_{i,t}c'_{i,t}\text{time}'_t)\varepsilon_{j,s}) = 0 \quad \text{for } \forall i, j, s \text{ and } t \qquad (4.4)$$

4.4.2 Description of the data set

We compiled a unique data set comprising yearly data on political decision makers and public deficits for the 10 West German states. Given the observation period from 1960 to 2009 and one missing value for Saarland in 1960, we obtain an unbalanced

13 In accordance with our data set (large T and small N), we use the Fisher-type unit-root test with the inverse Chi-square test statistic proposed by Choi (2001). We could reject the null hypothesis that all states have a unit root in real per capita deficit for both specifications of this test, either based on augmented Dickey-Fuller (ADF) or Phillips-Perron (PP) unit-root tests. However, we had also to reject the null hypothesis of the Hadri LM test that the entire panel is stationary. Applying ADF tests for the 10 states separately, we identify the city state Bremen and the Saarland to have a unit root. This result is not surprising at all, since these states experienced severe deficits until they received additional fiscal transfers from the federal government between 1994 and 2004. During this bailout time, both states enjoyed a budget surplus and could reduce their debt level. However, at the end of the temporary transfers both states again had the highest per capita deficits. Thus, our test results probably arise from the bailout. As the time series of the remaining states are stationary, we use the real deficit per capita as our dependent variable and control for the bailout period.

14 For a detailed discussion of different models see Beck and Katz (2011).

panel with 499 observations in levels and 489 observations in differences. We use data on credit market debt of the German states (within their core budget) and regional gross domestic product published by the German Federal Statistical Office. Deficits are calculated as debt changes. Both are deflated and normalized to real per capita terms using the consumer price index and regional population data (also published by the German Federal Statistical Office). Interest rate (discount rate) data is taken from Deutsche Bundesbank.

Furthermore, the data set captures the individual characteristics of all 110 finance ministers for the 10 West German states during the period under consideration. We compiled socio-demographic information of the finance ministers and their educational and occupational background based on the Munzinger biographical database (*Internationales Biographisches Archiv*) and other publicly available information (e.g., personal websites of politicians, government, and parliament websites). Table 4.1 presents an overview. The State Chancelleries provided data on government (coalitions) and cabinet structure as well as election dates.

We took February 1st as the cut-off date. Thus, the annual individual characteristics in our data set refer to the finance minister (or cabinet) in office on this day of the respective year. We chose this cut-off date as several states held regular elections in the last months of the year and the newly formed government quite often comes into office in January. This cut-off date allows us to consider the finance minister in office during the entire budgetary year and not the one who – by chance – stayed in office only until the end of January.[15]

Data description: The finance ministers' budgetary preference

The 110 finance ministers have a rather heterogeneous socio-demographic background. On average, they were appointed at the age of 51 while the earliest appointment was at the age of 34, the latest at 67. On average the finance ministers had 2.5 children; one finance minister had 11 children. However, they were predominantly male with only seven female finance ministers, who collectively served for around 24 years and account for 5 % of our observations.[16] Furthermore, we take into account the political orientation of the finance ministers with the dummy variable (left). It takes the value of one for 58 finance ministers who belong either to the Social Democratic Party or the Green Party.[17]

---

15 We challenge our results with respect to alternative cut-off dates in the robustness section (Table 4.5).

16 Generally, ministers in German state governments are predominantly male. The few female ministers usually head 'softer' ministries responsible for education, social or family policy (McKay, 2004).

17 For a finance minister belonging to the Left Party, the dummy variable (left) would also take the value of one. However, the first finance minister belonging to the Left Party came into office in November 2009 and is not included in our data set as we restrict our analysis to the West German states between 1960 and 2009.

Data description: The finance ministers' ability

We follow Jochimsen and Nuscheler (2011) and include a dummy variable for years when the finance minister in a coalition government has strong ties with the prime minister as they both belong to the same party (backing). This situation occurs in almost 40 % of our observations. Turning to the tenure of the finance ministers, we observe an average tenure of 3.5 years. While some ministers served only a few months, the finance minister with the longest tenure served for more than 16 consecutive years.

In our sample, all 110 finance ministers either passed the final secondary-education exam (the German 'Abitur') or a vocational training (apprenticeship). Three-quarters of the ministers (83) earned a university degree (edu_uni) and, out of those, 41 added a PhD (31 %, edu_phd). We use the remaining 27 ministers without a tertiary education as reference category. Most ministers who graduated from university studied law, namely 42 (law), 29 studied business or economics (economics), nine humanities or other social sciences (humanities) and four science or medicine (science).[18]

Moreover, we coded the ministers' work experience in different sectors prior to their appointment. Like the fields of study, the formed groups are not mutually exclusive.[19] Not surprisingly, a majority of 88 out of 110 ministers were members of parliament (mp) prior to their appointment (in either the state parliament, the federal parliament or the parliament of the European Union). The second largest group with 68 ministers worked in the public sector (public), thereof 60 in general public service (public_other) and 15 in the field of public finances, e.g., tax authorities or treasury (public_finance). A total of 47 ministers gained professional experience in the business sector (business), thereof 15 in the financial sector (business_finance) and 38 in other business sectors (business_other). In total, 40 finance ministers previously served as a spending minister (spending_minister). Eleven ministers worked in academia (academia), thereof six worked in economic or business research institutes or university departments. There are 15 ministers with other previous professional experience such as journalists, lawyers or party officers (others). Taking the finance-related subsectors of academia, the business and public sector altogether, a total of 30 ministers gained financial expertise

18 Note that one minister studied multiple subjects. As we coded all subjects, simply counting the numbers of graduates by subject would give a wrong number of 84 university graduates instead of the correct 83.

19 In their related work on members of central banks' monetary policy committees Göhlmann and Vaubel (2007) and Farvaque, Hammadou, and Stanek (2009, 2011) only consider the dominant professional experience, i.e., the longest experience. We do not follow this approach and instead use all available information to fully capture the professional career prior to their appointment. Thus, the dummy variables covering the sectors mentioned above will assume the value of one if a finance minister has any experience in the respective sector. Therefore, these dummy variables are not mutually exclusive and for a minister who gained experience in three sectors, for example, the sum of these variables will be three compared to one following the approach of Göhlmann and Vaubel (2007) and Farvaque, Hammadou, and Stanek (2009, 2011).

(finance_expertise).[20] We suppose that all the experiences that the finance ministers had over the course of their professional career are relevant for later performance.

Data description: Economic and political control variables

We control for the state of the economy by including the growth rate of regional gross domestic product in real terms per capita (gdp).[21] As the deficit may depend on the cost of borrowing, we also include the nationwide real interest rate (interest) in those specifications without time fixed effects. At first glance, it may be plausible to include the level of state indebtedness as well. We refrain, however, from including any lagged debt level as this basically equals the cumulated past deficits. Recall that we already estimate a dynamic model by including the first lagged deficit.

Even though we have normalized both public deficit and gdp to per capita values, we include the regional population (population) as a control variable, since the size of population varies significantly over the respective time period within single states. In particular, we expect states with a declining population to face increasing per capita expenditures and therefore higher borrowing because the maintenance of the existing public infrastructure becomes more expensive relative to the size of the population for them. As previously mentioned tax revenue per capita is due to the fiscal equalization scheme given. Consequently, additional expenditures caused by a shrinking population have to be financed via additional debt. This is reflected in our dependent variable deficit per capita. Therefore, population size is necessary to explain this variable. Furthermore, we acknowledge the financial support that Bremen and the Saarland received from the federal government with a time dummy (bailout) for both states during the respective years.

Additionally, we control for two effects described in the traditional political economy literature. First of all, we control for years with elections in the respective states (election).[22] Furthermore, we account for government fragmentation by including the probability that two randomly drawn ministers belong to different parties (fraction) as it is used, for example, in the well-established World Bank Database on Political Institutions. In pure single-party governments this variable takes the value of zero while higher values indicate more fragmented governments in which ministers belong to different parties. Table 4.1 presents the descriptive statistics of the control variables. Definitions and sources of all variables can be found in Table 4.7 in the appendix.

20 The variable finance_expertise is a summary variable taking the value of one if a minister gained financial expertise in one or more of the following sectors: academia, the business or public sector.

21 We do not control for employment or unemployment levels due to the fact that labor market-related expenditures are mainly born by the social security system and the local level.

22 The election dummy variable is based on the same cut-off date that we use to identify the relevant finance minister for a respective year. However, for the coding of the election dummies it should not matter whether we use the January 1st, February 1st or March 1st. Out of 122 state elections in our sample only five took place in January and eight in February.

Table 4.1: Descriptive statistics

	Obs.	Mean	Std. Dev.	Min	Max	No. of ministers
deficit	499	167.996	263.213	−852.894	1,552.622	–
		The finance ministers' budgetary preference				
left	499	0.429	0.495	0	1	58
age	499	54.467	6.412	34.717	70.617	–
agesq	499	3,007.712	705.185	1,205.279	4,986.810	–
female	499	0.046	0.210	0	1	7
kids	499	0.768	0.423	0	1	87
kids_n	499	2.465	2.146	0	11	–
		The finance ministers' ability				
backing	499	0.391	0.488	0	1	–
tenure	499	3.491	2.882	0.015	16.653	–
tenuresq	499	20.471	32.735	0.000	277.321	–
edu_uni	499	0.401	0.491	0	1	42
edu_phd	499	0.315	0.465	0	1	41
economics	499	0.253	0.435	0	1	29
law	499	0.381	0.486	0	1	42
humanities	499	0.076	0.266	0	1	9
science	499	0.030	0.171	0	1	4
finance_expertise	499	0.255	0.436	0	1	30
academia	499	0.078	0.269	0	1	11
academia_finance	499	0.042	0.201	0	1	6
academia_other	499	0.036	0.187	0	1	5
business	499	0.431	0.496	0	1	47
business_finance	499	0.116	0.321	0	1	15
business_other	499	0.375	0.485	0	1	38
mp	499	0.796	0.404	0	1	88
spending_minister	499	0.379	0.486	0	1	40
public	499	0.631	0.483	0	1	68
public_finance	499	0.142	0.350	0	1	15
public_other	499	0.551	0.498	0	1	60
other	499	0.146	0.354	0	1	15
		Economic and political control variables				
gdp	499	2.240	3.243	−6.717	13.556	–
interest	499	1.213	1.345	−2.069	3.922	–
population	499	6.107	5.085	0.654	18.080	–
bailout	499	0.044	0.205	0	1	–
election	499	0.240	0.428	0	1	–
fraction	499	0.245	0.218	0	0.778	–

Note: All information refers to February 1st of the respective year, i.e., the cabinet or the finance ministers in office on February 1st. Table 4.7 in the appendix provides a detailed description of variables and data sources.

4.4.3 Estimation methods

Given our state-specific effects μ_i and the inclusion of a lagged dependent variable (LDV) in the regression, the Ordinary Least Squares (OLS) estimator is inconsistent. Specific panel-data estimators like the Fixed Effects (FE or Least Square Dummy Variable (LSDV)), and the Random Effects (RE or Generalized Least Square (GLS)) estimator wipe out the unobserved time-invariant heterogeneity and thereby solve the omitted variable bias. However, they do not eliminate the LDV being correlated with the transformed error term (cf. Baltagi, 2008, ch. 8). According to Nickell (1981), the LSDV estimator is unbiased only as T approaches infinity and generates severely biased coefficients for finite T, i.e., in short panels. He shows that $\hat{\gamma}$ is downward biased for $\gamma > 0$ and the other coefficient estimates are upward biased if they are positively correlated with the LDV or vice-versa.[23]

Given our relatively long ($T = 50$), but small ($N = 10$) panel data set, one may argue that the bias of the LSDV estimator induced by the LDV is negligible.[24] However, given the low number of 499 observations, we regard it as necessary to examine alternative estimation methods. Two general procedures are used to resolve the Nickell bias either by using instruments to obtain unbiased estimates or by directly correcting for it (cf. Baltagi, 2008, ch. 8).

Following the first approach, the equation (4.1) is transformed to eliminate the time-invariant effects, e.g., Anderson and Hsiao (1981, 1982, AH estimator) and Arellano and Bond (1991, AB estimator) propose using first-differences. Then instruments are used for the transformed LDV in order to eliminate the correlation with the transformed error term. Anderson and Hsiao (1981, 1982), for example, use further lags of the difference of the dependent variable $\Delta d_{i,t-2} = d_{i,t-2} - d_{i,t-3}$ or of its level $d_{i,t-2}$ as instruments for $\Delta d_{i,t-1} = d_{i,t-1} - d_{i,t-2}$. Whereas Arellano and Bond (1991) argue that there are more instruments available and propose a generalized method of moments (GMM) procedure. As the AB estimator exploits all valid lags of the dependent variable as instruments, it is more efficient than AH. Blundell and Bond (1998, BB estimator) suggest using first-differenced instruments in the untransformed equation and instruments in levels for the first-differenced equation. However, the estimators discussed so far are well suited for large samples, but have poor finite sample properties and would generate biased estimates for small samples.

---

23 Nickell (1981) derives the approximation for the bias of $\hat{\gamma}$ for reasonably large values of T and in the absence of exogenous regressors as $plim_{N\to\infty}(\hat{\gamma}-\gamma) \approx \frac{-(1+\gamma)}{T-1}$. The bias of $\hat{\gamma}$ stays negative and becomes larger in absolute terms when exogenous regressors are included, but still approaches zero as T becomes sufficiently large.

24 And in fact using the approximation of Nickell (1981), the LSDV estimate $\hat{\gamma}$ might be downward biased by around 6 % for a real $\gamma = 0.5$ in a model without any other regressors.

The second approach relies on the standard fixed-effects estimator (LSDV), but uses an approximation of its bias to obtain a bias-corrected estimator (LSDVc).[25] The simulation studies of Judson and Owen (1999), Bruno (2005a), Kiviet and Bun (2001), and Bun and Kiviet (2006) show that the LSDVc estimator generates more accurate estimates and lower standard errors than the other estimators described above – particularly with long, but small panels. Given the properties of our data set ($T = 50$ and $N = 10$), we employ the LSDVc estimator for our analysis.

The correction procedure of the LSDVc estimator requires an initial consistent estimate of the coefficients, which can be obtained using one of the mentioned AB, AH, or BB estimators. We use the AB estimator as it is more efficient than AH (cf. Arellano and Bond, 1991) and appears to be more robust than BB (cf. Bruno, 2005a). In accordance with the results of Bruno (2005a) and Bun and Kiviet (2003, 2006), we base the bias correction on the bias approximation in powers of $T^{-2}N^{-1}$. The simulation study of Kiviet and Bun (2001) demonstrates that the bootstrap procedure for the estimation of the variance-covariance matrix of the LSDVc estimator often outperforms the analytical variance estimator. We follow their suggestion and apply the bootstrap procedure for the standard errors with 200 repetitions.

Furthermore, we use the Arellano-Bond test on first-order autocorrelation of the residuals for all our regressions and – as expected – cannot reject the null hypothesis. However, there is no second-order autocorrelation in the residuals. We can clearly reject the null hypothesis of the Sargan test of over-identifying restrictions.

4.4.4 Estimation results

Table 4.2, 4.3, and 4.4 illustrate the regression results. Before we turn to our hypotheses regarding the preferences and abilities of the finance minister, we briefly cover the base model shown in the first column of Table 4.2. Our base model includes the economic and political control variables only. The results indicate a rather strong path dependency of the deficit. The estimated coefficient of the lagged deficit is positive, larger than 0.5, and highly significant. The coefficient of gdp growth has a negative sign and is insignificant. This supports our argument against the deficit to gdp ratio as a dependent variable since state deficits and the regional gdp growth are only weakly related. Although an increase in regional gdp triggers higher regional tax revenue these regional tax gains are almost completely skimmed off by the fiscal equalization scheme. Furthermore, only a few business cycles-related expenditures are at the state level. The coefficient of the regional population has a negative sign and is highly significant. During the federal government bailout for Bremen and the Saarland, both states

25 Kiviet (1995) derives such an estimator by refining the bias approximation of Nickell (1981) in powers of T^{-1}. Bias approximations in powers of $(TN)^{-1}$ and $T^{-2}N^{-1}$ are suggested by Kiviet (1995, 1999). Simulation studies have shown that the bias approximation in powers of T^{-1} already accounts for more than 90 % of the bias in balanced (Bun and Kiviet, 2003, 2006) and unbalanced panels (Bruno, 2005a).

significantly reduced their annual deficits by roughly 250 Euro per inhabitant (bailout). Our base model does not provide evidence for the traditional political economy theories on political business cycles and weak governments. While the variable election has the expected positive sign, the variable fraction has an unexpected negative sign which, however, turns positive in the following estimation models. However, deficits are not significantly different in election years or when more fragmented governments are in office.

Budgetary preferences of the finance minister

The first part of our investigation addresses the preferences of the finance ministers. As a first step, we include her ideological leaning in model 2 in Table 4.2. Finance ministers belonging to the Social Democratic Party or the Green Party (left) do not exhibit significantly higher deficits. Thus, we reject hypothesis 4.1 on partisan behavior. This is consistent with the results of related studies on public finances in the German states that could not find partisan effects either for overall spending or for deficit (e.g., Seitz,

Table 4.2: Results for preference characteristics

	Dependent variable: deficit (real deficit per capita)					
	(1)	(2)	(3)	(4)	(5)	(6)
L.deficit	0.576***	0.577***	0.573***	0.574***	0.577***	0.576***
	(0.045)	(0.046)	(0.046)	(0.046)	(0.046)	(0.046)
gdp	−0.934	−0.903	−0.324	−0.470	−0.493	−0.539
	(5.540)	(5.556)	(5.541)	(5.543)	(5.565)	(5.581)
population	−61.377***	−60.839***	−73.904***	−71.606***	−73.189***	−74.172***
	(22.249)	(22.220)	(24.367)	(24.602)	(24.984)	(24.781)
bailout	−248.444***	−247.097***	−258.328***	−262.565***	−262.632***	−263.260***
	(47.294)	(47.231)	(46.811)	(47.287)	(47.611)	(47.379)
election	17.482	17.492	17.380	18.094	17.890	18.124
	(17.293)	(17.305)	(17.283)	(17.363)	(17.400)	(17.376)
fraction	−2.587	−1.790	4.902	4.605	8.524	7.141
	(40.323)	(41.757)	(42.100)	(42.142)	(43.678)	(42.531)
left		2.077	−1.531	−3.413	−4.054	−6.343
		(19.690)	(19.903)	(19.980)	(19.984)	(20.667)
age			−18.014	−15.292	−16.217	−15.591
			(19.539)	(19.266)	(19.514)	(19.472)
agesq			0.180	0.157	0.165	0.160
			(0.179)	(0.176)	(0.178)	(0.178)
female				31.324	30.004	30.250
				(37.108)	(37.678)	(37.318)
kids					−8.509	
					(21.378)	
kids_n						−2.140
						(4.093)
Observations	489	489	489	489	489	489
Number of states	10	10	10	10	10	10

Notes: The LSDVc estimator was applied with an initial Arellano-Bond estimate and 200 bootstrap repetitions. The estimates include both time fixed effects and state fixed effects that are not shown here. *** indicates significance at 1 % level, ** at 5 % level and * at 10 % level respectively. Standard errors are reported in parentheses.

Table 4.3: Results for ability including education

	Dependent variable: deficit (real deficit per capita)				
	(7)	(8)	(9)	(10)	(11)
L.deficit	0.570***	0.560***	0.558***	0.562***	0.565***
	(0.046)	(0.046)	(0.047)	(0.046)	(0.046)
gdp	−0.264	−0.666	−0.951	−0.665	−0.281
	(5.626)	(5.589)	(5.681)	(5.595)	(5.617)
population	−56.238**	−52.831**	−53.041**	−53.143**	−54.533**
	(22.450)	(22.547)	(22.541)	(22.724)	(23.226)
bailout	−258.788***	−265.379***	−270.900***	−264.890***	−266.687***
	(48.069)	(48.257)	(48.781)	(48.532)	(48.673)
election	17.345	14.908	14.260	14.962	15.362
	(17.289)	(17.439)	(17.434)	(17.457)	(17.454)
fraction	50.564	58.310	62.082	58.754	52.212
	(57.566)	(57.458)	(57.608)	(57.592)	(56.949)
left	11.346	15.086	14.239	14.816	10.963
	(20.997)	(21.379)	(21.411)	(21.439)	(21.690)
backing	−33.645	−35.895	−39.307*	−36.256	−34.404
	(21.937)	(22.053)	(22.263)	(22.213)	(21.951)
tenure		10.856	9.763	10.843	10.412
		(7.494)	(7.466)	(7.503)	(7.510)
tenuresq		−1.181*	−1.135*	−1.176*	−1.148*
		(0.649)	(0.646)	(0.648)	(0.650)
edu_uni			−8.438		
			(19.603)		
edu_phd			−28.418		
			(21.661)		
economics				3.030	−3.329
				(20.281)	(23.144)
law					−6.900
					(19.160)
humanities					−5.901
					(35.623)
science					−49.172
					(48.369)
Observations	489	489	489	489	489
Number of states	10	10	10	10	10

Notes: The LSDVc estimator was applied with an initial Arellano-Bond estimate and 200 bootstrap repetitions. The estimates include both time fixed effects and state fixed effects that are not shown here. *** indicates significance at 1 % level, ** at 5 % level and * at 10 % level respectively. Standard errors are reported in parentheses.

2000; Galli and Rossi, 2002; Jochimsen and Nuscheler, 2011). Instead of changing the borrowing patterns, state governments in Germany change the budget composition according to their ideological priorities (e.g., Schneider, 2010; Potrafke, 2011b).[26]

26 For the OECD countries, Potrafke (2011a) shows that government ideology hardly influences the budget composition on the expenditure side. However, Angelopoulos, Economides, and Kammas (2012) find significant effects on tax policies.

Table 4.4: Results for ability including professional background

	Dependent variable: deficit (real deficit per capita)				
	(12)	(13)	(14)	(15)	(16)
L.deficit	0.546***	0.559***	0.506***	0.521***	0.522***
	(0.046)	(0.046)	(0.048)	(0.047)	(0.047)
gdp	−1.408	0.626	0.853	−0.155	−0.515
	(5.551)	(5.651)	(5.583)	(5.577)	(5.503)
left	21.076	15.716	10.824	15.381	12.723
	(21.368)	(22.440)	(22.811)	(21.916)	(21.762)
backing	−35.819	−42.939*	−45.940**	−49.172**	−48.217**
	(22.000)	(22.701)	(22.674)	(22.175)	(21.970)
tenure	11.266	10.973	9.220	9.896	10.140
	(7.470)	(7.500)	(7.507)	(7.409)	(7.383)
tenuresq	−1.217*	−1.324**	−1.287*	−1.335**	−1.269**
	(0.647)	(0.657)	(0.659)	(0.649)	(0.644)
finance_expertise	−35.681**			−62.764***	−51.911***
	(17.933)			(20.748)	(19.390)
academia		−38.884			
		(33.529)			
academia_finance			−20.722		
			(44.367)		
academia_other			−9.932	−25.648	
			(43.805)	(42.948)	
business		1.860			
		(18.886)			
business_finance			−85.477***		
			(28.368)		
business_other			37.655**	33.266*	38.040**
			(18.253)	(18.201)	(16.885)
mp		−36.777	−64.928**	−65.052**	−62.900**
		(24.709)	(27.034)	(26.526)	(26.339)
spending_minister		−14.882	−24.314	−24.928	
		(18.541)	(18.553)	(18.468)	
public		−17.318			
		(19.372)			
public_finance			−18.730		
			(26.534)		
public_other			−11.049	−9.524	
			(18.246)	(18.275)	
other		−1.562	5.372	14.160	
		(26.255)	(24.841)	(24.858)	
Observations	489	489	489	489	489
Number of states	10	10	10	10	10

Notes: The LSDVc estimator was applied with an initial Arellano-Bond estimate and 200 bootstrap repetitions. The estimates include both time fixed effects and state fixed effects that are not shown here. Furthermore the variables population, bailout, election, and fraction are included but not shown for the sake of readability of the table. The estimates do not differ qualitatively from those in models 7 to 11 in the previous table. *** indicates significance at 1 % level, ** at 5 % level and * at 10 % level respectively. Standard errors are reported in parentheses.

Furthermore, we find no supporting evidence for our second hypothesis on the 'lame duck' effect either. We choose the age of the finance minister as an indicator for closeness to retirement. It is not significant in model 3 for neither the linear nor the quadratic term (age, agesq). This is well in line with the results of Dalle Nogare and Ricciuti (2011) who do not find evidence for higher or lower deficits when the head of government faces a term limit. Turning to gender and parenthood of the finance minister in models 4 to 6, one can see that these characteristics clearly do not affect public deficit. Female ministers do not incur significantly higher or lower deficits than their male colleagues and we cannot reject our hypothesis 4.3. Furthermore, we find no evidence that finance ministers with children incur significantly lower deficits than ministers without. Also, the number of children has no statistically significant effect on public deficits (hypothesis 4.4). These results do not necessarily imply that female finance ministers or finance ministers with children set the same priorities in specific policy areas as male finance ministers (as reported for the local level by Chattopadhyay and Duflo, 2004; Svaleryd, 2009) or those without children. Potential policy differences might cancel one another out or be limited in size and, therefore, might leave public deficits unaffected.

Our empirical examination above does not provide supporting evidence that any of the individual characteristics related to the finance ministers' preferences matters for the deficit.

Ability of the finance minister

The second part of our analysis focuses on individual characteristics related to the ability of the finance minister. To test our hypothesis 4.5, we include the variable backing that captures whether the finance minister in a coalition government belongs to the prime minister's party in the following models (models 7 to 16 in Tables 4.3 and 4.4). It always has the expected negative sign. Significance increases to the 5 % level with the inclusion of further ability related variables. Looking at the finance ministers' experience gained in office in model 8, we find longer-tenured finance ministers to issue significantly less new debt than the newly appointed. The linear term tenure has a positive sign, but is not significant while the quadratic term tenuresq is negative and significant.[27] In accordance with Feld and Schaltegger (2010), we cannot reject our sixth hypothesis. Newly appointed ministers need some time to build up experience and to use their authority within the cabinet to lower the deficit.

We now turn to the educational background of the finance ministers to test hypothesis 4.7. The regression models 9 to 11 indicate that their educational background does not affect public deficits. All educational variables are statistically insignificant –

27 Given the coefficients of the linear and the quadratic effect in model 8, we observe a turning point for tenure around 4.5 years. Ministers with a higher tenure incur significantly lower deficits.

both with respect to the highest educational level attained (model 9) and the field of studies (models 10 and 11). We also find no joint significance of these variables.

The remainder of our analysis addresses the professional experience of the finance minister. Results are shown in Table 4.4. As we are especially interested in the overall financial expertise gained by the finance minister prior to her appointment, we start with the summary variable finance_expertise in model 12. Recall that this variable captures all finance-related work experience in either the financial business sector, public finances or as professors in business or economics. As expected, the variable has a negative sign and is highly significant, indicating that finance ministers with financial expertise can realize lower deficits. In model 13, we consider the six main categories covering the previous profession of the finance minister: academia, business, mp (members of parliament), spending_minister, public, other. Unexpectedly, none of the categories is significant at the 10 % level.

To gain further insights, we decompose the professional categories academia, business, and public each into a finance-related and a not finance-related subcategory. Then, model 14 demonstrates that finance ministers with working experience in the financial business sector (business_finance) can reduce the public deficit (at the 1 % significance level). However, working experience in the non-finance business sector (business_other) increases public deficits significantly. While previous expertise as spending_minister does not affect deficits, former members of parliament (mp) also incur significantly lower deficits. All other subcategories are insignificant. The results remain unchanged when we include the summary variable finance_expertise instead of the finance-related subcategories in model 15.[28] In the final model 16, we dropped the insignificant professional categories and our main results remain.

As discussed in section 4.3.2, we do not regard reverse causality as a major issue with respect to the ability of the finance minister and the state of public finances. Since we cannot completely rule out a reverse relation, our results may be biased as the error term of the regression would then be correlated with the explanatory variable such as finance expertise. However, the effects of the finance ministers' financial expertise and their tenure as our main results are robust when we employ a GMM estimator, such as Arellano Bond, that also uses the first lags of these predetermined variables as instruments (see Section 4.4.5).

Overall, we find no evidence that the preference-related characteristics of the finance minister, i.e., ideological leaning, age, gender, or parenthood, affect the deficit. Furthermore, our results demonstrate that the ability of the finance minister to ensure sound budgeting does not depend on her educational attainment or her field of studies. However, we find that professional experience in the financial field prior to her appointment significantly reduces state deficits. Our findings are in line with results

28 An additional decomposition of the category other – into its three components: journalists, lawyers, and party officers – does not yield further significant results either. Results are available upon request.

from studies in monetary and economic policy (e.g., Dreher et al., 2009; Farvaque, Hammadou, and Stanek, 2009; Hau and Thum, 2009) that show professional experience to be more influential than educational background. Our results also indicate that political experience as a former spending minister does not affect the finance minister's ability. However, she achieves lower deficits when she had previously held a position as a member of parliament. Furthermore, a finance minister can overcome the weak-government problem in a coalition government when she has the full support of the prime minister due to the same party affiliation.

4.4.5 Robustness checks

We test the robustness of our main results derived in model 16 in several ways. First of all, we test alternative cut-off dates instead of our chosen cut-off date of February 1st. We obtain similar results for the tenure/tenuresq, mp, business_other, and the finance_expertise variables for various cut-off dates during the first half of a year and also for cut-off dates during the second half of the previous year (see Table 4.5). Furthermore, we implement two alternative specifications to capture time effects. The two estimations without any time effects and with dummy variables for specific events[29], respectively, yield similar results in size and significance for the variable finance_expertise and tenuresq. The results for mp and business_other vanish. The election dummy variable becomes significant as well (see Table 4.6). Given that both specifications do not include time fixed effects, we include the variable interest that captures the nationwide level of the real interest rate.

Additionally, we control for the robustness of our results with respect to alternative estimators like pooled OLS, the fixed effects estimator (LSDV) and the Arellano-Bond estimator. Rerunning the regressions, we find that our main results are robust to these alternatives.[30] It is not surprising that the significance of the finance_expertise variable vanishes with a p-value of 13.3 % for the pooled OLS estimation since no state fixed effects are included here. However, its coefficient is rather robust and the variable tenuresq stays significant with a p-value of 7.2 %. However, the pooled OLS estimates are inconsistent due to the lagged dependent variable and the unobserved state-specific effects (see above). We use the same specifications for the fixed effects (LSDV) and the Arellano-Bond estimator as we did for the LSDVc estimator and can replicate our results with both alternative estimators for most of the specifications (see Table 4.6).

---

29 Specifically, we use time dummies for both the first and second oil crises and the financial crisis (oil1, oil2, fin_crisis), for years after the German reunification (unific) and the inclusion of the East German states in the fiscal equalization scheme (equal). We also included a time dummy for the period of the federal government's bailout for Bremen and the Saarland to control for potential indirect effects on all states (bailout_period).

30 The estimated coefficient for the lagged deficit is higher with pooled OLS and lower with the fixed effects estimator than with LSDVc as discussed above.

Table 4.5: Robustness checks for alternative cut-off dates

	Cut-off date	Alternative cut-off dates in previous year			Alternative cut-off dates in same year			
	February 1st	July 1st	September 1st	November 1st	January 1st	March 1st	May 1st	July 1st
	Dependent variable: deficit (real deficit per capita)							
L.deficit	0.522***	0.542***	0.537***	0.531***	0.529***	0.527***	0.525***	0.530***
	(0.047)	(0.047)	(0.047)	(0.047)	(0.047)	(0.047)	(0.048)	(0.047)
gdp	−0.515	−0.368	−0.638	−1.017	−0.856	−0.197	0.432	0.283
	(5.503)	(5.541)	(5.535)	(5.498)	(5.493)	(5.487)	(5.505)	(5.468)
population	−54.756**	−55.102**	−54.086**	−54.482**	−54.165**	−54.426**	−54.139**	−52.687**
	(22.513)	(22.711)	(22.716)	(22.662)	(22.553)	(22.426)	(22.767)	(22.609)
bailout	−286.289***	−267.097***	−271.605***	−267.558***	−277.585***	−283.809***	−285.238***	−282.006***
	(49.335)	(48.796)	(49.017)	(48.996)	(49.250)	(49.204)	(49.947)	(49.846)
election	16.473	−0.685	−7.092	7.354	14.014	21.828	14.750	3.116
	(17.234)	(16.742)	(16.860)	(15.703)	(16.715)	(17.258)	(18.401)	(16.902)
fraction	73.102	81.048	78.066	59.805	66.192	73.297	81.972	102.341*
	(57.279)	(56.614)	(56.633)	(56.045)	(56.421)	(57.381)	(58.135)	(61.116)
left	12.723	−0.898	2.819	10.252	12.532	11.331	16.847	28.359
	(21.762)	(21.569)	(21.475)	(21.239)	(21.565)	(21.756)	(22.197)	(22.406)
backing	−48.217**	−54.163**	−49.580**	−44.986**	−48.076**	−47.978**	−51.219**	−62.538***
	(21.970)	(22.119)	(21.775)	(21.339)	(21.504)	(21.964)	(22.903)	(22.908)
tenure	10.140	11.974*	13.318*	13.576*	10.836	11.105	9.092	4.737
	(7.383)	(7.139)	(7.086)	(7.095)	(7.375)	(7.221)	(7.243)	(7.113)
tenuresq	−1.269**	−1.309**	−1.418**	−1.496**	−1.295**	−1.270**	−1.064*	−0.747
	(0.644)	(0.659)	(0.653)	(0.651)	(0.648)	(0.636)	(0.622)	(0.687)
finance_expertise	−51.911***	−38.023**	−40.677**	−49.120**	−47.074**	−49.452**	−48.551**	−50.661***
	(19.390)	(19.365)	(19.291)	(19.516)	(19.739)	(19.234)	(19.431)	(18.671)
business_other	38.040**	35.164**	31.501*	32.807*	37.444**	36.658**	35.870**	35.014**
	(16.885)	(17.254)	(16.992)	(16.938)	(16.837)	(16.961)	(17.266)	(17.476)
mp	−62.900**	−49.228*	−49.785*	−63.626**	−59.854**	−58.353**	−60.109**	−57.377**
	(26.339)	(25.419)	(25.596)	(26.274)	(26.734)	(26.080)	(26.735)	(26.976)
Observations	489	489	489	489	489	489	489	489
Number of states	10	10	10	10	10	10	10	10

Notes: Data on the individual characteristics of the finance minister (left, backing, tenure, tenuresq, finance_expertise, business_other, and mp) refer to the minister in office on the respective cut-off day. The LSDVc estimator was applied with an initial Arellano-Bond estimate and 200 bootstrap repetitions. The estimates include both time fixed effects and state fixed effects that are not shown here. *** indicates significance at 1 % level, ** at 5 % level and * at 10 % level respectively. Standard errors are reported in parentheses.

Table 4.6: Robustness checks for alternative estimators and time specifications

	Alternative estimators and time specifications									
	LSDVc	LSDVc		Pooled OLS	Fixed effects (LSDV)			Arellano Bond		
	Time FE	no Time FE	Events	no FE	no Time FE	Time FE	Events	no Time FE	Time FE	Events
	Dependent variable: deficit (real deficit per capita)									
L.deficit	0.522***	0.598***	0.626***	0.633***	0.548***	0.476***	0.574***	0.542***	0.466***	0.569***
	(0.047)	(0.043)	(0.041)	(0.076)	(0.077)	(0.055)	(0.071)	(0.074)	(0.045)	(0.069)
gdp	−0.515	−14.674***	−12.651***	−13.445***	−14.943***	−0.559	−12.775***	−14.701***	0.090	−12.607***
	(5.503)	(2.906)	(3.108)	(2.310)	(2.813)	(5.138)	(2.957)	(2.576)	(4.332)	(2.654)
interest		−3.568	14.002*	−4.544	−3.346		14.063**	−3.275		13.935***
		(6.550)	(7.452)	(3.989)	(3.805)		(4.769)	(3.192)		(4.757)
population	−54.756**	−20.711	−30.680	−6.425*	−20.249*	−59.512**	−33.067*	−19.449	−58.848**	−34.815*
	(22.513)	(21.173)	(24.494)	(3.013)	(10.777)	(23.549)	(16.054)	(13.758)	(26.044)	(18.761)
bailout	−286.289***	−211.564***	−218.413***	−116.769*	−224.952***	−307.672***	−237.189***	−232.709***	−327.517***	−248.023***
	(49.335)	(50.012)	(53.990)	(58.817)	(55.637)	(56.308)	(59.722)	(45.145)	(39.385)	(49.607)
election	16.473	39.778**	33.870*	40.051***	38.779***	16.446**	33.195**	39.382***	16.631***	33.864***
	(17.234)	(19.396)	(18.827)	(8.628)	(8.196)	(6.765)	(10.409)	(7.599)	(5.794)	(9.707)
fraction	73.102	−3.588	20.880	53.709	−8.280	77.377	14.193	−10.922	106.938*	13.660
	(57.279)	(63.032)	(60.475)	(47.904)	(33.679)	(58.686)	(33.541)	(43.925)	(61.875)	(40.018)
left	12.723	−3.291	4.087	23.681	−1.947	14.636	5.733	−12.195	8.954	−3.703
	(21.762)	(23.130)	(23.688)	(16.164)	(16.798)	(16.230)	(13.709)	(15.524)	(14.187)	(9.842)
backing	−48.217**	−12.575	−23.402	−40.826	−11.012	−50.105	−21.154	−9.368	−64.935*	−21.294
	(21.970)	(25.100)	(24.217)	(34.500)	(25.891)	(30.431)	(22.874)	(32.742)	(33.271)	(27.297)
tenure	10.140	18.937**	15.595*	12.533	19.940*	10.765	16.654*	18.069**	8.201	14.655**
	(7.383)	(8.609)	(8.324)	(7.105)	(10.358)	(8.411)	(8.794)	(8.447)	(8.244)	(7.310)
tenuresq	−1.269**	−1.696**	−1.516**	−1.137*	−1.785*	−1.339	−1.608*	−1.582**	−1.084	−1.390**
	(0.644)	(0.746)	(0.724)	(0.578)	(0.898)	(0.789)	(0.791)	(0.732)	(0.803)	(0.660)
finance_expertise	−51.911***	−47.572**	−47.644**	−28.899	−49.675*	−53.673	−49.558*	−47.509**	−53.047	−46.633**
	(19.390)	(22.734)	(22.423)	(21.903)	(22.485)	(37.504)	(22.685)	(20.859)	(34.022)	(21.510)
business_other	38.040**	9.840	13.822	11.315	9.451	39.531*	13.000	6.962	35.517*	8.848
	(16.885)	(18.844)	(18.047)	(12.440)	(17.763)	(19.836)	(14.071)	(17.109)	(18.347)	(13.320)
mp	−62.900**	−16.949	−26.436	6.459	−14.520	−63.540	−22.306	−17.345	−64.070*	−22.607
	(26.339)	(28.135)	(28.633)	(19.721)	(22.873)	(35.297)	(19.630)	(19.892)	(32.779)	(18.287)
bailout_period			20.179				22.099			26.418
			(35.880)				(30.885)			(28.749)
oil1			182.448***				181.406***			181.693***
			(46.573)				(46.705)			(45.063)
oil2			48.665				48.454			46.909*
			(33.263)				(29.906)			(28.351)
fin_crisis			101.931*				102.190**			99.747***
			(54.423)				(38.055)			(35.493)
unific			−86.491**				−90.846**			−88.009***
			(37.028)				(31.443)			(27.375)
equal			110.460**				117.384			114.313
			(42.908)				(76.627)			(71.453)
fedelection			66.102***				65.779***			67.104***
			(17.482)				(10.970)			(10.505)
euelection			−18.515				−16.486			−16.593
			(26.768)				(39.165)			(35.673)
constant				108.444**	238.193**	519.494***	259.962**	243.447***	429.480***	278.154***
				(39.484)	(80.704)	(109.633)	(95.338)	(92.657)	(153.927)	(101.667)
Observations	489	489	489	489	489	489	489	479	479	479
Number of states	10	10	10	(10)	10	10	10	10	10	10
R-squared				0.521	0.455	0.658	0.505			

Notes: Besides pooled OLS, all specifications include state fixed effects. Both, the state and – if included – the time fixed effects are not shown. The variable interest is only included in specifications without time fixed effects since it is not state specific. The LSDVc estimator was applied with an initial Arellano-Bond estimate and 200 bootstrap repetitions. Standard errors are robust and clustered at state level for OLS, fixed effects (LSDV) and Arellano Bond estimators. *** indicates significance at 1 % level, ** at 5 % level and * at 10 % level respectively. Standard errors are reported in parentheses.

We also challenge our implementation of the LSDVc estimator and used an alternative initial estimator (BB). Our results remain the same.[31]

4.5 Conclusion

Although there is a large theoretical and an increasing empirical literature on the political economy of public deficits, the role and responsibility of the finance minister has so far been neglected. This is particularly astonishing because in other policy areas, like economic policy, monetary policy, or corporate performance, the influence of individual characteristics on outcome and performance is already partly explored. By empirically analyzing the influence of the finance ministers' preferences and abilities on public deficits in 10 West German states from 1960 to 2009, we try to overcome this shortcoming in public finance.

Using a new and unique data set that includes the personal characteristics of all 110 relevant finance ministers, we employ several panel estimation techniques and report the following findings: There is strong evidence that the ability of the finance minister to ensure sound public finances depends on her professional experience prior to her nomination. Finance ministers who gained financial expertise, e.g., in the financial business sector, prior to their appointment, achieve significantly lower deficits than all others. However, ministers with previous experience in the non-financial business sector incur higher deficits. Furthermore, the finance minister's strength within the cabinet increases both with her previous political experience as a member of parliament and with her tenure as finance minister. If she is more than 4.5 years in office annual deficits decrease significantly. In coalition governments, the finance minister's position is further strengthened if she and the prime minister belong to the same party. We do not find evidence that her education affects her ability in any way. Apparently, it does not matter for the deficit if the finance minister has a university degree or which subject she studied. Our findings correspond with results from studies in monetary and economic policy showing professional experience to be more influential than educational background, too.

There is also no evidence that the socioeconomic characteristics of the finance minister affect the preferences of the finance minister: Neither the gender nor the parenthood of finance ministers affects public deficits. Female ministers do not issue more or less debt than their male colleagues, and children do not affect the attitude toward debt either. Moreover, we find no evidence for the lame duck argument as the age of the finance minister is irrelevant for public deficits. Finally, there is no support for the partisan theory, i.e., politically left finance ministers do not incur higher deficits than politically right ones.

31 Results are available upon request.

So what appear to be the characteristics of the 'perfect' finance minister? In times of fiscal stress and global fiscal uncertainties the 'perfect' finance minister should pay a great deal of attention to reaching a sound budget. It is more likely that she will succeed in doing so if she has significant professional experience in the field of business finance, if she stays in office for a long time, and if she has political experience as a former member of parliament. Moreover, in a coalition government she should belong to the same party as the prime minister. It does not matter how old she is or what (or if) she studied or, for that matter, whether the finance minister is male or female, with or without children.

4.A Appendix

Table 4.7: Variable description and sources

Variable	Description	Source
	General data	
deficit	Change of real state debt per capita in Euro for each *Land* (state)	Own calculation based on FSO*
gdp	Growth rate of real gdp per capita in percent for each *Land* (state)	Own calculation based on FSO*
interest	Real interest rate in percent (Central Bank discount rate until 2001 and base rate after 2002 respectively minus inflation rate)	Own calculation based on FSO* and Bundesbank
population	Inhabitants of each *Land* (state) in millions	FSO*
election	DV for each year with elections in the respective *Land* (state)	State chancelleries
fraction	Fractionalization of the cabinet members in percent based on their party affiliation calculated as in the World Bank Database on Political Institutions (Beck et al., 2001). It gives the probability that two randomly drawn ministers are affiliated with different parties (independent ministers are counted like an own party) and higher values indicate a more fragmented government	Own calculation based on state chancelleries
	Finance minister: General information	
age	Age of the finance minister in years	Various sources**
tenure	Experience of the finance minister in this position in years	State chancelleries
female	Dummy variable that takes the value 1 (DV) for a female finance minister	Various sources**
kids	DV for a finance minister with children	Various sources**
kids_n	Number of children of the finance minister	Various sources**
backing	DV only in coalition governments in which the finance minister belongs to the party of the prime minister	State chancelleries
left	DV when the finance minister belongs either to the Social Democratic Party or the Green Party	State chancelleries

Continued on next page...

Table 4.7: Variable description and sources (continued)

Variable	Description	Source
	Finance minister: Education	
edu_uni	DV when the finance minister has studied at an university or university of applied sciences	Various sources**
edu_phd	DV when the finance minister holds a PhD	Various sources**
economics	DV when the finance minister has studied economics or business	Various sources**
law	DV when the finance minister has studied law	Various sources**
science	DV when the finance minister has studied science, maths, or medicine etc.	Various sources**
humanities	DV when the finance minister has studied humanities or other subjects	Various sources**
	Finance minister: Professional background	
academia	DV when the finance minister has worked as a researcher or lecturer before	Various sources**
academia_finance	DV when the finance minister has worked as a researcher or lecturer in economics, finance or business before	Various sources**
academia_other	DV when the finance minister has worked as a researcher or lecturer in other fields than economics, finance or business before	Various sources**
business	DV when the finance minister has worked in the business sector before	Various sources**
business_finance	DV when the finance minister has worked in the finance sector before (e.g., private or public banks, insurance companies and central bank)	Various sources**
business_other	DV when the finance minister has worked in other business sectors than finance before	Various sources**
mp	DV when the finance minister has been a member of parliament (state/federal or European) before	Various sources**
spending_minister	DV when the finance minister has been a spending minister before	Various sources**
public	DV when the finance minister has worked in the public sector before	Various sources**
public_finance	DV when the finance minister has worked in the public finance sector before (e.g., ministry of finance, treasury, tax administration)	Various sources**
public_other	DV when the finance minister has worked in the public sector, not related to public finances, prior to her/his appointment	Various sources**
other	DV when the finance minister has other professional experience (e.g., journalist, lawyer, or party officer)	Various sources**
finance_expertise	DV when the finance minister has worked in any of the finance related fields covered by academia_finance, business_finance, or public_finance before	Various sources**

Continued on next page...

Table 4.7: Variable description and sources (continued)

Variable	Description	Source
	Time specific events	
fedelection	DV for each year with federal elections, same for all *Länder* (states)	Own coding
euelection	DV for each year with European elections, same for all *Länder* (states)	Own coding
oil1	DV for the first oil crisis during the years 1974 and 1975, same for all *Länder* (states)	Own coding
oil2	DV for the second oil crisis between the years 1978 to 1981, same for all *Länder* (states)	Own coding
fin_crisis	DV for the financial crisis during the years 2008 and 2009, same for all *Länder* (states)	Own coding
unific	DV for the years after reunification (1991 to 2009), same for all *Länder* (states)	Own coding
equal	DV for the years under equalization scheme (1995 to 2009), same for all *Länder* (states)	Own coding
bailout	DV for Saarland and Bremen during the federal government bailout (1994 to 2004)	Own coding
bailout_period	DV for the years with federal government bailout (1994 to 2004), same for all *Länder* (states)	Own coding

Notes: *Fso: Federal Statistical Office of Germany, **various sources: Munzinger Archive, state chancelleries and websites of politicians, parliaments and party archives.

Chapter 5: Finance ministers in Europe

5.1 Introduction[1]

In the aftermath of the collapse of Lehman Brothers in 2008, the global financial crisis has turned more and more into a debt crisis of several member states of the European Union (EU). The attempts of the EU to deal with the crisis granted the European finance ministers a more powerful position than other political actors. This development is reflected by an increased attention in the media and in the public debate.[2] Contrary to the high coverage in the business media, economic research has so far not really considered the relevance of the finance ministers and their individual characteristics for fiscal policy outcomes. However, several scholars have examined how individual characteristics of political decision makers affect other economic policy outcomes such as economic growth (e.g., the seminal contribution by Jones and Olken, 2005). They have concluded, for example, that the professional background of the head of government matters for the implementation of market-liberalizing reforms (Dreher et al., 2009) and that heads of government with a higher education stimulate economic growth (Besley, Montalvo, and Reynal-Querol, 2011). Furthermore, the composition of public budgets depends on the degree of female representation in the legislature (Chattopadhyay and Duflo, 2004; Svaleryd, 2009) and also on the socio-economic background of the head of government (Hayo and Neumeier, 2012). Similarly, it is shown for monetary policy that the educational and in particular the professional background of members of the central bank council affect inflation rates (Göhlmann and Vaubel, 2007; Farvaque, Hammadou, and Stanek, 2009, 2011).[3] In the field of fiscal policy, however, to date there has not yet been an in-depth exploration of how the finance minister as the central policy maker affects fiscal performance. Instead, it is common in the political economy literature to ascribe fiscal performance predominantly to institutional and political factors (e.g., Hagen and Harden, 1995; Kontopoulos and Perotti, 1999; Volkerink and Haan, 2001; Wehner, 2010). Even though, for instance, Hagen

1 I would like to thank Alberto Alesina, Giacomo Corneo, Ronny Freier, and Beate Jochimsen for helpful advice and thoughtful comments. In the same manner, comments from Enrique Moral-Benito and other participants of the 11th Journées d'Economie Publique Louis-André Gérard-Varet, Marseille, are gratefully acknowledged. Furthermore, I would like to thank the Friedrich Ebert Foundation for generous financial support of my research visit and my work on this project at Harvard University in February and March 2012. Kind research assistance was provided by Tina Dohrmann (biographies of finance ministers in Spain), Johanna Koskinen (Finland), Britta Labuhn (Portugal), and Melpomeni Skordou (Greece).

2 The Financial Times (FT), for example, publishes an annual ranking of European finance ministers. For the 2011 ranking see Atkins and Whiffin in the FT, November 22, 2011.

3 See Section 2.2 of this doctoral thesis for an in-depth review of the literature on the relevance of decision makers and their characteristics for policy outcomes.

and Harden (1995) emphasize the central role of the finance minister in the budgetary process, this decision maker and the relevance of her individual characteristics for sound public finances have not yet been well explored.

The present study addresses this gap and combines the well-established political economy approach with the innovative approach of Jones and Olken (2005) to focus on individual decision makers. In particular, this study investigates empirically if the individual characteristics of finance ministers affect the fiscal performance of European governments. Thereby, the study contributes to the scant but growing literature, to date, on the relevance of decision makers for public finances (see the literature review in Section 2.3). Two recent studies by Hayo and Neumeier (2011) and Mikosch (2012) examine if the characteristics of the head of government affect fiscal performance. The former study finds for German states that prime ministers from a poorer socio-economic background are associated with higher deficits. The latter study relies on data for OECD countries and reports lower deficits when the elected heads of government have had working experience outside politics. The latter study also shows that there are no general effects of specific professions, the education level, or the field of study.

For the finance minister herself, there are – according to the author's knowledge – only four studies that examine her individual characteristics: Feld and Schaltegger (2010) use data for Switzerland to show that finance ministers with a long tenure realize higher budget surpluses and lower expenditures; whereas Jochimsen and Nuscheler (2011) demonstrate that strong political ties between the finance minister and the prime minister improve fiscal performance in German states. Moessinger (2012) considers the educational background of finance ministers in 15 European countries and shows that the education and the political orientation of the finance minister are irrelevant for public finances. Furthermore, he finds evidence for lower debt growth when the finance minister stays in office for a long time or when she has served as a spending minister prior to her appointment. However, Moessinger (2012) does not consider the influence of other individual characteristics of the finance minister, such as previous professional experience outside politics, her gender, or her parental status. The first study that investigates how the finance minister's educational and professional background as well as her gender and parental status affect public finances is a companion paper for the German states, see Chapter 4 (or for an earlier version: Jochimsen and Thomasius, 2012). The main result is that finance ministers realize lower deficits when they have working experience in the field of finance.

According to the author's knowledge, so far there has not been a study that investigates the influence of the finance minister's education and previous professional experience outside politics in an international analysis. This study fills this gap and enriches the ongoing debate by examining these and further characteristics of the European ministers of finance. As in the companion study for Germany, this study distinguishes between characteristics that, first, affect her ability to overcome diverging interests and ensure sound budgeting and, second, shape her budgetary preferences.

Using dynamic panel estimations for 15 EU countries between 1970 and 2010, I find weak evidence that the finance minister's ability to ensure sound budgeting depends on her backing by the head of government and on her education. There is weak evidence, for instance, that the ratio of central government debt to GDP increases less when the finance minister belongs to the party of the prime minister in a coalition government. Furthermore, the growth of the debt ratio is higher when a former student of science, technology, engineering or mathematics is in charge of the budget. This result is predominantly driven by only a few observations from three countries and, hence, should be interpreted with care. However, there is no evidence that the debt growth is in any way affected by the professional background of the finance minister or by her political experience from previous positions as a spending minister or a member of parliament. With respect to the budgetary preferences of the finance ministers, this study finds supporting evidence that they do not act as partisans, i.e., a politically left finance minister does not incur higher or lower debt growth than others. Also the age and the parental status of the finance minister do not affect the debt ratio.

The remainder of this chapter is organized as follows. First, Section 5.2 highlights the traditional political economy perspectives on public debt. Then, specific hypotheses are derived with respect to the effect of the finance minister's characteristics on public debt. Section 5.3 outlines the empirical strategy and introduces the new data set with biographical information on the European ministers of finance. The results are discussed in Section 5.4 and Section 5.5 concludes.

5.2 Public finances and the European finance ministers

There are several circumstances in which a government should run a deficit to increase social welfare – for instance, to smoothen taxation and consumption over time (Barro, 1979). In light of the continued growth of government debt, the political economy literature, however, argues that the persistence of public deficits since the 1970s cannot solely result from welfare-optimizing policy measures (Alesina and Perotti, 1995). Instead, poor fiscal performance is predominatly ascribed to institutional and political factors. The seminal work by Roubini and Sachs (1989a), for example, identified government ideology and government instability as main drivers of public deficits in OECD countries. The political economy literature, both theoretical and empirical, suggests that there are three main causes for persistent public deficits:[4] First, opportunistic politicians may run public deficits to improve their reelection prospects and, thereby, create political business cycles (e.g., Rogoff, 1990; Alesina, Perotti, and Tavares, 1998; Persson and Tabellini, 1999). A second strand of the literature follows

4 Eslava (2011) provides a comprehensive review of the literature.

Hibbs (1977) and argues that party ideology (partisanship) and anticipated changes in political majorities induce higher spending and public deficits. However, the majority of empirical studies do not find supporting evidence that the government's ideology matters for the deficit (e.g., Haan and Sturm, 1994; Perotti and Kontopoulos, 2002). Furthermore, weak governments might be a third cause of high deficits because they are afflicted with a spending bias due to conflicts of interests and political fragmentation. Several empirical studies confirm this argument, for example, for fragmented coalition governments (e.g., Haan, Sturm, and Beekhuis, 1999; Perotti and Kontopoulos, 2002; Wehner, 2010). These concepts from the political economy literature will be included in the empirical analysis.

The remainder of this section is structured as follows. The first subsection discusses why the ability and the strength of the finance minister affect public finances and hypothesizes which individual characteristics matter for her ability to ensure sound public finances. The second subsection focuses on the budgetary preferences of the finance minister and hypothesizes which individual characteristics shape her preferences and, therefore, may matter for fiscal performance.

5.2.1 Public finances and the finance minister's ability

The weak government hypothesis gained much attention in the run-up phase to the Economic and Monetary Union (EMU) of the European Union in the early 1990s. In particular, Hagen and Harden (1995) demonstrate that governments succumb to a spending bias and enact a suboptimally large budget when the government is weak due to a decentralized budget process in which the spending ministers are free to determine the expenditures of their own portfolio. Furthermore, they argue that a strong minister of finance may resolve this spending bias. The finance minister is the pivotal cabinet member with respect to the deficit. While the spending ministers promote the interests of their own portfolio she is the only minister with an overall responsibility for the budget. Her political success depends on a good track record in public finances. However, the characteristics which strengthen the finance minister have so far not been either theoretically well defined nor empirically well examined. Yet, the literature considers her procedural rights (e.g., Hagen and Harden, 1995; Hallerberg, Strauch, and Hagen, 2007), her tenure (Feld and Schaltegger, 2010), her relationship with the prime minister (Jochimsen and Nuscheler, 2011), and the number of spending ministers in opposition to her (e.g., Kontopoulos and Perotti, 1999; Volkerink and Haan, 2001).

The companion study for finance ministers in German states in Chapter 4 of this doctoral thesis takes a different approach and investigates how individual characteristics of the finance minister, such as her educational and professional background, affect her ability to ensure sound public finances. Unexpectedly, the education of the finance minister does not matter for fiscal performance in German states – neither the level of education nor the field of study. Her political orientation has no significant effect either. However, the most important results of this study is that those finance ministers who have previously worked in the field of finance achieve significantly lower deficits. Moessinger (2012) takes a similar approach and considers the educational background of finance ministers in 15 European countries from 1981 through 2007 (see Section 2.3.2). His results confirm the above finding that the finance minister's education and political orientation are irrelevant for public finances. In addition, he finds evidence for lower debt when the finance minister stays in office for a long time or when she served as a spending minister before her appointment as finance minister. However, Moessinger (2012) does not consider the influence of other professional experiences gained before her appointment.[5]

In light of the promising results of the studies mentioned above, the present study enhances this approach even further. It examines which individual characteristics of the finance minister strengthen her ability to ensure sound budgeting in the EU countries. For the sake of clarity, the individual characteristics related to the minister's ability are clustered into three groups: The first group comprises characteristics that increase her political experience and her political standing, while the second group captures her educational background. The third group focuses on the professional experience of the minister which she gained before her appointment. The respective hypotheses for the three groups are derived in the following.

Political experience and standing

According to Feld and Schaltegger (2010), finance ministers who have been in office for several years are well grounded in the budget process and possess more political power then newly appointed finance ministers. Therefore, a finance minister with a high tenure may be more able to accomplish her budgetary goals and to reject spending inquiries from interest groups and the spending ministers.

Hypothesis 5.1 *Finance ministers with a higher tenure reduce the debt growth.*

The finance minister's ability to ensure sound budgeting will depend on her general political experience, too. It is argued that finance ministers with previous experience as a spending minister know very well the political strategies typically used by the spending ministers. Therefore, former spending ministers might be more able to avoid being cheated by spending ministers and interest groups (cf. ch. 4 and Moessinger, 2012).

5 Note that Moessinger (2012) considers – with the exception of Italy – only those members of the cabinet who hold the title 'finance minister'. He relies on the 'finance minister' even when there is an additional 'budget minister' with full rank in the cabinet besides this 'finance minister'. See the data description in Section 5.3.2 and Table 5.8 in the appendix. The table reports all those cases when a budget minister was a member of the cabinet with full rank and independent of the finance minister. Further differences regarding data and methodology between the present study and Moessinger (2012) are summarized in fn. 23 on p. 119.

Hypothesis 5.2 *The growth of public debt is decreased by finance ministers who served as a spending minister in the past.*

Similarly, the strength of the finance minister depends on her capabilities to ensure broad parliamentary support for the budget proposal. Former members of parliament will therefore enjoy an advantage compared to those ministers that have not been a member of parliament. This was first examined by the companion study for the German states (Jochimsen and Thomasius, 2012, see chapter 4 for an updated version).

Hypothesis 5.3 *Finance ministers that were members of parliament lower the growth of public debt.*

The majority of empirical studies show that weak governments, and especially coalition governments, incur higher deficits (see above). In this context, Jochimsen and Nuscheler (2011) examine another potential source of the finance minister's 'strength'. Using data for the German states, they show that a coalition government can overcome this weakness and realizes lower deficits when the finance minister and the prime minister belong to the same party. These close political ties assure the finance minister of the prime minister's support and therefore increase her political standing within the cabinet and allow her to achieve her budgetary goals.

Hypothesis 5.4 *Less debt is accumulated in a coalition government if the finance minister has the backing of the prime minister due to the same party affiliation.*

Educational background

Furthermore, it is argued, for example, in Moessinger (2012) and Chapter 4 that the strength of the finance minister is related to her level of education – either directly because of higher investments in her human capital (Mincer, 1958) or indirectly with higher education as a signal for generally higher ability (Spence, 1973). Therefore, I follow related studies on economic growth and inflation (e.g., Besley, Montalvo, and Reynal-Querol, 2011; Farvaque, Hammadou, and Stanek, 2009, 2011) and examine whether the public debt is affected if the finance minister has studied at a university or holds a PhD.

Hypothesis 5.5 *Finance ministers with a higher level of education incur less new debt.*

Not only the educational level, but also the field of study might be relevant here. For instance, Frey (1986) points out that trained economists often come up with different judgments than non-economists when they apply the economic concepts they incorporated during their education. Among others, the study by O'Roark and Wood (2011) provides supporting evidence. They show that in 2007 trained economists among the members of the U.S. Congress were less likely to vote for an increase of the minimum wage whereas they find no effect on the voting decision for other subjects. Hence, I follow Dreher et al. (2009) and Göhlmann and Vaubel (2007) and include the field of study as well. In the context of public finances, I expect finance ministers with an academic background in economics to be more concerned with intergenerational equality. Furthermore, it is likely that trained economist are perceived as more competent with respect to public finances than graduates from other subjects and are, hence, more able to convince others of their arguments in favor of a balanced budget.

Hypothesis 5.6 *Finance ministers who are trained economists achieve a lower debt growth.*

Professional experience

Studies on economic reforms by Dreher et al. (2009) and on inflation by Göhlmann and Vaubel (2007) and Farvaque, Hammadou, and Stanek (2009, 2011) demonstrate that the professional background of decision makers is much more relevant for policy outcomes than the educational background. A companion study for the German states in Chapter 4 yields the same result for the finance minister. I expect finance ministers who have working experience in the finance field, either in academia, in the public, or the private sector, to reduce public debt.

Hypothesis 5.7 *Finance ministers with financial expertise reduce the growth of debt.*

5.2.2 Public finances and the finance minister's preferences

This subsection discusses individual characteristics of the finance minister and hypothesizes how they shape her budgetary preferences and, thereby, matter for public debt.

The first aspect of the finance minister's personality that is likely to affect her attitude toward debt is her ideology. In his seminal contribution on unemployment and inflation, Hibbs (1977) argues that partisan politicians implement those policies that are in accordance with the preferences of their voters. The common assumption in the literature is that a politically left politician favors redistributional and expansionary policies compared to a politically right one (Cusack, 1997). Such partisan behavior on the spending side, however, does not necessarily affect the budget balance or the level of debt. And indeed, the majority of empirical studies do not find evidence that the government's ideology affects the deficit (e.g., Haan and Sturm, 1994; Perotti and Kontopoulos, 2002). Therefore, I do not expect politically left finance ministers to increase or decrease the growth of public debt.

Hypothesis 5.8 *There is no effect on public debt when a politically left finance minister is in office.*

The age of the finance minister might matter for public debt, too. An older finance minister can be expected to be more experienced than a younger one. Still, this effect that strengthens the finance minister might be better captured by her tenure than by her age and has, therefore, already been discussed in hypothesis 5.1. From an alternative perspective, an older minister who is close to retirement might appear as a 'lame duck' since she might have already reached her political peak (Barro, 1973) and may have no further political (career) ambitions. When Besley and Case (1995) discuss term limits in a reputation building model they find a similar effect. Politicans who face a binding term limit have only few incentives to continue building up their reputation. Applying this idea to the finance minister suggests that older ministers are less concerned with their reputation for sound public finances and, therefore, do not counter spending inquiries of interest groups or spending ministers as much as a younger finance minister would.

Hypothesis 5.9 *The level of public debt increases with the age of the finance minister.*

Furthermore, there are arguments that the gender of the finance minister influences her attitude toward public debt. For instance, the majority of studies in behavioral economics show that women are more risk averse than men (cf. Eckel and Grossman, 2008; Croson and Gneezy, 2009, who review of the related economic literature).[6] Therefore, the following hypothesis is derived.

Hypothesis 5.10 *The level of public debt is reduced by female finance ministers.*

The last hypothesis cannot be tested yet in the context of European central governments due to the low number of female finance ministers in the past (see the data description in Section 5.3.2). The companion study in Chapter 4 could not find significant differences in public deficits for female and male finance ministers in German states.

The parental status of the finance minister might influence her attitude toward debt, too. Intergenerational equality might be more important for a finance minister with (more) children and increase her awareness for fiscal sustainability and the implications of high public debt for future generations (cf. Barro, 1974).

Hypothesis 5.11 *Finance ministers with (more) children reduce the level of public debt.*

The hypotheses derived above and in Section 5.2.1 are targeted on the effect of specific characteristics of the finance minister on public debt. A potential concern for such an

6 See also the discussion on hypothesis 4.3 on page 78 in Chapter 4.

investigation is reverse causality (see the discussion at the end of Section 4.3.1). It cannot be ruled out that voters select candidates with specific characteristics in response to the economic or political circumstances. And indeed, a main result of the analysis of the determinants of electoral success in Chapter 3 was that voters care about the qualifications, in terms of education and professional experience, of candidates who run for a political office. Higher educated candidates received significantly higher votes and had a significantly higher probability of winning a mayoral election in Bavarian municipalities between 1950 and 2009. The same holds for candidates with specific professions. Related to this are studies for Italy which report increasing qualification levels among election candidates and elected politicians for more competitive political environments (Paola and Scoppa, 2011; Galasso and Nannicini, 2011). In light of these results, a regression discontinuity design (RDD) was employed in Chapter 3 to ensure a proper identification when the authors investigated the effects of the mayor's individual characteristics on fiscal policy. In the context of European finance ministers, however, reverse causality should be only a minor concern. As argued in Section 4.3.1 and in Dreher et al. (2009), a regression control framework should be a sufficient empirical strategy here for the following reason: The position of the finance minister in a European central government is not a public elective office, instead the finance minister is appointed by the head of government. The preceding selection process is neither transparent nor has it – according to the author's knowledge – yet been examined in the political economy literature. Hence, there are no general decision rules or specific criteria publicly available that establishes a functional relationship, i.e., a reverse causality, between the economic or political circumstances and the characteristics of the selected finance minister. On the contrary, when the head of government appoints the members of the cabinet she has to set up a well-diversified and balanced cabinet so that all relevant groups are represented, e.g., regions, parties or party wings, and genders. Since the number of candidates will be limited it is rather unlikely that the head of government will consider their age, their educational or professional background or their parental status as key selection criteria. Given these constraints, reverse causality does not appear to be a severe issue in the following analysis.

5.3 Data set and empirical model

The hypotheses derived in the preceeding section are tested for a panel of European countries. The underlying empirical model is outlined in the following part of this section, while the data set is described thereafter.

5.3.1 Specification of the econometric model

The following empirical analysis extends the standard political economy approach and considers the change in public debt in country in i at time t as a function not only of the economic and political circumstances but also of the characteristics of the respective minister in charge of the budget. I follow the related empirical literature on public debt and focus on the change of the debt-to-GDP ratio and include the first lag of the dependent variable (LDV) to capture the persistence of debt accumulation (cf. Haan and Sturm, 1994; Hallerberg, Strauch, and Hagen, 2007). However, I deviate from the literature and rely on the central government debt instead of the general government debt. The reason is straightforward: The national finance minister is accountable for the budget and debt of the central government. Relying on general government data would include fiscal data of subnational levels that cannot be influenced by the national finance minister or – depending on the fiscal autonomy of subnational entities – can only be influenced to a limited extent.[7]

The empirical model is specified as follows:

$$y_{i,t} = \gamma y_{i,t-1} + x'_{i,t}\beta_1 + z'_{i,t}\beta_2 + \text{time}'_t\beta_3 + \mu_i + \varepsilon_{i,t} \tag{5.1}$$

in which $y_{i,t}$ represents the annual change in the ratio of central government debt to GDP in country $i = 1,\ldots,N$ at time $t = 1,\ldots,T$ and $y_{i,t-1}$ represents its first lag. The vector $x_{i,t}$ contains all variables referring to the minister in charge of the budget whereas the vector $z_{i,t}$ captures the economic and political control variables. Global fixed year effects are captured with the vector time_t. Finally, μ_i represents time-invariant country fixed effects and $\varepsilon_{i,t}$ is the error term.

Estimating the model in equation 5.1 with the standard OLS estimator yields inconsistent and biased estimates due to the unobserved time-invariant heterogeneity across countries, i.e., the country-specific effects μ_i, and due to the correlation between the LDV and the error term, i.e., the Nickell bias (1981). While the fixed-effects panel data estimator takes the former issue into account, it does not eliminate the Nickell bias. This bias disappears only for long panels, i.e., only when T goes to infinity.[8]

There are basically two categories of estimators available that take this bias into account. The first category directly corrects for the bias while the second category relies

7 The change in the central government debt ratio is stationary for most of the EU countries considered here. I could to reject the null hypothesis of the Fisher-type unit-root test with the inverse Chi-square test statistic proposed by Choi (2001) that all countries have a unit root in the change of the debt ratio (for both specifications of this unit-root test, i.e., the augmented Dickey-Fuller (ADF) and the Phillips-Perron (PP) specifications). However, I had to reject the null hypothesis of the Hadri Lagrange Multiplier test that the entire panel is stationary, too. Applying ADF tests for the 15 countries separately, I identify the United Kingdom to have a unit root. However, this should be a minor issue since the time series of the other 14 countries are stationary.

8 According to Nickell, $\hat{\gamma}$ is downward biased for $\gamma > 0$, whereas the estimates for the other explanatory variables are upward biased if they are positively correlated with the LDV or vice-versa. Applying the approximation of Nickell (1981), the fixed effects estimate for $\hat{\gamma}$ might be downward biased by around nine percent for $T = 40$ and a real $\gamma = 0.44$ for the sample used in this study (in a model without any other regressors).

on the use of instruments to obtain unbiased estimates.[9] The latter comprises the standard dynamic panel estimators proposed by Anderson and Hsiao (1981, 1982), Arellano and Bond (1991), and Blundell and Bond (1998). Still, these estimators are not well-suited for small samples and would generate biased estimates for the sample used in the present analysis. Consequently, I rely on the first category of estimators and employ the bias corrected least squares dummy variable estimator (LSDVc). This estimator was proposed by Kiviet (1995) and (Bruno, 2005a,b) for dynamic panel data models with small N.[10]

This estimator is based on the fixed-effects estimator and directly corrects for the approximated Nickell bias using an initial, consistent estimate. One of the above mentioned standard dynamic panel estimators can be employed to obtain this initial estimate. I use the Arellano and Bond (1991) estimator because it is more efficient and appears to be more robust than the estimators proposed by Anderson/Hsiao and Blundell/Bond (see Bruno, 2005a).[11]

The Arellano-Bond test for autocorrelation confirms the chosen specification. The test results show that the residuals of the estimations exhibit autocorrelation of the first order for all models estimated. However, the test does not indicate second-order autocorrelation for almost all estimations. I can also clearly reject the null hypothesis of the Sargan test of over-identifying restrictions.

5.3.2 Description of the data set

The analysis is based on a panel with annual data for 15 member countries of the European Union over the period from 1970 to 2010.[12] The panel is unbalanced due to missing data for some countries at the beginning and at the end of the investigated period and consists of 480 observations in total. The data set comprises three types of variables: first, fiscal and economic indicators and, second, variables covering general political economy aspects and, third, variables regarding the individual characteristics of the ministers in charge of the budget. Table 5.1 summarizes the variables employed

9 See Behr (2003) or Baltagi (2008, ch. 8) for a general discussion.

10 Several simulation studies demonstrate that the LSDVc estimator yields more accurate estimates and has lower standard errors, especially for small panels, than the estimators from the second category, cf. Judson and Owen (1999); Kiviet and Bun (2001); Bun and Kiviet (2006); Bruno (2005a).

11 In accordance with Bruno (2005a) and Bun and Kiviet (2003, 2006), I base the bias correction on the bias approximation in powers of $T^{-2}N^{-1}$. Furthermore, I follow the suggestion of Kiviet and Bun (2001) who show that the bootstrap procedure for the estimation of the variance-covariance matrix of the LSDVc estimator outperforms the analytical variance estimator and, hence, I undertake 200 repetitions of the procedure to bootstrap the standard errors. However, employing 50, 100 or 300 repetitions does not yield qualitatively different results.

12 The panel includes the so-called EU-15 countries, i.e., those countries that were member states of the EU before the enlargement in 2004. These are Austria, Belgium, Denmark, Finland, France, Germany, Greece, Ireland, Italy, Luxembourg, the Netherlands, Portugal, Spain, Sweden, and the United Kingdom.

Table 5.1: Descriptive statistics

	Observations	Mean	Std. Dev.	Minimum	Maximum
Dependent and control variables					
debt	480	0.887	4.389	−11.100	24.700
gdp	480	2.475	2.376	−8.539	10.917
unemployment	480	7.769	4.069	0.699	24.171
cost	480	0.771	2.099	−6.518	10.458
openness	480	69.588	45.195	18.464	307.663
population	480	26.775	25.101	0.395	82.502
emu	480	0.356	0.479	0	1
RR_currency	480	0.088	0.283	0	1
RR_inflation	480	0.013	0.111	0	1
RR_stock	480	0.269	0.444	0	1
RR_banking	480	0.146	0.353	0	1
election	480	0.285	0.452	0	1
majority	480	0.558	0.087	0.292	0.858
govfrac	480	0.334	0.265	0	0.828
Ability: Political experience and standing					
tenure	480	2.502	2.233	0.031	11.515
tenure_spending	480	1.425	2.234	0	11.293
tenure_mp	480	7.342	7.222	0	39.989
backing	480	0.450	0.498	0	1
Ability: Education					
university_phd	480	0.910	0.286	0	1
university	480	0.620	0.486	0	1
phd	480	0.281	0.450	0	1
economics	480	0.490	0.500	0	1
law	480	0.329	0.470	0	1
stem	480	0.083	0.277	0	1
other_fields	480	0.288	0.453	0	1
Ability: Professional experience					
finance	480	0.390	0.488	0	1
academia	480	0.198	0.399	0	1
academia_finance	480	0.125	0.331	0	1
business	480	0.223	0.417	0	1
business_finance	480	0.092	0.289	0	1
central_bank	480	0.046	0.209	0	1
lawyer	480	0.113	0.316	0	1
outsider	480	0.308	0.462	0	1
party_officer	480	0.040	0.195	0	1
public	480	0.194	0.396	0	1
public_finance	480	0.102	0.303	0	1
union_officer	480	0.056	0.231	0	1
Preferences					
left	480	0.438	0.497	0	1
age	477	50.703	7.760	30.765	80.903
female	480	0.021	0.143	0	1
kids	397	0.975	0.157	0	1
kids_n	397	2.718	1.423	0	9

Note: All information refer to January 1st of the respective year, i.e., the cabinet or the budget ministers who were in office on January 1st. Table 5.10 in the appendix provides a detailed description of variables and data sources.

in the analysis and Table 5.10 in the appendix presents the sources. Table 5.9 in the appendix compares the mean values for the individual characteristics by country.

The data on the change in the ratio of central government debt to GDP (*debt*) are taken from Reinhart and Rogoff (2011, henceforth RR). This data source allows us to include additional years in the analysis compared to the OECD debt data that is available with gaps only from 1980 onward.[13] The mean value in Table 5.1 shows that the debt-to-GDP ratio increased on average by 0.9 percentage points per year in the sample. In accordance with the above mentioned literature, the growth rate of real GDP (gdp) and the unemployment rate (unemployment) are included as well to control for the state of the economy. I expect a negative effect of GDP growth on the debt ratio and a positive one for the unemployment rate. The variable openness captures the participation in the globalization and is calculated as the sum of exports and imports as a share of the GDP. I expect a negative effect on the debt ratio due to higher consolidation activities in more open economies. Furthermore, the costs of debt service (cost) is controlled for. This variable is defined as the product of the debt ratio and the difference between the real long-term interest rate and the growth rate of real GDP (as in Hallerberg, Strauch, and Hagen, 2007).[14] The population size is included, too, and captures different patterns over time (*population*).[15]

Additionally, specific event-related dummy variables are included in the analysis. The first, emu, captures the participation in the EMU. It is a dummy variable (DV) that takes the value of 1 in the year 1999 and thereafter for the 11 founding members and from 2001 onward for Greece when the country joined the EMU. The author expects a negative relationship between this variable and the debt ratio. Furthermore, country-specific dummy variables are employed to control for financial crises. They are provided by Reinhart and Rogoff (2011) and capture country-specific years with inflation rates over 20 % (RR_inflation), years with currency depreciations of 15 % or more versus the respective anchor currency (RR_currency), years with stock market crashes (RR_stock), or banking crises (RR_banking).[16] The first two crisis types should have a negative effect on the debt ratio. On the contrary, the latter types are expected to affect the debt ratio positively.

---

13 The OECD data on central government debt is used only for Italy, Luxembourg, and the Netherlands over the entire period since the RR data is incomplete or starts much later than the OECD data.

14 The cost of debt servicing reflects the effect of interest payments on government debt relative to the economic growth. If the economy exhibits a higher real growth rate than the real long-term interest rate the cost of serving the debt of the past becomes negative. This has been the case for most EMU member states in Southern Europe following the introduction of the Euro.

15 In this case, it is difficult to derive a hypothesis on the direction of the effect on the debt ratio. There are good arguments for both directions.

16 Since there is no data included for Luxembourg in the RR data set, I have used the crises indices of Belgium instead as both countries formed an economic and monetary union, the *union économique belgo-luxembourgeoise*, before the introduction of the Euro.

The second group of variables controls for traditional political economy aspects. They are taken from the World Bank Database of Political Institutions (DPI) that is provided by Beck et al. (2001, December 2010 version).[17] Among these three variables, the variable election controls for political business cycles. It is a DV for upcoming elections at the national level within the next 13 months and a positive effect on the debt ratio is expected. Weak governments are captured by two variables that measure, first, how politically fragmented the government is (govfrac) and, second, how much parliamentary support the government has (majority). The former gives the probability that two randomly drawn members of parliament who support the government belong to different parties. The value of the variable can range from 0 to 1 and is 0 for single party governments. The latter variable represents the share of seats in the parliament supporting the government. According to the political economy theories presented in the previous section, the debt ratio should increase with more government fragmentation and decrease with the share of seats in the parliament.

The third group of variables relates to the minister in charge of the budget and her individual characteristics that are likely to affect her ability to achieve a balanced budget and to shape her preferences toward debt. The hypotheses on the impact of the respective variables were derived in Section 5.2. The data was collected by the author based on publicly available sources such as the websites of the politicians or their parties and information provided by the government or parliamentary information offices. The data refer to the minister in office on January 1st of the respective year.

In most countries the finance minister takes the responsibility for all areas of public finances such as the treasury, the budget, the fiscal and tax policy as well as the financial regulation. However, it is worth mentioning that these tasks have repeatedly been shared among different cabinet members in the Kingdom of Belgium, the Kingdom of Denmark, the French Republic, the Italian Republic, and the Grand Duchy of Luxembourg. In this study the focus is on the minister who is responsible for the budget – as long as this person is a minister of full rank within the cabinet or at least equally ranked as the finance minister. The finance minister is only considered in those cases when the budget minister works as a state secretary or junior minister. See Table 5.8 in the appendix for a list of all budget ministers considered here.[18] However, the term 'finance minister' is, for the sake of clarity, used for all ministers in charge of the budget in the following.

The average tenure of the finance ministers in the sample amounts to 2.50 years, but differs across countries, with between 1.45 in Portugal and 3.41 in Austria. The finance minister with the highest tenure in the sample served for more than 11 years. The finance minister served on average for 1.43 years as a spending minister

17 The data base contains data since 1975. The data for earlier years was compiled by the author.

18 In his related analysis, Moessinger (2012) relies on the finance minister irrespective of an equally ranked budget minister, see fn. 5 on p. 105.

(tenure_spending) before their appointment and for 7.34 years as a member of parliament (tenure_mp). In 45 % percent of observations it was the case that the finance minister and the prime minister belonged to the same party in a coalition government (backing). While this has never occured in Finland, it holds for all observations for Luxembourg.[19]

The education of the minister is described by seven different variables. The variable university_phd captures whether the minister has participated in a tertiary education program. The variables university and phd differentiate further between tertiary programs at bachelor or master level and doctoral programs. The finance minister has studied or even holds a PhD in 91 % of the observations. While this holds for only 62 % of observations for Belgium, there are seven countries in which all finance ministers participated in a tertiary education.

Additionally, the author has collected information about the field of study and differentiates between the so-called STEM subjects (i.e., science, technology, engineering, and mathematics, stem with 8.3 % of observations), programs related to business or economics (economics with 49 %), legal studies (law with 32.9 %), and all other subjects, i.e., mainly the remaining social sciences, humanities, and arts (other_fields with 28.8 %). Note that some ministers studied several subjects and are coded respectively.

The professional experience is covered by several dummy variables that take the value of 1 if a minister had worked for at least five years in the respective sector before her appointment (as in Mikosch, 2012, ch. 5). In almost 20 % of observations the finance ministers have working experience in academia or research (*academia*) and for 12.5 % of observations this was related to economics, business, or finance. Around 22.3 % gained professional experience as an employee or manager in the private sector or as an entrepreneur (business), thereof 9.2 % were related to finance. Work experience in a central bank or international financial institutions such as the IMF or the World Bank was gained by finance ministers in 4.6 % of observations (central_bank). Around 11.3 % were lawyers or judges (lawyer). A further 4 % gained experience as a party officer (party_officer) and 5.6 % as a trade union officer (union_officer). Work experience in the public sector characterizes 19.4 % of observations, thereof 10.2 % in the field of public finances. In 30.8 % of observations, the finance minister can be considered as an outsider (outsider) because she had worked for more than five years outside of politics and the public sector, i.e., she worked in academia, in the private sector, as a lawyer, for a central bank or at an international financial institution. At the same time, these outsiders had not worked for more than five years in politics, in the public sector, as a lobbyist, or as a party or trade union officer. In 39 % of observation, there is a finance minister in office who has significant work experience in the field

19 Note that the variable takes the value 0 for all single party governments. Therefore, the mean value of backing for the United Kingdom (UK) amounts 0.03 in Table 5.9 despite the fact that the finance and the prime minister belonged to the same party in almost all UK governments.

of finance (finance), either in the public or private sector, in academia or in a central bank or an international institution.

Among the variables related to the budgetary preferences of the finance minister, the dummy variable left indicates that she belongs to or is nominated by a politically left party in 43.8 % of observations.[20] While there was a politically left finance minister in 94 % of observations for Portugal, there was not a single one for Luxembourg. Furthermore, the variable age measures the age of the finance ministers who were on average 51 years old while – on average – Italy has the oldest and Luxembourg the youngest finance ministers. Her gender is recorded by the dummy variable female. As mentioned in the discussion of the finance minister's budgetary preferences above, there have so far been only a few female finance ministers in European central governments. In the entire data set of 167 finance ministers, there are only seven women in total. Out of those, three served for less than 18 months and four were in office for three years or less.[21] Looking at the cut-off date of January 1st, the number declines to only six women in the sample representing only 2.1 % of observations. This is far too low to allow any statistical inference.

The parenthood status of the finance minister is also included in the analysis. The variables kids and kids_n indicate that the finance ministers have at least one child in 97.5 % of observations and have on average 2.7 children.

5.4 Results and robustness checks

This section highlights the regressions results based on a panel of 15 EU member states between 1970 and 2010. In the first part the empirical findings are discussed for the base model and for the models that focus on the finance minister's characteristics related to her ability (tables 5.2, 5.3, and 5.4). The following part presents the results related to her budgetary preferences (Table 5.5). The robustness of the empirical findings is examined with respect to alternative estimators and alternative cut-off dates in the last part (tables 5.7 and 5.6).

5.4.1 Results related to the finance minister's ability

The base model of this analysis explains changes in the debt ratio with standard variables covering the economic and political situation without including any individual characteristics of the respective finance minister. The results are shown in column 1

20 The author relies on the party classification used in the DPI to generate this variable.

21 Note that Christine Lagarde, the French minister of finance from June 2007 to June 2011, was not in charge of the government budget and, therefore, is not included in the analysis. Instead, Éric Woerth and François Baroin who served as budget ministers of equal rank in the cabinet in that period are considered (see Table 5.8).

Table 5.2: Base model and results for political experience and standing (ability I)

	Dependent variable: *debt* (change in debt-to-GDP ratio)						
	(1)	(2)	(3)	(4)	(5)	(6)	(7)
L.debt	0.443***	0.444***	0.444***	0.436***	0.441***	0.435***	0.434***
	(0.045)	(0.045)	(0.045)	(0.045)	(0.046)	(0.045)	(0.045)
gdp	−0.347***	−0.347***	−0.340***	−0.353***	−0.346***	−0.363***	−0.363***
	(0.113)	(0.113)	(0.113)	(0.113)	(0.114)	(0.113)	(0.113)
unemployment	0.088	0.090	0.096	0.109	0.112	0.094	0.092
	(0.077)	(0.077)	(0.078)	(0.079)	(0.079)	(0.077)	(0.077)
cost	0.275**	0.274**	0.281**	0.277**	0.278**	0.299**	0.300**
	(0.134)	(0.133)	(0.134)	(0.134)	(0.133)	(0.131)	(0.131)
openness	−0.006	−0.006	−0.008	−0.008	−0.009	−0.006	−0.006
	(0.017)	(0.017)	(0.017)	(0.017)	(0.017)	(0.017)	(0.017)
population	0.051	0.050	0.060	0.055	0.060	0.045	0.045
	(0.058)	(0.059)	(0.059)	(0.058)	(0.060)	(0.058)	(0.058)
emu	−0.856	−0.875	−0.929	−0.847	−0.942	−0.690	−0.674
	(2.089)	(2.088)	(2.098)	(2.198)	(2.187)	(2.082)	(2.084)
RR_currency	−0.114	−0.119	−0.108	−0.105	−0.112	−0.221	−0.217
	(0.697)	(0.701)	(0.696)	(0.697)	(0.702)	(0.698)	(0.694)
RR_inflation	−2.627*	−2.622*	−2.658*	−2.549*	−2.585*	−2.481*	−2.484*
	(1.482)	(1.486)	(1.482)	(1.483)	(1.488)	(1.474)	(1.470)
RR_stock	0.729	0.733	0.721	0.740	0.738	0.795*	0.792*
	(0.456)	(0.460)	(0.457)	(0.455)	(0.460)	(0.460)	(0.457)
RR_banking	0.875	0.883	0.844	0.905	0.888	0.822	0.816
	(0.565)	(0.569)	(0.563)	(0.568)	(0.573)	(0.569)	(0.564)
election	0.623*	0.620*	0.622*	0.617*	0.613	0.599	0.601
	(0.375)	(0.374)	(0.375)	(0.375)	(0.374)	(0.373)	(0.374)
majority	−2.148	−2.149	−2.095	−1.685	−1.775	−2.309	−2.309
	(2.347)	(2.349)	(2.346)	(2.389)	(2.401)	(2.343)	(2.341)
govfrac	0.110	0.114	0.113	−0.169	−0.083	0.416	0.413
	(1.085)	(1.089)	(1.084)	(1.150)	(1.167)	(1.091)	(1.087)
tenure		0.011			0.021	0.009	
		(0.082)			(0.083)	(0.082)	
tenure_spending			0.085		0.065		
			(0.078)		(0.086)		
tenure_mp				0.035	0.025		
				(0.032)	(0.034)		
backing						−0.706*	−0.707*
						(0.385)	(0.384)
Observations	480	480	480	480	480	480	480
Countries	15	15	15	15	15	15	15

Notes: The LSDVc estimator was applied with an initial Arellano-Bond estimate and 200 bootstrap repetitions. The estimates include both time fixed effects and country fixed effects that are not shown here. *** indicates significance at 1 % level, ** at 5 % level and * at 10 % level respectively. Standard errors are reported in parentheses.

of Table 5.2. As expected, there is a strong and significant path dependency in the debt-to-GDP ratio (debt). An increase of 1 percentage point in the previous years is associated with a further increase of 0.44 percentage points in the current year. Out of the four economic control variables, the growth rate of real GDP and the cost of debt servicing have a significant effect on the debt ratio. The estimate for the former variable has a negative sign as expected. When real GDP grows by 1 % the debt ratio is reduced by 0.35 percentage points. The estimate for the latter variable has a positive sign but its interpretation is more complex. Given the point estimate, the change in the debt-to-GDP ratio would increase by an additional 0.28 percentage points, for instance, if the country has a debt-to-GDP ratio of 50 % and the real long-term interest rate exceeds its real growth of GDP by 2 percentage points and vice versa. This is well in line with the results in Hallerberg, Strauch, and Hagen (2007).

As expected, there is a positive, but insignificant effect of the unemployment rate on the debt ratio. The base model, however, does not provide evidence for an effect of globalization measured by the countries' participation in international trade (openness) or an effect of the size of the population measured in million inhabitants. The respective coefficients are neither relevant in size nor are they significant. The estimated coefficient of the variable capturing the membership in the EMU has a negative sign but is not significant. The four RR crises indices have the expected signs. However, only the negative estimate for inflation crises is significant. Out of the three variables that cover the political situation, only the estimate for the dummy variable capturing pre-election periods is significant with an expected positive sign. The result indicates that the change in the debt ratio is on average 0.62 percentage points higher in a pre-election year. Also, the estimates for the fragmentation variable and the share of members of parliament supporting the government have the expected positive or respectively negative sign but are insignificant. Hence, the base model only provides support for one political economy hypothesis, namely, the hypothesis on political business cycles around elections. However, this effect is not robust to the inclusion of further variables and significance falls slightly below the 10 % level in the following models.

The remainder of this section highlights the results for the three groups of individual characteristics that are hypothesized to increase the ability of the finance minister. The discussion is structured as in Section 5.2.1.

Political experience and standing

The empirical results for the first group of characteristics related to the political experience and the political standing of the finance minister are rather mixed. Models 2 to 5 in Table 5.2 do not provide supporting evidence for the first three hypotheses which claim that the growth of debt is reduced if the finance minister has already served for a long time (hypothesis 5.1), if she served as a spending minister before her appointment (5.2), or if she has been a member of parliament (5.3). The estimates for all three tenure variables are not only insignificant but also have an unexpected positive sign. Hence the three hypotheses are rejected. The result for the tenure as finance minister is unexpected as it contradicts the findings for German states in Chapter 4, and Feld and Schaltegger (2010) for the Swiss central government.[22]

Moreover, these results differ from the related study by Moessinger (2012) who finds a negative and highly significant effect of the finance minister's tenure and her tenure

22 The inclusion of the squared tenure of the finance minister – as in Chapter 4 – yields a positive estimate for the linear term and a negative for the quadratic term, but none of the two is significant.

as a previous spending minister on debt growth in Europe. There are several methodological differences between his investigation and this study which might explain these different results.[23]

Which of the different features generates the opposing results can only be hypothesized. The most likely explanation is the inclusion of a country-specific linear time trend, the (linear) variable age, and the (linear) variable tenure at the same time in Moessinger (2012) which might cause biased estimates due to multicollinearity. Replicating the specification of Moessinger (2012) in the dynamic panel model with tenure, age and a country-specific linear time trend included at the same time, the estimate for tenure turns negative as in Moessinger (2012), but remains insignificant. Nevertheless, the author rejects hypothesis 5.1 that the tenure of the finance minister affects the debt growth in European countries based on the results of the specification reported in model 2. The same applies to hypotheses 5.2 and 5.3 for the tenure as a previous spending minister or as a former member of parliament.[24] When all three tenure variables are included in model 5, they are not jointly significant given a p-value of 59.9 % for the F-test.

Looking at the political ties between the finance minister and the head of government, models 6 and 7 provide supporting evidence for hypothesis 5.4. The finance minister can reduce the debt growth by 0.71 percentage points when she belongs to the party of the head of government and, therefore, enjoys the political backing of the head of government. This confirms previous results for the German states of Jochimsen and Nuscheler (2011) and Jochimsen and Thomasius (2012, see also ch. 4).

23 Both, Moessinger (2012) and the present study investigate the effect of individual characteristics of the finance minister on the change in central government as a share of the GDP. However, they differ in mainly five aspects related to data and methods. First of all, Moessinger (2012) uses data for 14 EU member states and Norway between 1981 and 2009, whereas this study analyzes data for the EU-15 countries between 1970 and 2010. In comparison with this study, Moessinger (2012) includes additional data for Norway, while he does not include data for Belgium. Second, he analyzes the cabinet members with the title 'finance minister' whereas this study focuses on the minister in charge of the budget (Table 5.8 in the appendix reports those cases in which, besides the 'finance minister', an own budget minister of equal rank was in charge of the budget). Only when the budget minister is a junior minister or state secretary of lower rank is the finance minister referred to in this study. The third difference is related to the data used for the dependent variable. While Moessinger (2012) uses OECD data for the central government debt to GDP ratio that is available for years after 1980, this study uses the data from Reinhart and Rogoff (2011) who provide longer historical time series. Fourth, Moessinger (2012) estimates a panel model and uses the fixed effects estimator. This study relies on a dynamic panel model and employs the LSDVc estimator. How time effects are captured is the fifth difference. Moessinger (2012) uses time fixed effects and includes a country-specific linear trend in addition. This study employs time fixed effects as well, and includes additional country-specific dummy variables for years with financial crises provided by Reinhart and Rogoff (2011) and for EMU membership. However, the present study does not include a linear time trend since the dependent variable does not exhibit a clear linear trend.

24 Results do not change when dummy variables for former spending ministers or former members of parliament are used instead of the respective tenure variables. Both estimates are also positive, but remain insignificant.

Educational background

The second group of characteristics that might strengthen the finance minister relates to her education. Hypothesis 5.5 states that higher educated ministers reduce debt growth, hypothesis 5.6 focuses on field of study. It claims that debt growth is lower when trained economists are in office. The empirical results presented in Table 5.3 support neither of the two hypotheses. Ministers that participated in a bachelor or master program or earned a PhD do not realize signficantly lower debt growth in comparison to the reference group without such tertiary education. Moreover, the point estimate in model 1 has a positive sign. The same applies when it is further distinguished between ministers who participated in a bachelor or masters program and those who earned a PhD in model 2. The companion study for the German states in Chapter 4 reports negative point estimates for the education level. However, they are also not significant. The study by Mikosch (2012, ch. 5) analyzes how the education of the head of government affects the change in the ratio of general government debt to GDP. It also reports a positive but insignificant estimate for tertiary education.

Looking at the field of study in models 3 to 8, a negative effect on debt growth is identified for trained economists. However, hypothesis 5.6 is rejected as it is far from being significant. Models 5, 7, and 8 yield an unexpected result for former students of science, technology, engineering, and mathematics (stem). These finance ministers are associated with a significantly higher change of 1.8–1.9 percentage points in the ratio of debt-to-GDP. The significance of the negative estimate for former students of other subjects (mainly humanities) in model 6 vanishes as soon as other subject dummies are included. The four subject dummy variables in model 8 are jointly significant at 0.6 % level (F-test). However, this significance is solely driven by the variable stem. The other three subject dummy variables are not jointly significant with a p-value of 47.1 %. Note that the result for the variable stem relies predominantly on data from France, Greece, and Italy. The three countries have the highest share of finance ministers who have studied these subjects with 23–29 % of observations while there are eight countries that do not have more than one observation each for these fields of study (thereof, six countries do not have a single observation, see also Table 5.9 in the appendix). Since these three countries are not well known for balanced budgets the result for these subjects should not be generalized for all EU-15 countries.

In his related study, Moessinger (2012) does not find any significant effect for trained economists and lawyers either. Since his analysis is focused on these two subjects, there are no results reported for former students of stem subjects or other_fields. The companion study in Chapter 4 does not yield any significant effects for the four subjects examined, but the reported estimates for trained economists and other subjects are negative as in model 8 of this study. Looking at the head of government and the general government debt ratio, Mikosch (2012, ch. 5) does not find any significant effects for the four subject groups either. Note that the p-value of the variable backing passes the 10 % significance threshold as soon as the variable stem is included.

Table 5.3: Results for education (ability II)

	Dependent variable: *debt* (change in debt-to-GDP ratio)							
	(1)	(2)	(3)	(4)	(5)	(6)	(7)	(8)
L.debt	0.434***	0.433***	0.435***	0.436***	0.430***	0.434***	0.430***	0.433***
	(0.045)	(0.044)	(0.045)	(0.045)	(0.045)	(0.045)	(0.044)	(0.045)
emu	−0.730	0.977	−0.724	−0.666	1.573	−0.479	−0.068	1.596
	(2.095)	(2.114)	(2.070)	(2.089)	(2.104)	(2.075)	(2.069)	(2.109)
backing	−0.703*	−0.688*	−0.690*	−0.699*	−0.548	−0.776**	−0.612	−0.614
	(0.386)	(0.388)	(0.383)	(0.387)	(0.378)	(0.384)	(0.379)	(0.381)
university_phd	0.260							
	(0.586)							
university		0.441						
		(0.554)						
phd		0.664						
		(0.644)						
economics			−0.327					−0.213
			(0.358)					(0.383)
law				−0.056				0.059
				(0.376)				(0.399)
stem					1.925***		1.837***	1.795***
					(0.577)		(0.582)	(0.640)
other_fields						−0.696*	−0.589	−0.613
						(0.409)	(0.408)	(0.417)
Observations	480	480	480	480	480	480	480	480
Countries	15	15	15	15	15	15	15	15

Notes: The LSDVc estimator was applied with an initial Arellano-Bond estimate and 200 bootstrap repetitions. The control variables gdp, unemployment, cost, openness, population and the four RR crises indices as well as election, majority and govfrac are included. They do not differ qualitatively from the base model in Table 5.2 and are not shown here for the sake of clarity. The estimates include both time fixed effects and country fixed effects that are not shown here. *** indicates significance at 1 % level, ** at 5 % level and * at 10 % level respectively. Standard errors are reported in parentheses.

Taking the results all together, there is no evidence that the finance minister's level of education affects debt growth in the EU-15 countries. The same holds for the field of study, with one exception: Former students of science, technology, engineering, and mathematics realize a significant growth in the debt-to-GDP ratio.

Professional experience

The third group of characteristics that are hypothesized to enhance the ability of the finance minister refer to the professional experience she gained before her appointment. The empirical results highlighted in Table 5.4 do not provide supporting evidence for hypothesis 5.7. This hypothesis claims that ministers with professional experience in finance-related areas reduce the growth of public debt. The variable finance in model 1 takes the value of 1 for ministers with at least five years working experience in a finance-related field. Even though the estimate for this variable has the expected negative sign, it is not statistically significant and the hypothesis is rejected for this sample of EU-15 countries. Also, the decomposition of the professional experience into three subgroups of finance- or economics-related work experience in academia (academia_finance), business (business_finance), or the field of public fin-

Table 5.4: Results for professional experience (ability III)

	Dependent variable: *debt* (change in debt-to-GDP ratio)				
	(1)	(2)	(3)	(4)	(5)
L.debt	0.433***	0.438***	0.430***	0.440***	0.429***
	(0.044)	(0.045)	(0.044)	(0.046)	(0.044)
emu	−0.778	−0.743	−0.678	−0.694	1.151
	(2.083)	(2.084)	(2.079)	(2.216)	(2.134)
backing	−0.690*	−0.778*	−0.732*	−0.679	−0.696*
	(0.384)	(0.399)	(0.385)	(0.425)	(0.384)
finance	−0.321				
	(0.378)				
academia_finance		0.539			
		(0.638)			
business_finance		0.163			
		(0.603)			
public_finance		−0.310			
		(0.596)			
public			−0.505		
			(0.394)		
academia				0.665	
				(0.553)	
business				0.007	
				(0.420)	
union_officer				−0.325	
				(0.865)	
lawyer				0.213	
				(0.549)	
party_officer				0.256	
				(0.697)	
central_bank				−0.084	
				(0.808)	
outsider					0.463
					(0.389)
Observations	480	480	480	480	480
Countries	15	15	15	15	15

Notes: The LSDVc estimator was applied with an initial Arellano-Bond estimate and 200 bootstrap repetitions. The control variables gdp, unemployment, cost, openness, population and the four RR crises indices as well as election, majority and govfrac are included. They do not differ qualitatively from the base model in Table 5.2 and are not shown here for the sake of clarity. The estimates include both time fixed effects and country fixed effects that are not shown here. *** indicates significance at 1 % level, ** at 5 % level and * at 10 % level respectively. Standard errors are reported in parentheses.

ance (public_finance) does not yield a different result in model 2. Nevertheless, the estimate for public_finance has a negative sign, while the estimates for the other two variables are positive. The three variables are also jointly insignificant with a p-value of 78.9 %. Contrary to these results, the companion study in Chapter 4 finds a negative and significant effect of finance ministers with finance experience on public deficits in the German states.

The third model focuses on public sector employees and yields a negative estimate. But again, the estimate is insignificant. In model 4 all six professional groups are included besides the reference category public sector employees. Former researchers (academia), lawyers (lawyer), and party officers (party_officer) are associated with a positive and former central bank staff (central_bank) with a negative effect on the debt growth. Contrary to conventional wisdom, former trade union officials (union) are associated with a negative effect on debt growth whereas former private sector employees, managers or entrepreneurs (business)are found to have a positive effect. However, the single variables are not significant and they are also not jointly significant with a p-value of 94.2 %.

The last model in Table 5.4 captures the effect of former 'outsiders' who gained more than five years professional experience outside politics and the public sector and at the same time did not work for more than five years in the public sector or politics before their appointment. The estimate for the variable outsider is positive but insignificant. The sign corresponds to the mirror-inverted analysis in Mikosch (2012, ch. 5). He finds a negative and significant effect on the growth of public debt when the head of government is a former career politician without any outside experience.

Altogether, the professional background of finance ministers had no significant effect on changes in the debt ratio in the considered EU-15 countries. Hence, this study cannot confirm the respective results of Chapter 4 for finance ministers in German states.

The preceding section presented the empirical results for the finance minister's ability to influence the debt growth along three categories of individual characteristics. With respect to the first categories, political experience and standing, only the political ties between the finance minister and the prime minister have proved to matter for fiscal performance in the central governments of EU-15 countries. The change in the debt-to-GDP ratio will be 0.7 percentage points lower when both belong to the same party in a coalition government. There are no significant effects for political experience gained as a former spending minister or member of parliament. The second category refers to the education of the finance minister. It is shown that her level of education does not affect the debt ratio. The field of study also does not matter – with only one exception: Former students of science, technology, engineering, or mathematics increase (STEM) the growth of debt by 1.8–1.9 percentage points. However, this effect is mainly driven by observations from three countries that are not well known for sound budgeting. Therefore, the author refrains from generalizing this result for all EU-15 countries. Moreover, the significance of the prime minister's backing vanishes as soon as the STEM subjects are included. The analysis of the finance minister's professional experience before her appointment yields no significant results at all. Neither experience in the field of finance, nor experience in specific sectors or professions affects the ability of the finance minister with respect to debt growth.

5.4.2 Results related to the finance minister's preferences

The following part highlights the empirical results for the hypotheses on the budgetary preferences of the finance minister from section 5.2.2. Table 5.5 summarizes the results.

Looking at the party affiliation, model 1 provides supporting evidence that the change in the debt ratio does not follow a significantly different pattern when the minister in charge belongs to or is nominated by a politically left party (as classified in the DPI). Hence, the hypothesis 5.8 that her ideological orientation is irrelevant for the debt ratio is confirmed.

The age of the finance minister is included in models 2 and 3. Neither the linear nor the quadratic specification are significant and hypothesis 5.9 is rejected. However, the point estimates for the linear term in model 2 and for the quadratic term in model 3

Table 5.5: Results for preferences

	Dependent variable: *debt* (change in debt-to-GDP ratio)				
	(1)	(2)	(3)	(4)	(5)
L.debt	0.443***	0.439***	0.437***	0.426***	0.422***
	(0.045)	(0.051)	(0.051)	(0.072)	(0.072)
emu	−0.663	−1.255	−1.246	0.707	1.496
	(2.092)	(2.005)	(2.013)	(3.367)	(3.428)
RR_inflation	−2.683*	−2.647*	−2.678*	0.541	0.573
	(1.480)	(1.538)	(1.538)	(3.466)	(3.516)
govfrac	0.480	−0.016	0.106	0.928	0.891
	(1.103)	(1.155)	(1.171)	(2.016)	(1.979)
left	0.494				
	(0.331)				
age		−0.028	0.126		
		(0.028)	(0.207)		
age_sq			−0.001		
			(0.002)		
kids				0.610	
				(2.055)	
kids_n					−0.072
					(0.197)
Observations	480	477	477	397	397
Countries	15	15	15	15	15

Notes: The LSDVc estimator was applied with an initial Arellano-Bond estimate and 200 bootstrap repetitions. The control variables gdp, unemployment, cost, openness, population and the three other RR crises indices as well as election and majority are included. They do not differ qualitatively from the base model in Table 5.2 and are not shown here for the sake of clarity. The estimates include both time fixed effects and country fixed effects that are not shown here. *** indicates significance at 1 % level, ** at 5 % level and * at 10 % level respectively. Standard errors are reported in parentheses.

are negative and not positive as expected.[25] Moessinger (2012) reports a negative, but insignificant estimate for the finance minister's age, too.

As mentioned earlier, it is not possible to test whether female and male finance ministers differ with respect to the change in the debt ratio. The number of observations is with only six women out of 167 ministers simply too low to draw upon any statistical inference (see p. 116). Hence, hypothesis 5.10 cannot be challenged empirically in this investigation. The companion study in Chapter 4 finds no significant difference between female and male finance ministers with respect to public deficits in German states.

Models 4 and 5 present the results for the parenthood status. Neither the dummy variable for finance ministers who have children in model 4 and the number of children in model 5 are significant and, hence, hypothesis 5.11 is rejected. The point estimate for the dummy variable has an unexpected positive sign while the estimate for the number of children has the expected negative sign. The companion study in Chapter 4 does not find significant results either.

The above analysis of the characteristics related to the budgetary preferences of the finance minister does not provide supporting evidence for any of the preference related hypotheses introduced in Section 5.2.2. Neither the ideological leaning of the finance minister, her age nor her parental status have a statistically significant effect on the growth of central government debt relative to GDP in the EU-15 countries.

5.4.3 Robustness checks

Only the analysis of characteristics related to the finance minister's ability identifies specific characteristics that affect the growth of central government debt in EU-15 countries. The estimation result of model 7 in Table 5.2 demonstrates that the political backing of the prime minister matters for the finance minister's ability to ensure sound public finances. Model 5 in Table 5.3 shows that finance ministers who have studied one of the STEM subjects incur higher debt growth than others. Recall that the latter results should not be generalized since it is mainly driven by three countries. As the latter effect also cancels out the former, the robustness of both models is challenged individually. In the following subsection, the robustness of these two empirical results is first examined with respect to alternative implementations of the bias corrected least squares dummy variable (LSDVc) estimator, to alternative estimators and to waiving the time fixed effects. Furthermore, the robustness to alternative cut-off dates is tested to avoid the results from being driven by the choice of the cut-off date. Results which infer that professional experience does not matter is examined with respect to the creation of the respective dummy variables, too.

25 Irrespective of the lack of significance, model 3 gives at least an indication that finance ministers are associated with lower debt growth when they are older than 63 years.

Table 5.6: Robustness checks for alternative estimators and time specifications

	Alternative estimators and time specifications						
	LSDVc	LSDVc	Pooled OLS	Fixed effects (LSDV)		Arellano Bond	
	Time FE	no Time FE	no FE	Time FE	no Time FE	Time FE	no Time FE
	Dependent variable: *debt* (change in debt-to-GDP ratio)						
	Panel 1: Inclusion of backing only						
L.debt	0.434***	0.468***	0.451***	0.377***	0.417***	0.377***	0.417***
	(0.045)	(0.041)	(0.067)	(0.072)	(0.078)	(0.066)	(0.074)
constant			1.207	1.506	4.352***	1.446	4.352***
			(0.708)	(2.441)	(1.312)	(2.327)	(1.166)
backing	−0.707*	−0.740**	−0.553	−0.756	−0.784	−0.756	−0.784
	(0.384)	(0.362)	(0.445)	(0.558)	(0.552)	(0.508)	(0.525)
Obs.	480	480	480	480	480	467	467
Countries	15	15	(15)	15	15	15	15
R-squared			0.480	0.539	0.487		
	Panel 2: Inclusion of backing and stem						
L.debt	0.430***	0.472***	0.451***	0.374***	0.420***	0.374***	0.420***
	(0.045)	(0.040)	(0.068)	(0.073)	(0.080)	(0.066)	(0.076)
constant			1.457*	1.478	4.445***	1.975	4.445***
			(0.812)	(2.415)	(1.265)	(2.244)	(1.117)
backing	−0.548	−0.548	−0.466	−0.584	−0.584	−0.584	−0.584
	(0.378)	(0.358)	(0.478)	(0.624)	(0.603)	(0.568)	(0.572)
stem	1.925***	1.813***	1.757***	1.967**	1.834***	1.967***	1.834***
	(0.577)	(0.568)	(0.477)	(0.710)	(0.521)	(0.645)	(0.495)
Obs.	480	480	480	480	480	467	467
Countries	15	15	(15)	15	15	15	15
R-squared			0.491	0.550	0.498		

Notes: Besides pooled OLS, all specifications include country fixed effects. Both, the country and – if included – the time fixed effects are not shown. Also the control variables gdp, unemployment, cost, openness, population, emu, the four crises indices, election, majority, and govfrac are included but not shown here for the sake of clarity. The LSDVc estimator was applied with an initial Arellano-Bond estimate and 200 bootstrap repetitions. Standard errors are robust and clustered at country level for OLS, fixed effects (LSDV) and Arellano Bond estimators. *** indicates significance at 1 % level, ** at 5 % level and * at 10 % level respectively. Standard errors are reported in parentheses.

The above analyses rely on the Arellano-Bond estimator as an initial estimate for the implemented LSDVc estimator (see Section 5.3.1). The results remain unchanged when the Blundell-Bond estimator is used instead (Kiviet and Bun, 2001; Bruno, 2005b).[26]

The robustness to alternative estimators is challenged in Table 5.6. Again, the first panel tests the robustness for the variable backing in the specification of model 7 in Table 5.2 and panel 2 relies on model 5 as in Table 5.3. The results in panel 1 indicate that the significance of the variable backing is not robust to alternative estimators. Only

26 The results are not shown here, but are available upon request.

when the bias corrected least squares dummy variable estimator for dynamic panels is employed is a significant effect found. The same applies when the variables backing and stem are examined in panel 2. However, the point estimates are rather stable across the different estimators and also the exclusion of the time fixed effects does not change the results in both panels.

Table 5.7 presents the results for the alternative cut-off dates separated in two panels. Panel 1 relies on model 7 from Table 5.2 while model 5 from Table 5.3 is reestimated in panel 2. The significance of the variable backing in panel 1 does not hold for all alternative cut-off dates. However, the point estimate remains rather stable. Also the significance of the variable stem is not entirely robust to the alternative cut-off dates in panel 2 and, moreover, the estimated coefficient exhibits a strong variation.

The dummy variables that capture the professional background of the finance minister take the value of 1 if the finance minister has work experience of at least five years in the respective field, e.g., public sector or academia. Changing the required work experience from five to three, four and six or seven years does not affect the results.

Table 5.7: Robustness checks for alternative cut-off dates

		Alternative cut-off dates					
	Cut-off date	in previous year		in same year			
	January 1st	October 1st	December 1st	February 1st	April 1st	June 1st	August 1st
	Dependent variable: *debt* (change in debt-to-GDP ratio)						
	Panel 1: Inclusion of backing only						
L.debt	0.434***	0.439***	0.434***	0.434***	0.430***	0.432***	0.433***
	(0.045)	(0.045)	(0.045)	(0.045)	(0.045)	(0.045)	(0.045)
backing	−0.707*	−0.436	−0.666*	−0.658*	−0.588	−0.661*	−0.688*
	(0.384)	(0.367)	(0.378)	(0.390)	(0.382)	(0.383)	(0.403)
	Panel 2: Inclusion of backing and stem						
L.debt	0.430***	0.427***	0.420***	0.431***	0.425***	0.430***	0.430***
	(0.045)	(0.045)	(0.045)	(0.045)	(0.046)	(0.045)	(0.045)
backing	−0.548	−0.399	−0.632	−0.514	−0.497	−0.612	−0.641
	(0.378)	(0.395)	(0.406)	(0.383)	(0.376)	(0.379)	(0.399)
stem	1.925***	1.230*	1.044	1.745***	1.522**	1.067	0.792
	(0.577)	(0.667)	(0.659)	(0.587)	(0.610)	(0.651)	(0.665)
Observations	480	479	479	480	480	480	480
Countries	15	15	15	15	15	15	15

Notes: Data on the individual characteristics of the finance minister (backing and stem) refer to the minister in office on the respective cut-off day. The LSDVc estimator was applied with an initial Arellano-Bond estimate and 200 bootstrap repetitions. The estimates include both time fixed effects and country fixed effects that are not shown here. Also the control variables gdp, unemployment, cost, openness, population, emu, the four crises indices, election, majority, and govfrac are included but not shown here for the sake of clarity. *** indicates significance at 1 % level, ** at 5 % level and * at 10 % level respectively. Standard errors are reported in parentheses.

Hence, these alternative definitions of the dummy variables confirm that the professional background does not matter for the debt ratio in the EU-15 countries.[27]

The above robustness checks demonstrate that the estimates for the variable backing are robust (in size) to alternative cut-off dates and also to alternative estimators. The estimates also remain significant for most alternative cut-off dates. However, the significance vanishes as soon as alternative estimators are employed. On the contrary, the size of the estimated coefficients for stem is not robust to alternative cut-off dates, but the estimates remain significant for most alternative cut-off dates and for all alternative estimators.

5.5 Conclusion

This paper contributes to the growing literature that includes the characteristics of political decision makers in the analysis of policy outcomes. It examines if the growth of central government debt is affected by individual characteristics of the finance minister and focuses, in particular, on characteristics that may matter for her ability to ensure sound public finances and characteristics that may shape her budgetary preferences. The analysis employs dynamic panel estimations based on data for 15 member states of the European Union between 1970 and 2010.

Essentially, the empirical results show that the individual characteristics of finance ministers have almost no influence on the growth of central government debt in Europe. First, preference related characteristics, such as her political orientation, her age, or the existance of children, do not affect debt growth at all. The effect of the finance minister's gender could not be examined here due to the very low number of female ministers in the sample, which precludes any empirical analysis. Second, the results are mixed for the ability related characteristics which are examined along three groups. The first group covers the political experience and the standing within the cabinet. The results show that the political experience from previous positions as a spending minister or member of parliament is irrelevant for public debt. But there is weak evidence that the political ties with the prime minister matter for the finance minister's standing within the cabinet: Debt growth is lower when the finance minister belongs to the same party as the prime minister in a coalition government. This confirms the results for the German states in Jochimsen and Nuscheler (2011) and the companion study in Chapter 4 (and the earlier version: Jochimsen and Thomasius, 2012). However, its significance depends on the estimator employed and the chosen cut-off date. The second group captures the finance minister's education. Neither the level nor the field of study prove to be relevant for public debt – with only one exception. Debt growth is higher when

27 Results are available upon request.

the finance minister is a former student of science, technology, engineering, or mathematics. The significance of this effect is robust to alternative estimators and most alternative cut-off dates, but its reason remains opaque.

One explanation could be that the estimates rely predominately on observations from three countries that are not well known for sound budgeting while more than half of the countries contribute with no more than one observation each. It is likely that the dummy variable captures the general fiscal situation in these three countries rather than a causal effect of the finance ministers' background in the STEM subjects. Hence, this result should not be generalized to all countries in the sample. Nevertheless, the overall result that the finance minister's education does not matter for debt growth is well in line with Chapter 4 and the related study by Moessinger (2012). The examination of the third group of characteristics which is related to her ability to ensure sound budgeting does not yield significant results either. Contrary to Chapter 4 (and Jochimsen and Thomasius, 2012), there is no evidence that finance ministers with previous working experience in the finance area reduce the growth of central government debt in the EU-15 countries.

Public debt is also not affected by other professional experiences. These results for the professional background might be explained by opposing effects for different political orientations within one group of professional experience. Similarly, the effects of the professional background on the strength of the finance minister might differ across countries – due to different fiscal cultures or different budgeting procedures – and as a result might cancel each other out. These aspects require further exploration as they go far beyond the scope of this study. In addition to this, future research should examine how ministers with specific professional and educational backgrounds affect fiscal performance in crisis situations such as financial market crises. This approach could also include whether the ideological orientation of the finance minister becomes relevant in times of financial distress.

Even though the evidence is weak, this study suggests that fiscal performance is improved when the finance minister has the backing of the prime minister due to the same party affiliation. Hence, ruling or designated heads of coalition governments should be emphatic about retaining the finance ministry for their political party to ensure sound budgeting.

5.A Appendix

Table 5.8: Budget ministers of equal rank besides the finance minister

Name	Position (official language)	Start date	End date
Belgium			
A. Cools	Minister van Begroting	17.06.1968	21.02.1971
M. Denis	—	22.02.1971	19.01.1972
L. Tindemans	—	26.01.1973	24.04.1974
C. Geens	Minister van Begroting en Wetenschapsbeleid	08.12.1976	02.06.1977
G. Spitaels	Minister van Begroting	03.04.1979	17.05.1980
G. Geens	—	18.05.1980	21.10.1980
G. Mathot	Minister van Binnenlandse Zaken en Begroting	22.10.1980	16.12.1981
P. Maystadt	Minister van Begroting en Wetenschapsbeleid	17.12.1981	27.11.1985
G. Verhofstadt	Minister van Begroting en Wetenschappelijk Onderzoek	28.11.1985	09.05.1988
H. Schiltz	Minister van Begroting en Wetenschapsbeleid	09.05.1988	28.09.1991
W. Demeester	—	29.09.1991	04.03.1992
M. Van De Wiele	Minister van Begroting	07.03.1992	05.09.1993
H. Van Rompuy	—	05.09.1993	12.07.1999
J. Vande Lanotte	Minister van Begroting, Sociale integratie en Sociale economie , (later: Begroting en Overheidsbedrijven)	12.07.1999	15.10.2005
F. Van den Bossche	Minister van Begroting en Overheidsbedrijven	16.10.2005	20.12.2007
Y. Leterme	Minister van Begroting, Mobiliteit en Institutionele Hervormingen	21.12.2007	19.03.2008
G. Vanhengel	Minister van Begroting	17.07.2009	06.12.2011
France			
M. Papon	Ministre du Budget	03.04.1978	03.05.1981
M. Charasse	—	02.04.1992	01.10.1992
M. Malvy	—	02.10.1992	28.03.1993
N. Sarkozy	Ministre du Budget, porte-parole du Gouvernement	29.03.1993	11.05.1995
É. Woerth	Ministre du Budget, des Comptes publics, de la Fonction publique et de la Réforme de l'État	17.05.2007	19.03.2010
F. Baroin	—	20.03.2010	28.06.2011
Italy			
B. Andreatta	Ministro del Bilancio e della Programmazione Economica	02.08.1979	03.04.1980
—	—	21.02.1993	27.04.1993
G. La Malfa	—	04.04.1980	30.11.1982
G. Bodrato	—	01.12.1982	03.08.1983
P. Romita	—	04.08.1983	16.04.1987
G.G. Goria	—	17.04.1987	28.07.1987
E. Colombo	—	29.07.1987	12.04.1988
A. Fanfani	—	13.04.1988	21.07.1989
P. Cirino Pomicino	—	22.07.1989	27.06.1992
F. Reviglio	—	28.06.1992	20.02.1993
L. Spaventa	—	28.04.1993	09.05.1994

Continued on next page...

Table 5.8: Budget ministers of equal rank besides the finance minister (continued)

Name	Position (official language)	Start date	End date
G. Pagliarini	—	10.05.1994	16.01.1995
R. Masera	—	17.01.1995	15.02.1996
M. Arcelli	—	16.02.1996	16.05.1996
C.A. Ciampi	Ministro del Tesoro, del Bilancio e della Programmazione Economica	17.05.1996	14.05.1999
G. Amato	—	15.05.1999	21.04.2000
V. Visco	—	22.04.2000	10.06.2001
Luxembourg			
M. Fischbach	Ministre de la Justice and Ministre du Budget	26.01.1995	03.02.1998
L. Frieden	Ministre de la Justice, Ministre du Trésor et du Budget (temporarily in addition: Ministre de la Défense)	04.02.1998	22.07.2009

Notes: The table presents ministers that were responsible for the budget besides the finance minister. Only ministers with full or at least equal rank in the cabinet are listed here and used in the analysis, i.e., budget ministers working as a state secretary or junior minister in the finance ministry are not included. The position or title of the minister is given in the local language. For multi-lingual countries, the most common language is used. In the case of Luxembourg, the author relies on the language used on the respective government websites. *Source*: Government and parliamentary information offices and websites.

Table 5.9: Minister characteristics by country (mean values)

Country	AT	BE	DE	DK	ES	FI	FR	GR	IE	IT	LU	NL	PT	SE	UK
Begin	1980	1971	1971	1980	1980	1980	1971	1992	1977	1980	1992	1971	1980	1980	1971
End	2010	2009	2010	2010	2008	2010	2010	2008	2010	2010	2006	2010	2010	2010	2010
Observed years	31	39	40	31	29	31	40	17	34	31	15	40	31	31	40
Observed ministers	10	18	11	10	6	9	17	7	13	17	3	10	13	10	9
Ability: Political experience and standing															
tenure	3.41	1.94	2.82	2.32	2.83	2.63	2.03	1.72	1.92	1.83	5.13	3.29	1.45	2.2	2.93
tenure_spending	1.39	0.98	1.44	3.14	1.18	0.69	0.53	1.95	3.65	1.17	2.1	0.32	0.38	1.87	1.56
tenure_m[illegible]	0.87	3.87	10.17	12.4	4.66	9.41	4.03	7.12	14.44	11.16	2.8	2	1.96	6.02	15.99
backing	0.68	0.31	0.9	0.87	0.14	0	0.63	0.12	0.74	0.39	1	0.4	0.06	0.58	0.03
Ability: Education															
university_phd	1	0.62	0.98	0.94	1	0.77	1	1	0.85	1	1	0.83	1	0.84	0.98
university	0.74	0.38	0.43	0.94	0.24	0.77	0.95	0.29	0.76	0.61	0.8	0.65	0.48	0.42	0.73
phd	0.26	0.23	0.55	0	0.76	0	0.05	0.71	0.09	0.39	0.2	0.18	0.52	0.29	0.25
economics	0.81	0.23	0.4	0.45	0.9	0.1	0.38	0.82	0.5	0.39	0.53	0.68	0.84	0.32	0.33
law	0.13	0.41	0.25	0.13	0.48	0.29	0.6	0.12	0.35	0.58	1	0.13	0.26	0.06	0.38
stem	0	0.03	0.03	0.16	0.1	0.16	0.23	0.29	0.09	0.26	0	0	0	0	0
other_fields	0.06	0.41	0.33	0.23	0.24	0.23	0.65	0.41	0.03	0.13	0	0.1	0.06	0.55	0.63
Ability: Professional experience															
finance	0.16	0.31	0.15	0.23	0.86	0.29	0.6	0.41	0.21	0.71	0	0.5	0.97	0.48	0.35
academina	0	0.49	0.2	0.03	0.62	0	0.1	0.41	0.15	0.48	0	0	0.94	0.03	0
academia_finance	0	0.23	0.03	0.03	0.52	0	0.1	0.41	0	0.32	0	0	0.74	0	0
business	0.29	0.03	0.03	0.61	0.24	0.42	0.53	0.12	0.41	0.06	0	0.33	0.26	0.13	0.1
business_finance	0.16	0	0.03	0.13	0	0.26	0.18	0	0.21	0.06	0	0.18	0.19	0	0.1
central_bank	0.06	0	0	0	0.38	0.03	0.08	0	0	0.19	0	0.18	0.1	0	0
lawyer	0	0.15	0.03	0	0	0.23	0.05	0.12	0.12	0.19	0.73	0.05	0	0	0.38
outsider	0.1	0.18	0.03	0.06	0.34	0.65	0.23	0.35	0.32	0.71	0.53	0.08	0.35	0.03	0.35
party_officer	0.1	0.05	0	0.03	0	0.1	0.15	0	0	0	0	0.03	0	0.19	0.13
public	0.19	0.18	0.57	0.03	0.24	0.06	0.55	0	0.18	0.1	0	0.48	0.52	0.58	0
public_finance	0.06	0	0	0	0.24	0	0.38	0	0	0	0	0.48	0.42	0.26	0
union_officer	0.29	0	0.13	0.23	0	0.06	0	0	0	0	0	0.13	0	0.03	0
Preferences															
left	0.68	0.31	0.57	0.35	0.62	0.26	0.38	0.65	0.09	0.26	0	0.3	0.94	0.68	0.45
age	45.67	45.23	56.36	50.95	50.46	50.05	54.97	50.67	47.52	59.26	41.14	47.57	49.63	50.9	53.58
female	0	0.1	0	0.03	0	0	0	0	0	0	0	0	0.06	0.1	0
kids	1	1	0.9	1	1	1	1	1	0.97	0.96	0.67	1	1	1	1
kids_n	1.82	3.44	2.2	2.23	2.55	3.23	3	2.42	4.15	2.22	1.33	2.52	2.33	2.61	3.08

Note: Mean values for age and tenure are calculated based on all observations, i.e., one minister that serves for three years, for example, enters into the calculation of tenure with 3 different values and not with a single value. Hence, the mean of tenure does not correspond to the mean of the maximum tenure of the finance ministers. All information refer to the budget minister who was in office on January 1st. Table 5.10 provides a detailled description of variables and data sources.

Table 5.10: Variable description and sources

Variable	Description	Source
Dependent and control variables		
debt	Change in the ratio of central government debt to GDP in percentage points	Reinhart and Rogoff (2011) and OECD National Accounts Statistics (for Italy, Luxembourg, and the Netherlands only)
gdp	Growth rate of (real) gross domestic product in percent	OECD National Accounts Statistics
unemployment	Unemployment rate among civilian labor force in percentage points	OECD Employment and Labour Market Statistics
cost	Cost of debt servicing defined as Hallerberg, Strauch, and Hagen (2007): difference between the real long-term interest rate and the growth rate of real GDP multiplied with the ratio of government debt to GDP	Own calculation based on Reinhart and Rogoff (2011) and OECD National Accounts Statistics
openness	Sum of exports and imports relative to GDP in percent	Own calculation based on OECD National Accounts Statistics
population	Number of inhabitants in million people	OECD Employment and Labour Market Statistics
emu	DV for participation in the Economic and Monetary Union of the EU, i.e., equal to 1 for the 11 founding members since 1999 and for Greece since 2001	Own coding
RR_currency	DV for years with an annual depreciation of 15 percent or more versus the U.S. dollar, the *Deutsche Mark*, or the Euro	Reinhart and Rogoff (2011)
RR_inflation	DV for years with an annual inflation rate of 20 percent or more	Reinhart and Rogoff (2011)
RR_stock	DV for years with a stock market crash	Reinhart and Rogoff (2011)
RR_banking	DV for years with bank-runs or bank closure, mergers, takeovers or large-scale government assistance of an important financial institution	Reinhart and Rogoff (2011)
election	DV for national (executive or legislative) elections within the next 13 months	Database on Political Institutions (Beck et al., 2001, version December 2010) for years 1976–2009, own computation for remaining years based on information offices of governments and parliaments

Continued on next page...

Table 5.10: Variable description and sources (continued)

Variable	Description	Source
majority	Share of parliament seats held by parties that support the government in percent	Database on Political Institutions (Beck et al., 2001, version December 2010) for years 1976–2009, own computation for remaining years based on information offices of governments and parliaments
govfrac	Fractionalization of government measured by the probability that two randomly drawn members of parliament who support the government are affiliated with different parties (it takes the value 0 for single party governments and higher values indicate a more fragmented government)	Database on Political Institutions (Beck et al., 2001, version December 2010) for years 1976–2009, own computation for remaining years based on information offices of governments and parliaments
Ability: Political experience and standing		
tenure	Experience in the position of a budget and/or finance minister in the central government in years	Various sources*
tenure_spending	Previous experience as spending minister in the central government in years	Various sources*
tenure_mp	Previous experience as member of parliament in years	Various sources*
backing	DV for same party affiliation of the finance minister and the prime minister in coalition governments	Various sources*
Ability: Education		
university_phd	DV for ministers who have participated in a tertiary education program such as bachelor or master (level 6 or higher according to the International Standard Classification of Education, ISCED-2011)	Various sources*
university	DV for ministers who have participated in a tertiary education program but not in a doctoral program (ISCED-2011 levels 6 or 7)	Various sources*
phd	DV for ministers who hold a PhD (ISCED-2011 level 8)	Various sources*
economics	DV for economics or business as field of study	Various sources*
law	DV for law as field of study	Various sources*
stem	DV for medicine as field of study or any of the so-called STEM subjects, i.e., science, technology, engineering, and mathematics	Various sources*
other_fields	DV for any other field of study, e.g., the remaining social sciences or humanities and arts	Various sources*

Continued on next page...

Table 5.10: Variable description and sources (continued)

Variable	Description	Source
Ability: Professional experience		
finance_expertise	DV for work experience of at least five years (in total) in any finance related field such as academia, business, or public sector	Various sources*
academia	DV for work experience of at least five years as a researcher or lecturer	Various sources*
academia_finance	DV for work experience of at least five years as a researcher or lecturer in economics, finance or business	Various sources*
business	DV for work experience of at least five years in the business sector	Various sources*
business_finance	DV for work experience of at least five years in the private finance sector, e.g., banks and insurance companies	Various sources*
central_bank	DV for work experience of at least five years in a central bank or in international finanical institutions, e.g., the IMF, the World Bank, or the EBRD	Various sources*
lawyer	DV for work experience of at least five years as a lawyer or judge	Various sources*
outsider	DV for work experience of at least five years outside politics and outside the public sector, e.g., in academia, in the private sector, as a lawyer, for a central bank or an international financial institution, and at the same time not more than five years of cumulated work experience in politics, in the public sector, as a lobbyist, or as a party or trade union officer	Various sources*
party_officer	DV for work experience of at least five years as a party officer	Various sources*
public	DV for work experience of at least five years in the public sector	Various sources*
public_finance	DV for work experience of at least five years in the public finance sector, e.g., ministry of finance, treasury, tax administration	Various sources*
union_officer	DV for work experience of at least five years as a trade union official	Various sources*
Ability: Preferences		
left	DV for budget ministers who belong to a politically left party (based on the party classification in the Database on Political Institutions (Beck et al., 2001, version December 2010))	Various sources*
age	Age of the minister in years	Various sources*
female	DV for a female minister	Various sources*
kids	DV for a minister with children	Various sources**
kids_n	Number of children of the minister	Various sources**

Notes: * Government information offices, biographical archives and websites of parliaments, parties, and politicians.

Chapter 6: Conclusion

This doctoral thesis amalgamates three empirical studies to investigate the relevance of political decision makers and their personal characteristics for public finances. The thesis combines the well-established approach of tracing the evolution of public finances to political-economy aspects using the innovative approach of Jones and Olken (2005) to focus on individual decision makers. Thereby, it contributes to the growing literature on the relevance of a political decision maker's personal characteristics for policy outcomes (for a review see Chapter 2).

The first empirical study is concerned with the qualification of politicians at the local level in Germany (Chapter 3). In particular, the study focuses on direct mayoral elections and examines the effects of the candidates' qualification, i.e., education and experience as indicated on the ballot sheet, for electoral success and for fiscal policy outcomes. The analysis is based on data covering the outcomes of mayoral elections, information about the candidates, and municipality budgets for a large panel of 2,031 municipalities in Germany's federal state of Bavaria between 1950, respectively 1984, and 2009. This study employs the regression discontinuity methodology and uses close elections to identify causal effects of the mayor's qualification on local fiscal performance.

The relevance of the finance minister's personal characteristics for public deficits in German states is examined in the second study (Chapter 4). It uses dynamic panel estimations and is based on a new and unique data set for the 10 West German states. The data set comprises information on the educational, the professional, and the political background as well as on the gender and the parental status of all 110 respective ministers of finance between 1960 and 2009.

The third study focuses on the European finance ministers and examines whether their personal characteristics affect the evolution of central government debt (Chapter 5). The analysis relies on dynamic estimation techniques and employs another new and unique data set. This panel data set covers the 167 central-government ministers in charge of the budget in the EU-15 countries between 1970 and 2010.

The remainder of this last chapter proceeds as follows. The next section highlights the main results of the three empirical studies and their contribution. Section 6.2 first provides explanations for the different results of the three studies and then discusses the different empirical methods used. Policy implications are presented in Section 6.3. Section 6.4 presents an outlook for future research and Section 6.5 concludes.

6.1 Main results and contribution

This thesis contributes to the literature in several ways. First of all, it examines the relevance of political decision makers for fiscal performance across three different government levels comprising the Bavarian municipalities at the local level, German states at the subnational level and the EU-15 countries at the national level.

Before the main results of the studies and their contribution are highlighted in the following section, it should be noted that the fiscal performance and, in particular, the amount of public deficits or debt do not fully capture the quality of political decisions. First of all, there are several circumstances in which governments should run a deficit to maximize social welfare, for instance, by smoothening taxation and consumption over time (for a discussion on tax policy see Corneo, 2009b). Hence, public deficits or debt do not indicate sub-optimal political decisions with respect to welfare maximization *per se*. Nevertheless, the political economy literature argues that politicians face many incentives to exceed the optimal degree of deficit financing and accumulate more than the welfare-maximizing level of debt. In addition to this, the optimal size of the deficit can hardly be determined in reality. This precludes a comparison of the realized levels and the theoretically optimal levels of fiscal outcomes. Therefore, the empirical analyses in this thesis can only consider the realized levels of fiscal outcomes.

The first empirical study in Chapter 3 contributes two main innovations. The first innovation is the use of real election data from Germany to examine whether voters prefer more qualified candidates not only with respect to the incumbency status but also the expected education level based on the candidate information stated on the ballot sheet. For mayoral elections in Bavaria, it is shown that candidates enjoy a bonus of 1.7–2.2 percentage points in vote share if the profession stated on the ballot sheet signals a university education. Furthermore, there is strong evidence for the well-known incumbency advantage. Mayors that run again for reelection receive an additional bonus of 15–18 percentage points in vote share.

Chapter 3 goes beyond related studies on election outcomes and links election outcomes to fiscal outcomes. According to the author's knowledge, it is the first empirical study that relies on close elections to identify the causal effects of the mayor's qualification on local public finances.

In light of the strong results for election outcomes, the results of this regression discontinuity design (RDD) are intriguing. They show that the mayor's qualification only has significant effects on some measures of local fiscal policy. The mayor's education, for instance, does not significantly affect local debt level, spending, tax rates or specific spending and revenue categories. The estimates exhibit a large variation in size and signs, too.

However, the study suggests that mayors that spent some time in office prior to their election decrease the municipalities level of debt and total expenditures as well as lower local tax rates. While the estimates are not thoroughly significant, they have the expected sign across different implementations of the RDD. However, the analysis of particular professions does not yield significant results. Local public debt is not affected if the mayor belongs to any of the five professional groups under investigation (entrepreneurs, farmers, finance sector professionals, lawyers, and public employees). On the contrary, the study yields a surprising result for the group of farmers and shows that they increase the local tax rates – including the tax on agricultural property.

The results of Chapter 3 are surprising and raise the question of why voters care so much about the mayor's qualification in terms of education and experience if it does not matter much for fiscal outcomes such as debt, expenditures and tax rates.

Chapters 4 and 5 contribute to the growing literature on the relevance of the finance minister for public finances (see the review in Section 2.3) and investigate whether the personal characteristics of the minister in charge of the budget[1] affect the evolution of public debt in German states and in the EU-15 countries. Both studies introduce new and unique data sets that comprise information on the finance minister's characteristics that are related to her ability to ensure sound budgeting, such as her educational and professional background, political experience and standing, as well as to her budgetary preferences, such as her age, gender, and ideological leaning. While Chapter 4 is – according to the author's knowledge – the first ever study to examine the relevance of the educational and professional background of finance ministers' in German states, Chapter 5 includes the previous professional work experience of finance ministers outside of politics for the first time in an analysis of European finance ministers.

Both studies demonstrate that the finance minister's characteristics which might shape her budgetary preferences affect neither the public deficit in German states nor the change of central government debt relative to the GDP in the EU-15 countries. Apparently, it does not matter for fiscal performance whether the finance minister has children or how many, how old she is, or whether she belongs to or was nominated by a left party.

Similarly to Chapter 3, the two studies do not find any supporting evidence that the education of the finance minister affects public finances at all. Neither her education level nor her field of study matter for the evolution of public debt of German states or European central governments. There is only one exception for the European finance ministers. The change of the central government debt-to-GDP ratio is higher when the finance minister is a former student of science, technology, engineering, or mathematics (STEM). However, this result relies on only few observations from mainly three countries that are not well known for sound public finances while more than half of the

1 In most countries the finance minister takes the responsibility for all areas of public finances (treasury, budget, fiscal and tax policy and regulation of financial markets). In some countries, however, these tasks have repeatedly been spread across different ministries, see table 5.8 on p. 130. For the sake of clarity, the term 'finance minister' is used for all ministers in charge of the budget in the following.

countries in the sample contribute with one or even less observations each. Therefore, this result has to be interpreted with care and should not be generalized to all countries.

With respect to other personal characteristics related to the finance minister's political experience and her political standing, the results of the two studies are mixed. While the tenure in office does not matter at the central government level in Europe, the finance ministers with higher tenures realize significantly lower deficits in German states. The latter result is well in line with Chapter 3 which suggests that local debt decreases when the mayor was reelected.

A similar effect is found for finance ministers in German states who have been members of parliament whereas this does not hold for the central-government finance ministers. Nevertheless, both studies suggest that the political backing of the finance minister matters especially in coalition governments. In particular, the deficit or the change in the debt-to-GDP ratio is lower when the finance minister and the prime minister belong to the same party in a coalition government. The statistical significance of this effect is, however, more robust in the analysis for the German states.

The two studies yield different results for the finance ministers' professional background, too. For the German states, there is strong and robust evidence that ministers with previous work experience in the field of finance incur lower deficits. On the contrary, previous work experience in the non-finance related business sector is associated with higher deficits. The second study for the EU-15 countries, however, cannot confirm these results and finds no significant effects of previous work experience at all. These mixed results correspond to the study for Bavarian municipalities in Chapter 3. There, only one professional group, namely farmers, is identified to significantly affect tax rates. Whereas no results are found for other professional groups or other fiscal indicators.

Beside these mixed results, all three studies have one finding in common: Women are considerably underrepresented in politics. Within the first study, there are 3 percent female candidates running for mayoral elections in Bavaria and even less women among the elected mayors. Looking at the finance ministers, the picture does not change much. While seven out of 110 finance ministers in the German states were female (5 percent of observations), there were only seven women among the 167 finance ministers in the central governments of the EU-15 countries (2 percent of observations). Moreover, the study for Bavarian municipalities reports a strong and significant electoral disadvantage for female candidates in mayoral elections who receive a malus of 5 percentage points in vote share. The low number of female mayors and finance ministers in Europe precludes any statistical interference with respect to any potential effects of the gender on fiscal outcomes in Chapters 3 and 5. Nevertheless, this analysis is possible for the German states with roughly 5 percent of observations in which women served as the finance minister. The study in Chapter 4 finds no evidence that the finance minister's gender affects fiscal performance in any way.

In a nutshell, the first study for mayors in Bavarian municipalities (Chapter 3) identifies a discrepancy between the high weight that voters put on a politician's qualification and the limited evidence that their qualification affects local fiscal outcomes. Also, the two studies for finance ministers in German states and European central governments provide evidence that only some personal characteristics of the political decision makers matter for public finances. In particular, the studies on Germany (Chapter 4) and the EU-15 countries (Chapter 5) provide no evidence that characteristics of the finance ministers related to her budgetary preferences, such as age, parental status, and ideological leaning, affect the fiscal performance.

Where data availability permits the analysis, there is also no evidence for different fiscal outcomes between female and male finance ministers (Chapter 4). By and large, the education of political decision makers does not affect fiscal outcomes across all government levels considered either. However, the political experience of the decision makers matters in German states with significantly lower deficits when the finance minister has been in office for a long time (Chapter 4). Similarly, the study for Bavarian municipalities suggests declining local debt when a mayor was reelected (Chapter 3). Apparently, the previous work experience matters only to some extent. Finance ministers in German states achieve lower deficits when they had been working in the field of finance before their appointment whereas experience in the non-finance business sector is associated with higher deficits (Chapter 4). The study for Bavarian municipalities reports that those mayors who were previously farmers increase local tax rates (Chapter 3).

The studies for the German states and the EU-15 countries report that the backing of the head of government (same party affiliation) allows the finance minister to ensure sound budgeting in a coalition government.

Altogether, the three studies only find some evidence that the individual characteristics of politicians affect fiscal performance. Depending on the government level considered, they identify the previous work or political experience of the political decision makers and their political standing within a coalition government as three things that matter for public finances.

6.2 Critical appraisal of different results and methods

The following two sections address the differences across the three empirical studies. The first section focuses on fiscal institutions and fiscal cultures and, thereby, discusses possible explanations for the different results. The second section reconsiders the different empirical methods employed.

6.2.1 Different results and fiscal institutions and attitudes

Taking the results of the three empirical studies of this thesis altogether, two features stand out. First of all, it is noteworthy how much voters care about the qualification of politicians in terms of (expected) education and experience in office (Chapter 3) while their qualification affects fiscal outcomes only to some extent (Chapter 3, 4, and 5).

The second feature that attracts attention are the different results with respect to the professional background of the finance minister in the studies for German states (Chapter 4) and European central governments (Chapter 5). The former study finds strong empirical evidence for an effect on public deficits, while the latter does not find significant effects.

The discrepancy between the high weight that voters put on the politicians' qualification and the limited evidence that their qualification affects local fiscal outcomes is intriguing at first glance. Nevertheless, this might reflect an institutional peculiarity of German municipalities. German municipalities have very little leeway in fiscal decision-making due to limited control over their expenditures and revenues (see Bundesministerium der Finanzen, 2012). The different results with respect to the relevance of the finance minister's professional experience for the German states and the EU-15 countries might also be driven by different institutional settings. It is plausible that the background of the finance minister in a German state is more important for political decisions than in European central governments given that the finance ministries in Germany states are smaller and therefore have less analytical capacities than the Federal Ministry of Finance. Analogically, the individual background of the finance minister might be less relevant at the central government level given that she is equipped with more resources and has better access to advisers than her colleagues at the regional level.

In addition to these institutional factors, the fiscal culture, i.e., the general assessment of or general attitude of the society toward fiscal performance, might explain the few and also different findings, too. For instance, the background of the mayor might be less relevant for fiscal policy within the state of Bavaria if all citizens (or at least all politicians) have the same stable attitude toward fiscal performance. This could explain the few significant effects on fiscal outcomes for the mayor's education and experience in Chapter 3. Analogically, the individual characteristics might become (more) important when the attitudes toward fiscal performance are not (or less) stable and aligned. Then, the individual characteristics would become decisive. Correspondingly, the strong empirical evidence that the professional background of the finance minister matters for public deficits in German states (Chapter 4) might be traced to less stable or less aligned fiscal attitudes in German states.

Very much related to this discussion is the potential heterogeneity across European countries with respect to the effects of the educational and professional background of the finance ministers. In particular, the zero findings for previous work experience in Chapter 5 might reflect opposing effects on the debt ratio. For instance, if the effect of previous finance-related work experience is negative for some countries and positive for other countries, then both effects might cancel each other out and yield insignificant results. This is less likely within a single country such as Germany but might materialize in an international study. Accordingly, the different results for the professional experience in German states (Chapter 4) and EU-15 countries (Chapter 5) might be traced to the heterogeneity of this effect across European countries. The same argument would apply for other individual characteristics if their effects on fiscal performance differ in their direction across countries – or over time.

The preceding discussion shows how differences in the institutional setting and attitudes toward fiscal performance can affect the results of the three empiricial studies in Chapters 3, 4, and 5. Consequently, the few and partially different findings of the empirical studies do not necessarily contradict each other nor do they conclusively indicate that the individual characteristics of decision makers play no role or just a minor one in fiscal policy. On the contrary, the preceding discussion demonstrates that the role of the individual characteristics of political decision makers requires further investigation (see Section 6.4).

6.2.2 Different empirical methods

Although all three studies examine the effects of the individual characteristics of political decision makers on public finances they rely on two different empirical methodologies. The two studies on the finance ministers in German states (Chapter 4) and in European central governments (Chapter 5) rely on a standard regression control framework[2] whereas the study on mayors in Bavarian municipalities (Chapter 3) employs the RDD method.

The estimation of causal effects based on a standard regression control framework may suffer from an omitted variable or selection bias. In particular, unobserved variables that could affect the nomination of a specific finance minister would be of concern as they would be correlated with the outcome variable under consideration in Chapters 4 and 5. However, the authors consider it unlikely that their results suffer from a substantial selection bias as the qualification and the professional experience do not as yet play a crucial role in the nomination process of finance ministers.[3]

The RDD used in Chapter 3 analyzes the effect of the individual characteristics of local political decision makers in a "quasi-experimental" setting by including data on the outcomes of mayoral elections.

2 In fact, a dynamic model with the first lag of the outcome variable as an additional regressor is used to capture the persistence of fiscal performance.

3 See the discussion in Chapter 4, pp. 80 and 93, and Chapter 5, p. 109.

In contrast to the regression control framework, this RDD methodology allows us – based on credible assumptions – to argue that neither the omitted variable nor the selection bias are any longer of concern for the identification of the effects.

Similar to the allocation rule in which commendations are awarded to students in Thistlethwaite and Campbell (1960), the victory in the mayoral elections depends deterministically on the vote share of the candidates and whether the candidate passes the decisive 50 percent threshold. The large number of elections in the data set allows the use of the RDD method to investigate the causal effects of having a mayor in office with specific attributes – with respect to her educational, her experience in office, or her professional background.

However, the superior identification of the RDD comes at the cost of limited applicability. Firstly, this methodology can only be used when there is a known deterministic selection process at work. Therefore, the RDD cannot be applied in the two studies on finance ministers in German state and European central governments. The selection process of these finance ministers is neither entirely known nor is it likely to be deterministic or to follow any specific rules that could be used in an RDD setting. Secondly, the RDD requires a sample of sufficient size to evaluate the effects as it relies mainly on observations close to the threshold. And thirdly, the RDD will generally only identify a local average treatment effect such that the external validity of the results is an entirely different question.

The preceding disussion of the two methods employed in the empirical studies in this thesis highlights that the RDD is the preferable methodology to preclude any potential omitted variable or selection bias *a priori* by the choice of the empirical design. However, this methodology could only be employed in the study on mayors in Bavaria (Chapter 3). Given the indispensable prerequisites, i.e., a deterministic decision rule that is known and a large sample size, the RDD method could not be applied in the two studies on finance ministers in German states (Chapter 4) and European central governments (Chapter 5). Nevertheless, both studies rely on fixed-effects estimations to capture unobserved effects that do not vary over time and, additionally, include a set of control variables to capture observable influences. Moreover, there is no publicly-known, deterministic rule for the selection of a finance minister that, indeed, would cause a selection bias. Therefore, the potential omitted variable and the selection bias can be reckoned to be a minor issue in the two studies for the German states and the EU-15 countries.

6.3 Policy implications

In light of the on-going debt crisis in Europe and increasing levels of debt in almost all OECD countries, sound public finances will be of high priority in the future. The investigation of political decision makers in fiscal policy reveals that their individual characteristics affect fiscal performance to some extent. Therefore, the empirical results should well be taken into account in the appointment process of key positions in fiscal policy in order to realize sound budgeting. In particular, the empirical studies suggest that the growth of debt is reduced with political decision makers in office who, first, have gained professional experience in the field of finance (finance ministers in German states) or, second, stay in office for a long period of time (mayors in Bavarian municipalities and finance ministers in German states).

The third feature that supports the reduction of debt growth is that the finance minister has the backing of the head of government, i.e., both belong to the same party if the government is formed by more than one party (finance ministers in German states and EU-15 countries). Thus, ruling or designated heads of coalition governments should claim the finance ministry for their political party in order to reduce the growth of public debt.

Apparently, the education of political decision makers does not affect fiscal performance. Preference-related characteristics do not matter either. In particular, the finance minister's age and parental status or whether she belongs to or is nominated by a left party have no effect on the evolution of debt (German states and EU-15 counties). The same holds for the gender. There is no evidence for better or worse fiscal performance with female political decision makers – where data availability allows the analysis.

6.4 Further research

This thesis sheds light on the relevance of individual decision makers for public finances. Drawing the results together, some questions remain unanswered and some new directions emerge for further research. Although they go far beyond the scope of this thesis they appear interesting and promise further insights.

There are three evident extensions for further research in the field of public finances.

First of all, the approach taken here can be extended by examining the characteristics of political decision makers conditional on specific situations or environments. For instance, the previous work experience of a finance minister or her education might become more important for fiscal performance in times of high unemployment or economic crises. Future research could therefore examine such interaction terms of the finance minister's characteristics with certain economic indicators. The same holds for interactions with the political leaning of the finance minister herself, or of the entire government, to investigate whether the effects of specific characteristics such as education or work experience differ across political camps (as, for instance, Mikosch, 2012, does for the heads of governments in ch. 5 of his doctoral thesis).

A further possible extension is to broaden the perspective from an assessment of the finance minister to an assessment of the educational and professional background of the government. In particular, there are two starting points: One could be to consider the entire cabinet and construct competence indices based on the educational and/or professional background of the members of government (as Hau and Thum, 2009, do for supervisory boards of banks). A second starting point could be to look at the top-level positions within the finance ministry, i.e., the state secretaries or the head of the directorate-general in charge of the budget.

Besides looking at decision makers in top or central positions, a third extension could investigate whether the resources available to the finance minister affect fiscal performance. For instance, it can be hypothesized that a finance minister has more power within the government and can accomplish her goal much more easily when she has a well-equipped ministry with a high number of high-skilled employees or civil servants.

In addition to these three promising extensions, the effect of a politician's gender requires further analyses as data availablity so far only permits an assessment for the German states. Furthermore, the innovative approach taken in this thesis could be extended to analyze the relevance of political decision makers and their characteristics on outcome variables in other fields as well. For instance, it would be interesting to know whether former teachers attain a higher share of the government budget for education purposes when they serve as a minister of education. The same question could be asked for changes in health care spending when a former physician becomes minister of health. As it turns out, the assessment of political decision makers and their individual characteristics offers several interesting and promising new directions for future research.

6.5 Concluding remarks

As a last remark it should be noted that this thesis identifies two more general aspects with need for action. The first aspect is gender equality in top-level political positions. The empirical studies reveal that women are underrepresented among political decision makers across all three government levels considered.

However, what justifies this underrepresentation of women is at least questionable with respect to gender equality. If their underrepresentation in fiscal policy is based on a lack of confidence in their strength to ensure sound budgeting, the study for the German states demonstrates that this is unjustified as female ministers of finance do not realize higher deficits than male ones.

Hence, potential barriers that have kept women away from top positions in fiscal policy should be removed to achieve fair shares of both genders among political decision makers in the future.

The second aspect refers to transparency about political decision makers and their individual backgrounds. In Germany, the discussion about the political background of politicians has so far been focused on the declaration of their moonlight activities in order to avoid potential conflicts of interest. However, the study in Chapter 3 demonstrates that voters care a great deal about the individual characteristics of politicians. More transparency on their individual backgrounds would allow the electorate to make better informed decisions in the voting booth. The collection of detailed biographical information about the political decision makers investigated in this thesis was rather difficult and time consuming – even for politicians that are still active or were active during the last decade. Therefore, not only their current moonlight activities should be declared, but also their education and previous work experience should be publicized in a standardized and objective way to increase transparency about the qualification of politicians. This would not merely enable further research in this area, but would also allow well-informed decision making by the electorate.

References

Adams, Renée B. and Daniel Ferreira. 2009. 'Women in the boardroom and their impact on governance and performance.' *Journal of Financial Economics* 94 (2):291–309.

Ade, Florian. 2013. *Local Public Choice: Five Essays on Fiscal Policy, Interest Rates, and Elections*. Baden-Baden: Nomos.

Ade, Florian and Ronny Freier. 2011a. 'Divided government versus incumbency externality effect: Quasi-experimental evidence on multiple voting decisions.' *DIW Discussion Paper* No. 1121.

———. 2011b. 'When can we trust population thresholds in regression discontinuity designs?' *DIW Discussion Paper* No. 1136.

Alesina, Alberto. 1988. 'Macroeconomics and politics.' In *NBER Macroeconomics Annual*, vol. 3, edited by Stanley Fischer. Cambridge MA: MIT Press, 13–62.

Alesina, Alberto and Roberto Perotti. 1995. 'The political economy of budget deficits.' *IMF Staff Papers* 42 (1):1–31.

Alesina, Alberto, Roberto Perotti, and José Tavares. 1998. 'The political economy of fiscal adjustments.' *Brookings Papers on Economic Activity* 1998 (1):197–266.

Anderson, T. W. and Cheng Hsiao. 1981. 'Estimation of dynamic models with error components.' *Journal of the American Statistical Association* 76 (375):598–606.

———. 1982. 'Formulation and estimation of dynamic models using panel data.' *Journal of Econometrics* 18 (1):47–82.

Angelopoulos, Konstantinos, George Economides, and Pantelis Kammas. 2012. 'Does cabinet ideology matter for the structure of tax policies?' *European Journal of Political Economy* 28 (4):620–635.

Arellano, Manuel and Stephen Bond. 1991. 'Some tests of specification for panel data: Monte Carlo evidence and an application to employment equations.' *The Review of Economic Studies* 58 (2):277.

Ashworth, John, Benny Geys, and Bruno Heyndels. 2005. 'Government weakness and local public debt development in Flemish municipalities.' *International Tax and Public Finance* 12 (4):395–422.

Atkins, Ralph and Andrew Whiffin. November 22, 2011. 'Striker amid stumblers: A traumatic year has tested the resourcefulness of the continent's Treasury chiefs to the limit - with surprising results.' *The Financial Times (London, England)* .

Atkinson, Stanley M., Samantha Boyce Baird, and Melissa B. Frye. 2003. 'Do female mutual fund managers manage differently?' *Journal of Financial Research* 26 (1):1–18.

Baltagi, Badi H. 2008. *Econometric Analysis of Panel Data.* Chichester: John Wiley, 4 ed.

Barro, Robert J. 1973. 'The control of politicians: An economic model.' *Public Choice* 14 (1):19–42.

———. 1974. 'Are government bonds net wealth?' *Journal of Political Economy* 82 (6):1095–1117.

———. 1979. 'On the determination of the public debt.' *Journal of Political Economy* 87 (5):940–971.

Bartels, Larry M. 1996. 'Uninformed votes: Information effects in presidential elections.' *American Journal of Political Science* 40 (1):194–230.

Beck, Nathaniel and Jonathan N. Katz. 2011. 'Modeling dynamics in time-series–cross-section political economy data.' *Annual Review of Political Science* 14 (1):331–352.

Beck, Thorsten, George Clarke, Alberto Groff, Philip Keefer, and Patrick Walsh. 2001. 'New tools in comparative political economy: The database of political institutions.' *World Bank Economic Review* 15 (1):165–176.

Behr, Andreas. 2003. 'A comparison of dynamic panel data estimators: Monte Carlo evidence and an application to the investment function.' *Economic Studies Discussion Paper, Deutsche Bundesbank* No. 5.

Benmelech, Efraim and Carola Frydman. 2012. 'Military CEOs.' mimeo.

Berggren, Niclas, Henrik Jordahl, and Panu Poutvaara. 2010. 'The looks of a winner: Beauty and electoral success.' *Journal of Public Economics* 94 (1-2):8–15.

Bertrand, Marianne and Antoinette Schoar. 2003. 'Managing with style: The effect of managers on firm policies.' *The Quarterly Journal of Economics* 118 (4):1169–1208.

Besley, Timothy. 2005. 'Political selection.' *The Journal of Economic Perspectives* 19 (3):43–60.

Besley, Timothy and Anne Case. 1995. 'Does electoral accountability affect economic policy choices? Evidence from gubernatorial term limits.' *The Quarterly Journal of Economics* 110 (3):769–798.

Besley, Timothy, Jose G. Montalvo, and Marta Reynal-Querol. 2011. 'Do educated leaders matter?' *The Economic Journal* 121 (554):F205–227.

Blundell, Richard and Stephen Bond. 1998. 'Initial conditions and moment restrictions in dynamic panel data models.' *Journal of Econometrics* 87 (1):115–143.

Bönke, Timm, Beate Jochimsen, and Carsten Schröder. 2011. 'Fiscal equalization and regions' (un)willingness-to-tax: Evidence from Germany.' *Economics Working Paper / Christian-Albrechts-Universität Kiel* No. 06.

Brender, Adi and Allan Drazen. 2009. 'Do leaders affect government spending priorities?' *NBER Working Paper Series* No. 15368.

Bruno, Giovanni S.F. 2005a. 'Approximating the bias of the LSDV estimator for dynamic unbalanced panel data models.' *Economics Letters* 87 (3):361–366.

———. 2005b. 'Estimation and inference in dynamic unbalanced panel-data models with a small number of individuals.' *Stata Journal* 5 (4):473–500.

Buchanan, James M. and Gordon Tullock. 1962. *The Calculus of Consent*. Ann Arbor: University of Michigan Press.

Bun, Maurice J. G. and Jan F. Kiviet. 2003. 'On the diminishing returns of higher-order terms in asymptotic expansions of bias.' *Economics Letters* 79 (2):145–152.

———. 2006. 'The effects of dynamic feedbacks on LS and MM estimator accuracy in panel data models.' *Journal of Econometrics* 132 (2):409–444.

Bundesministerium der Finanzen. 2012. 'Bundespolitik und Kommunalfinanzen.' *Monatsbericht* 9:33–44.

Calmfors, Lars. 2003. 'Fiscal policy to stabilise the domestic economy in the EMU: What can we learn from monetary policy?' *CESifo Economic Studies* 49 (3):319–353.

Campa, Pamela. 2011. 'Gender quotas, female politicians and public expenditures: Quasi-experimental evidence.' *Econpubblica Working Paper* No. 157.

Carter, David A., Betty J. Simkins, and W. Gary Simpson. 2003. 'Corporate governance, board diversity, and firm value.' *Financial Review* 38 (1):33–53.

Caughey, Devin and Jasjeet S. Sekhon. 2011. 'Elections and the regression discontinuity design: Lessons from close U.S. house races, 1942-2008.' *Political Analysis* 19 (4):385–408.

Chappell, Henry W., Thomas M. Havrilesky, and Rob Roy McGregor. 1995. 'Policy-makers, institutions, and central bank decisions.' *Journal of Economics and Business* 47 (2):113–136.

Chattopadhyay, Raghabendra and Esther Duflo. 2004. 'Women as policy makers: Evidence from a randomized policy experiment in India.' *Econometrica* 72 (5):1409–1443.

Choi, In. 2001. 'Unit root tests for panel data.' *Journal of International Money and Finance* 20 (2):249–272.

Congleton, Roger D. and Yongjing Zhang. 2009. 'Is it all about competence? The human capital of U.S. presidents and economic performance.' *SSRN Working Paper* No. 1684151.

Corneo, Giacomo G. 2009a. *Öffentliche Finanzen: Ausgabenpolitik*. Tübingen: Mohr Siebeck, 3 ed.

———. 2009b. 'Steuerpolitik in finanzkritischen Zeiten.' *Wirtschaftsdienst* 89 (5):282–283.

Croson, Rachel and Uri Gneezy. 2009. 'Gender differences in preferences.' *Journal of Economic Literature* 47 (2):448–474.

Cusack, Thomas R. 1997. 'Partisan politics and public finance: Changes in public spending in the industrialized democracies, 1955–1989.' *Public Choice* 91 (3/4):375–395.

Dalle Nogare, Chiara and Roberto Ricciuti. 2011. 'Do term limits affect fiscal policy choices?' *European Journal of Political Economy* 27 (4):681–692.

Debrun, Xavier, David Hauner, and Manmohan S. Kumar. 2009. 'Independent fiscal agencies.' *Journal of Economic Surveys* 23 (1):44–81.

Deutsche Bundesbank. 2007. 'Zur Entwicklung der Gemeindefinanzen seit dem Jahr 2000.' *Monatsbericht* Juli:29–49.

Dezsö, Cristian L. and David G. Ross. 2008. ''Girl power': Female participation in top management and firm performance.' *Working Paper, Columbia Business School* August 2008.

Downs, Anthony. 1957. 'An economic theory of political action in a democracy.' *Journal of Political Economy* 65 (2):135–150.

Dreher, Axel, Michael J. Lamla, Sarah M. Lein, and Frank Somogyi. 2009. 'The impact of political leaders' profession and education on reforms.' *Journal of Comparative Economics* 37 (1):169–193.

Eagly, Alice H., Steven J. Karau, and Mona G. Makhijani. 1995. 'Gender and the effectiveness of leaders: A meta-analysis.' *Psychological Bulletin* 117 (1):125–145.

Eckel, Catherine C. and Philip J. Grossman. 2008. 'Men, women and risk aversion: Experimental evidence.' In *Handbook of Experimental Economics Results*, vol. 1, edited by Charles R. Plott and Vernon L. Smith. Amsterdam: North-Holland, 1061–1073.

Eslava, Marcela. 2011. 'The political economy of fiscal deficits: A survey.' *Journal of Economic Surveys* 25 (4):645–673.

Farvaque, Étienne, Hakim Hammadou, and Piotr Stanek. 2009. 'Select your committee: The impact of central bankers background on inflation.' *Economie Internationale* 117 (1):99–129.

———. 2011. 'Selecting your inflation targeters: Background and performance of monetary policy committee members.' *German Economic Review* 12 (2):223–238.

Feld, Lars P. and Christoph A. Schaltegger. 2010. 'Political stability and fiscal policy: Time series evidence for the Swiss federal level since 1849.' *Public Choice* 144 (3):505–534.

Ferreira, Fernando and Joseph Gyourko. 2011. 'Does gender matter for political leadership? The case of U.S. mayors.' *NBER Working Paper Series* No. 17671.

Foschi, Martha. 2000. 'Double standards for competence: Theory and research.' *Annual Review of Sociology* 26 (1):21–42.

Freier, Ronny. 2011. 'Incumbency as the major advantage: The electoral advantage for parties of incumbent mayors.' *DIW Discussion Paper* No. 1147.

Freier, Ronny and Sebastian Thomasius. 2012. 'Voters prefer more qualified mayors, but does it matter for public finances? Evidence for Germany.' *DIW Discussion Paper* No. 1262.

Frey, Bruno S. 1986. 'Economists favour the price system who else does?' *Kyklos* 39 (4):537–563.

Gagliarducci, Stefano and Tommaso Nannicini. 2013. 'Do better paid politicians perform better? Disentangling incentives from selection.' *Journal of the European Economic Association* 11 (2):369–398.

Galasso, Vincenzo and Tommaso Nannicini. 2011. 'Competing on good politicians.' *The American Political Science Review* 105 (1):79–99.

Galli, Emma and Stefania P. S. Rossi. 2002. 'Political budget cycles: The case of the western German Länder.' *Public Choice* 110 (3):283–303.

Gehlbach, Scott, Konstantin Sonin, and Ekaterina Zhuravskaya. 2010. 'Businessman candidates.' *American Journal of Political Science* 54 (3):718–736.

Goemans, Hein E. 2008. 'Which way out? The manner and consequences of losing office.' *Journal of Conflict Resolution* 52 (6):771–794.

Göhlmann, Silja and Roland Vaubel. 2007. 'The educational and occupational background of central bankers and its effect on inflation: An empirical analysis.' *European Economic Review* 51 (4):925–941.

Haan, Jakob de and Jan-Egbert Sturm. 1994. 'Political and institutional determinants of fiscal policy in the European Community.' *Public Choice* 80 (1):157–172.

Haan, Jakob de, Jan-Egbert Sturm, and Geert Beekhuis. 1999. 'The weak government thesis: Some new evidence.' *Public Choice* 101 (3):163–176.

Hagen, Jürgen von and Ian J. Harden. 1994. 'Budget processes and fiscal performance.' In *Towards Greater Fiscal Discipline*, *European Economy*, vol. 3. Luxembourg, 311–418.

———. 1995. 'Budget processes and commitment to fiscal discipline: Papers and Proceedings of the Ninth Annual Congress European Economic Association.' *European Economic Review* 39 (3-4):771–779.

Hahn, Jinyong, Petra Todd, and Wilbert Klaauw. 2001. 'Identification and estimation of treatment effects with a regression-discontinuity design.' *Econometrica* 69 (1):201–209.

Hallerberg, Mark and Jürgen von Hagen. 1999. 'Electoral institutions, cabinet negotiations, and budget deficits within the European Union.' In *Fiscal Institutions and Fiscal Performance*, edited by James M. Poterba and Jürgen von Hagen. Chicago: University of Chicago Press, 209–232.

Hallerberg, Mark, Rolf Strauch, and Jürgen von Hagen. 2007. 'The design of fiscal rules and forms of governance in European Union countries.' *European Journal of Political Economy* 23 (2):338–359.

Hau, Harald and Marcel Thum. 2009. 'Subprime crisis and board (in-) competence: private versus public banks in Germany.' *Economic Policy* 24 (60):701–752.

Hayo, Bernd and Florian Neumeier. 2011. 'Political leaders' socioeconomic background and fiscal performance in Germany.' *MAGKS Joint Discussion Paper Series* No. 41.

———. 2012. 'Leaders' impact on public spending priorities: The case of the German Laender.' *Kyklos* 65 (4):480–511.

Hayo, Bernd and Stefan Voigt. 2013. 'Endogenous constitutions: Politics and politicians matter, economic outcomes don't.' *Journal of Economic Behavior & Organization* 88:47–61.

Hibbs, Douglas A. Jr. 1977. 'Political parties and macroeconomic policy.' *The American Political Science Review* 71 (4):1467–1487.

Imbens, Guido W. and Karthik Kalyanaraman. 2012. 'Optimal bandwidth choice for the regression discontinuity estimator.' *The Review of Economic Studies* 79 (3):933–959.

Imbens, Guido W. and Thomas Lemieux. 2008. 'Regression discontinuity designs: A guide to practice.' *Journal of Econometrics* 142 (2):615–635.

Jochimsen, Beate. 2012. 'Wohlstand messen.' *Aus Politik und Zeitgeschichte* 62 (27/28):19–23.

Jochimsen, Beate and Robert Nuscheler. 2011. 'The political economy of the German Länder deficits: Weak governments meet strong finance ministers.' *Applied Economics* 43 (19):2399–2415.

Jochimsen, Beate and Sebastian Thomasius. 2012. 'The perfect finance minister: Whom to appoint as finance minister to balance the budget?' *DIW Discussion Paper* No. 1188.

———. 2014. 'The perfect finance minister: Whom to appoint as finance minister to balance the budget?' *European Journal of Political Economy* (forthcoming).

Johnson, Johnnie E.V. and Philip L. Powell. 1994. 'Decision making, risk and gender: Are managers different?' *British Journal of Management* 5 (2):123–138.

Jones, Benjamin F. and Benjamin A. Olken. 2005. 'Do leaders matter? National leadership and growth since World War II.' *The Quarterly Journal of Economics* 120 (3):835–864.

———. 2009. 'Hit or miss? The effect of assassinations on institutions and war.' *American Economic Journal: Macroeconomics* 1 (2):55–87.

Jong-A-Pin, Richard and Jochen Mierau. 2011. 'No country for old men: Aging dictators and economic growth.' *KOF Working Paper* No. 289.

Judson, Ruth A. and Ann L. Owen. 1999. 'Estimating dynamic panel data models: a guide for macroeconomists.' *Economics Letters* 65 (1):9–15.

Kiviet, Jan F. 1995. 'On bias, inconsistency, and efficiency of various estimators in dynamic panel data models.' *Journal of Econometrics* 68 (1):53–78.

———. 1999. 'Expectations of expansions for estimators in a dynamic panel data model; some results for weakly exogenous regressors.' In *Analysis of Panels and Limited Dependent Variable Models*, edited by Cheng Hsiao, Kajal Lahiri, Lung-Fei Lee, and M. Hashem Pesaran. Cambridge: Cambridge University Press, 199–225.

Kiviet, Jan F. and Maurice J. G. Bun. 2001. 'The accuracy of inference in small samples of dynamic panel data models.' *TI Discussion Paper* No. 006/4. Tinbergen Institute, Amsterdam.

Klaauw, Wilbert van der. 2008. 'Regression–Discontinuity Analysis: A Survey of Recent Developments in Economics.' *Labour* 22 (2):219–245.

Kontopoulos, Yianos and Roberto Perotti. 1999. 'Government fragmentation and fiscal policy outcomes: Evidence from OECD countries.' In *Fiscal Institutions and Fiscal Performance*, edited by James M. Poterba and Jürgen von Hagen. Chicago: University of Chicago Press, 81–102.

Lee, David S. 2008. 'Randomized experiments from non-random selection in U.S. House elections.' *Journal of Econometrics* 142 (2):675–697.

Lee, David S. and Thomas Lemieux. 2010. 'Regression discontinuity designs in economics.' *Journal of Economic Literature* 48 (2):281–355.

Lee, David S., Enrico Moretti, and Matthew J. Butler. 2004. 'Do voters affect or elect policies? Evidence from the U. S. House.' *The Quarterly Journal of Economics* 119 (3):807–859.

Lott, John R. and W. Robert Reed. 1989. 'Shirking and sorting in a political market with finite-lived politicians.' *Public Choice* 61 (1):75–96.

Lyness, Karen S. and Madeline E. Heilman. 2006. 'When fit is fundamental: Performance evaluations and promotions of upper-level female and male managers.' *Journal of Applied Psychology* 91 (4):777–785.

McCrary, Justin. 2008. 'Manipulation of the running variable in the regression discontinuity design: A density test.' *Journal of Econometrics* 142 (2):698–714.

McDermott, Monika L. 1998. 'Race and gender cues in low-information elections.' *Political Research Quarterly* 51 (4):895–918.

———. 2005. 'Candidate occupations and voter information shortcuts.' *The Journal of Politics* 67 (1):201–219.

McKay, Joanna. 2004. 'Women in German politics: Still jobs for the boys?' *German Politics* 13 (1):56–80.

Mechtel, Mario. 2011 'It's the occupation, stupid! Explaining candidates' success in low-information elections.' mimeo.

Mikosch, Heiner. 2012. *Rigidities, Institutions and the Macroeconomy*. Ph.D. thesis, KOF Swiss Economic Institute, ETH Zurich, Zurich.

Mincer, Jacob. 1958. 'Investment in human capital and personal income distribution.' *Journal of Political Economy* 66 (4):281–302.

Moessinger, Marc-Daniel. 2012. 'Do personal characteristics of finance ministers affect the development of public debt?' *Paper presented at the IIPF conference,* August 2012.

Nickell, Stephen. 1981. 'Biases in dynamic models with fixed effects.' *Econometrica* 49 (6):1417–1426.

O'Roark, J. Brian and William C. Wood. 2011. 'Determinants of congressional minimum wage support: The role of economic education.' *Public Choice* 147 (1-2):209–225.

Paola, Maria de and Vincenzo Scoppa. 2011. 'Political competition and politician quality: Evidence from Italian municipalities.' *Public Choice* 148 (3-4):547–559.

Perotti, Roberto and Yianos Kontopoulos. 2002. 'Fragmented fiscal policy.' *Journal of Public Economics* 86 (2):191–222.

Persson, Petra and Ekaterina Zhuravskaya. 2011. 'Elite capture in the absence of democracy: Evidence from backgrounds of Chinese provincial leaders.' *SSRN Working Paper* No. 1506709.

Persson, Torsten, Gérard Roland, and Guido Tabellini. 1997. 'Separation of powers and political accountability.' *The Quarterly Journal of Economics* 112 (4):1163–1202.

Persson, Torsten and Guido Tabellini. 1999. 'Political economics and macroeconomic policy.' In *Handbook of Macroeconomics*, vol. 1, edited by John B. Taylor and Michael Woodford. North Holland: North-Holland, 1397–1482.

Pettersson-Lidbom, Per. 2008. 'Do parties matter for economic outcomes? A regression-discontinuity approach.' *Journal of the European Economic Association* 6 (5):1037–1056.

Potrafke, Niklas. 2011a. 'Does government ideology influence budget composition? Empirical evidence from OECD countries.' *Economics of Governance* 12 (2):101–134.

———. 2011b. 'Public expenditures on education and cultural affairs in the West German States: Does government ideology influence the budget composition?' *German Economic Review* 12 (1):124–145.

Reinhart, Carmen M. and Kenneth S. Rogoff. 2011. 'From financial crash to debt crisis.' *The American Economic Review* 101 (5):1676–1706.

Reskin, Barbara F. and Denise D. Bielby. 2005. 'A sociological perspective on gender and career outcomes.' *The Journal of Economic Perspectives* 19 (1):71–86.

Rogoff, Kenneth S. 1990. 'Equilibrium political budget cycles.' *The American Economic Review* 80 (1):21–36.

Rogoff, Kenneth S. and Anne Sibert. 1988. 'Elections and macroeconomic policy cycles.' *The Review of Economic Studies* 55 (1):1–16.

Roubini, Nouriel and Jeffrey D. Sachs. 1989a. 'Government spending and budget deficits in the industrial countries.' *Economic Policy* 4 (8):100–132.

———. 1989b. 'Political and economic determinants of budget deficits in the industrial democracies.' *European Economic Review* 33 (5):903–933.

Sachverständigenrat zur Begutachtung der gesamtwirtschaftlichen Entwicklung. 2012. *Stabile Architektur für Europa – Handlungsbedarf im Inland: Jahresgutachten 2012/13*. Wiesbaden.

Sajons, Christoph J. 2011. *Essays in immigration economics and political economy*. Ph.D. thesis, Universitat Pompeu Fabra, Departament d'Economia i Empresa, Barcelona.

Schaltegger, Christoph A. and Lars P. Feld. 2009. 'Do large cabinets favor large governments? Evidence on the fiscal commons problem for Swiss cantons.' *Journal of Public Economics* 93 (1-2):35–47.

Schneider, Christina J. 2010. 'Fighting with one hand tied behind the back: Political budget cycles in the West German states.' *Public Choice* 142 (1-2):125–150.

Seitz, Helmut. 2000. 'Fiscal policy, deficits and politics of subnational governments: The case of the German Laender.' *Public Choice* 102 (3):183–218.

———. 2008. 'Die Bundesbestimmtheit der Länderausgaben.' *Wirtschaftsdienst* 88 (5):340–348.

Spence, Michael. 1973. 'Job market signaling.' *The Quarterly Journal of Economics* 87 (3):355–374.

Svaleryd, Helena. 2009. 'Women's representation and public spending.' *European Journal of Political Economy* 25 (2):186–198.

Thistlethwaite, Donald L. and Donald T. Campbell. 1960. 'Regression-discontinuity analysis: An alternative to the ex post facto experiment.' *Journal of Educational Psychology* 51 (6):309–317.

Thomasius, Sebastian. 2012. 'Der Stabilitätsrat: Ein fiskalpolitisches Gremium zwischen Kontinuität und Neuanfang.' In *Staatsverschuldung in Deutschland nach der Föderalismusreform II - eine Zwischenbilanz, Schriften der Bucerius Law School*, vol. 11, edited by Clemens Hetschko, Johannes Pinkl, Hermann Pünder, and Marius Thye. Hamburg: Bucerius Law School Press, 189–222.

Tirole, Jean. 1994. 'The internal organization of government.' *Oxford Economic Papers* 46 (1):1–29.

Tversky, Amos and Daniel Kahneman. 1974. 'Judgment under uncertainty: Heuristics and biases.' *Science* 185 (4157):1124–1131.

Volkerink, Bjørn and Jakob de Haan. 2001. 'Fragmented government effects on fiscal policy: New evidence.' *Public Choice* 109 (3):221–242.

Wehner, Joachim. 2010. 'Cabinet structure and fiscal policy outcomes.' *European Journal of Political Research* 49 (5):631–653.

Wissenschaftlicher Beirat beim Bundesministerium der Finanzen. 2005. *Haushaltskrisen im Bundesstaat, Schriftenreihe des Bundesministeriums der Finanzen*, vol. 78. Berlin.

Wyplosz, Charles. 2005. 'Fiscal policy: Institutions versus rules.' *National Institute Economic Review* 191 (1):64–78.

Kurzfassung in deutscher Sprache

Motivation der Arbeit

In der öffentlichen Diskussion werden politische Erfolge und Misserfolge häufig einzelnen Politikern[1] zugeschrieben und auf deren Kompetenz und Fertigkeiten zurückgeführt. Die besondere Stellung einzelner politischer Entscheidungsträger verdeutlichen u. a. das bei den Bundestags- und den meisten Landtagswahlen zur Anwendung kommende personalisierte Verhältniswahlrecht sowie die Direktwahl der Bürgermeister auf kommunaler Ebene.[2]

Auch im Verlauf der europäischen Staatsschuldenkrise zeigte sich der hohe Stellenwert, der einzelnen politischen Entscheidungsträgern und ihrem jeweiligen Hintergrund zugemessen wird, als die bisherigen Regierungen Griechenlands und Italiens im November 2011 durch so genannte Technokratenregierungen abgelöst wurden. Beide Staaten sahen sich deutlichen Vertrauensverlusten in ihre finanzielle Stabilität ausgesetzt. Die Einsetzung der aus parteipolitisch unabhängigen Experten bestehenden Regierungen unter Loukas Papadimos in Griechenland bzw. Mario Monti in Italien wurde dabei als wichtiger Lösungsschritt betrachtet.

Im Gegensatz zu dem hohen Stellenwert in der öffentlichen Debatte haben politische Entscheidungsträger selbst und ihr jeweiliger fachlicher Hintergrund in der ökonomischen und politökonomischen Literatur bisher kaum Beachtung gefunden. Stattdessen werden bei der Analyse wirtschaftlicher Vorgänge insbesondere institutionelle Aspekte und die sich daraus ergebenden Anreize für einzelne Akteure betrachtet. Besley stellt in diesem Zusammenhang fest, dass "öffentliche Institutionen nicht funktionsfähig sein können, wenn die Eignung derjenigen, die öffentliche Ämter übernehmen, und deren Überzeugungen außer Acht gelassen werden." (Besley, 2005, S. 58, Übers. d. Verf.)

Sofern theoretische Modelle politische Entscheidungsträger einbeziehen, wird üblicherweise zwischen zwei Typen von Politikern unterschieden, die entweder über ein hohes oder ein niedriges Kompetenzniveau verfügen. In diesen Modellen wird dann angenommen, dass die Politiker diese Informationsasymmetrie dazu nutzen, die Wahrscheinlichkeit ihrer (Wieder-)Wahl zu erhöhen. Rogoff und Sibert (1988) erklären anhand eines solchen Modells politische Konjunkturzyklen im Umfeld von Wahlen.

1 Aus Gründen der besseren Lesbarkeit werden Personenbezeichnungen im Folgenden lediglich in der grammatikalisch männlichen Form verwendet. Es sind aber immer beide Geschlechter gemeint.

2 In anderen Ländern wie Finnland, Irland, den Niederlanden, Schweden sowie der Schweiz finden sich noch stärker personalisierte Wahlsysteme, bei denen die Wahlberechtigten innerhalb der Parteilisten ihre Stimme(n) frei vergeben können. In Brasilien, Finnland und Frankreich wird auch das Staatsoberhaupt direkt gewählt.

Aus der ökonomischen und politökonomischen Theorie heraus ergibt sich jedoch nicht, welche spezifischen Eigenschaften einen kompetenten oder weniger kompetenten Politiker auszeichnen.

Bei einer Betrachtung der Fiskalpolitik und der öffentlichen Finanzen wird typischerweise der Finanzminister als entscheidendes Mitglied des Regierungskabinetts angesehen. Unter anderem veranschaulicht dies das alljährlich von der Financial Times (London) veröffentlichte Ranking der europäischen Finanzminister, das die Haushaltslage der europäischen Staaten den jeweiligen Finanzministern zurechnet (vgl. das Ranking dür 2011 bei Atkins und Whiffin, 2011). Im Gegensatz dazu werden Haushaltsentwicklungen in der politökonomischen Literatur weniger auf den Finanzminister selbst, sondern vielmehr auf institutionelle und politische Gründe zurückgeführt. Gleichwohl Hagen und Harden (1995) zeigen, wie wichtig ein 'starker' Finanzminister für solide Staatsfinanzen ist, definieren sie 'Stärke' ausschließlich über die Stellung im Budgetprozess und lassen die fachliche Kompetenz oder andere individuelle Charakteristika außer Acht.

Der Literaturüberblick in Kapitel 2 verdeutlicht, dass die Bedeutung der politischen Entscheidungsträger und ihrer individuellen Charakteristika für die öffentlichen Finanzen bisher nur unzureichend wissenschaftlich untersucht worden, so dass ausgehend von der veröffentlichten Literatur nicht klar ist, ob und ggf. welche individuellen Eigenschaften der Finanzpolitiker die Fiskalpolitik beeinflussen. Jedoch werden die individuellen Charakteristika von politischen Entscheidungsträgern bereits bei der Analyse anderer Politikbereiche einbezogen.

Wegweisend waren hierbei insbesondere die Arbeiten von Jones und Olken (2005) und Göhlmann und Vaubel (2007), die den Einfluss einzelner Regierungsoberhäupter auf das Wirtschaftswachstum bzw. der Ausbildung und Berufserfahrung von Mitgliedern des Zentralbankrates auf die Inflationsrate betrachtet haben. Die vorliegende Dissertationsschrift nimmt diesen innovativen Ansatz auf und erweitert den etablierten politökonomischen Ansatz zur Analyse der öffentlichen Finanzen entsprechend. Das übergreifende Ziel dieser Arbeit ist ein Erkenntnisgewinn darüber, ob die persönlichen Charakteristika fiskalpolitischer Entscheidungsträger die Entwicklung der öffentlichen Finanzen beeinflussen. Dieses Ziel wird im Rahmen von drei empirischen Studien verfolgt, bei denen jeweils neue Datensätze und innovative Methoden zum Einsatz kommen.

Aufbau der Arbeit

Die vorliegende Arbeit ist in sechs Kapitel gegliedert. Das erste Kapitel führt in die Arbeit ein, bevor in Kapitel 2 die bestehende Literatur vorgestellt wird, die sich mit dem Einfluss der individuellen Charakteristika von Politikern sowohl auf deren Abschneiden bei Wahlen als auch auf Politikergebnisse befasst. Darüber hinaus wird die bedeutende Rolle des Finanzministers als zentraler fiskalpolitischer Entscheidungsträger herausgearbeitet.

Die Kapitel 3, 4 und 5 stellen den Hauptteil der Arbeit dar und präsentieren die empirischen Studien zur Bedeutung der persönlicher Charakteristika für die öffentlichen Finanzen in den drei betrachteten Regierungsebenen.

Kapitel 3 beginnt mit einer Betrachtung der Rolle der Bürgermeister für die Kommunalfinanzen in Bayern und entstand in Koautorenschaft mit Ronny Freier.[3] Die regionalstaatliche Ebene wird im vierten Kapitel anhand von Daten zu den westdeutschen Bundesländern und den Landesfinanzministern untersucht. Das Kapitel wurde gemeinsam mit Beate Jochimsen verfasst.[4]

Kapitel 5 widmet sich der nationalstaatlichen Ebene und analysiert die Bedeutung der nationalen Finanzminister für die zentralstaatliche Verschuldung in 15 Mitgliedsländern der Europäischen Union.

Das Schlusskapitel fasst die wesentliche Ergebnisse und den Forschungsbeitrag zusammen (Abschnitt 6.1). Ebenso werden Gründe für die zum Teil unterschiedlichen Ergebnisse der drei empirischen Studien und die unterschiedlichen empirischen Methoden diskutiert (Abschnitt 6.2). Darüber hinaus werden Implikationen für die Politik abgeleitet (Abschnitt 6.3) und Ansatzpunkte für weitere Forschungsarbeiten in diesem Feld skizziert.

Bürgermeister und Kommunalfinanzen in Bayern

Die erste empirische Studie (Kapitel 3) untersucht, welchen Einfluss die Qualifikation des Bürgermeisters auf die Kommunalfinanzen in Bayern hat. Die Analyse basiert auf einem umfangreichen Datensatz für die 2.031 bayerischen Kommunen (ohne kreisfreie Städte). Der Datensatz beinhaltet die Wahlergebnisse der Bürgermeisterwahlen und Informationen zu den dabei angetretenen Kandidaten zwischen 1950 und 2009 sowie die Haushaltsdaten der entsprechenden Kommunen seit 1984. Eine Analyse der Kommunalpolitik ist von besonderem Interesse, da diese viel näher am Alltagsleben der Bürger ist als die höheren Regierungsebenen. So obliegen den Kommunen in Deutschland wichtige Aufgaben wie die Bereitstellung der lokalen Infrastruktur, des öffentlichen Personennahverkehr sowie von Kinderbetreuungsplätzen.

Die Studie zeichnet sich insbesondere durch zwei Innovationen aus. Die erste Innovation ist die Untersuchung anhand von Daten aus deutschen Kommunen, ob höher qualifiziertere Kandidaten – im Sinne von Erfahrung im Amt und Ausbildungsniveau –

3 Eine gekürzte Fassung ist als Diskussionspapier erschienen (Freier und Thomasius, 2012).

4 Die Studie wurde vom *European Journal of Political Economy* zur Veröffentlichung angenommen (Jochimsen und Thomasius, 2014). Eine frühere Version wurde bereits als Diskussionspapier veröffentlicht (Jochimsen und Thomasius, 2012).

bei der Bürgermeisterwahl mehr Stimmen erhalten. Es zeigt sich, dass Wähler denjenigen Kandidaten ihre Stimme geben, die bereits über Erfahrung im Amt des Bürgermeisters oder über eine akademische Ausbildung verfügen. So profitieren amtierende Bürgermeister von einem Amtsinhaberbonus und erzielen einen um 15–18 Prozentpunkte höheren Stimmanteil. Einen um 1,7–2,2 Prozentpunkte höheren Stimmanteil erhalten dagegen Kandidaten, deren Berufsangabe auf dem Stimmzettel eine höhere Ausbildung signalisiert.

Die Studie in Kapitel 3 geht jedoch über eine einfache Analyse der Wahlergebnisse hinaus. Erstmalig werden Wahlen mit knappem Ausgang dazu genutzt, den Effekt der Qualifikation des Bürgermeisters auf die Kommunalfinanzen empirisch zu untersuchen. Die Nutzung der Wahlergebnisse erlaubt die Identifikation eines kausalen Zusammenhanges im Rahmen der so genannten *regression discontinuity design* Methode. Da die Qualifikation des Wahlgewinners bei einer knappen Wahl mehr oder weniger zufällig ist, ermöglicht die Fokussierung auf knappe Wahlen eine quasi-experimentelle Untersuchung.

Angesichts des großen Einflusses der Qualifikation auf das Wahlergebnis überraschen die Untersuchungsergebnisse der *regression discontinuity design* Methode. Ihnen zufolge beeinflusst die Qualifikation des Bürgermeisters nur einzelne Finanzkennzahlen.

So hat das Ausbildungsniveau des Bürgermeisters keinen signifikanten Effekt auf die kommunale Verschuldung, Ausgaben, die Hebesätze der Kommunalsteuern oder spezifische Ausgaben- und Einnahmekategorien. Die geschätzten Koeffizienten variieren über verschiedene Schätzspezifikationen hinweg stark in ihrer Größe und weisen auch wechselnde Vorzeichen auf.

Gleichwohl deuten die Ergebnisse darauf hin, dass Bürgermeister die kommunale Verschuldung, die Ausgaben und auch Hebesätze reduzieren, wenn sie wiedergewählt werden. Die Schätzwerte sind zwar nicht durchgängig signifikant, haben aber konsistent über alle *regression discontinuity design* Spezifikationen das gleiche Vorzeichen.

Die Analyse einzelner Berufsgruppen liefert keine signifikanten Ergebnisse. Somit macht es für die kommunalen Finanzen insgesamt keinen Unterschied, ob der Bürgermeister zu einer der untersuchten Berufsgruppen gehört (Beschäftigte des Öffentlichen Dienstes, Beschäftigte im Finanzbereich, Landwirte, Rechtsanwälte, Unternehmer und Manager). Jedoch deckt die Studie einen unerwarteten Zusammenhang für die Hebesätze der kommunalen Steuern auf. Nach der Wahl eines Landwirts zum Bürgermeister kommt es zu einem Anstieg der Hebesätze für die Gewerbesteuer und für beide Arten der Grundsteuer (für landwirtschaftlich genutzte Grundstücke sowie für bebaute oder bebaubare Grundstücke).

Die Ergebnisse des dritten Kapitels überraschen und werfen die Frage auf, warum die Qualifikation der Kandidaten – im Sinne von Erfahrung im Amt und Ausbildungsniveau – bei der Wahl des Bürgermeisters das Wahlergebnis so stark beeinflussen, wenn die Qualifikation des Bürgermeisters gleichzeitig auf die Kommunalfinanzen und insbesondere die Verschuldung, die Ausgaben und die Hebesätze keinen Einfluss hat.

Finanzminister und Haushaltsdefizite in den Bundesländern

Die Bedeutung der individuellen Charakteristika der Finanzminister für das Haushaltsdefizit in den westdeutschen Bundesländern wird in der zweiten empirischen Studie analysiert (Kapitel 4). Die Untersuchung basiert auf einem neuen und selbst erhobenen Paneldatensatz und nutzt dynamische Schätzverfahren. Der Datensatz umfasst Informationen zu den 110 Landesfinanzministern, die zwischen 1960 und 2009 in den zehn westdeutschen Bundesländern amtierten.

Die Analyse betrachtet insbesondere diejenigen individuellen Charakteristika, die für die fiskalpolitischen Präferenzen des Finanzministers relevant sind, und diejenigen, die seine Fähigkeit zur Durchsetzung einer soliden Haushaltspolitik beeinflussen.

Zur ersten Gruppe (Präferenzen) zählen insbesondere das Alter, das Geschlecht und die parteipolitische Zugehörigkeit des Finanzministers sowie ob er Kinder hat und ggf. wie viele. Zur zweiten Gruppe (Fähigkeiten) zählen die Ausbildung (erreichtes Bildungsniveau sowie ggf. Studienrichtung) und die Berufserfahrung sowie die Erfahrung im Amt des Finanzministers (Amtsdauer). Diese Studie analysiert erstmals welche Relevanz der Bildungshintergrund und die Berufserfahrung des Finanzministers für die deutschen Bundesländer haben. Ebenso wird betrachtet, ob der Finanzminister gestärkt ist, wenn er in einer Koalitionsregierung der Partei des Ministerpräsidenten angehört.

Hinsichtlich seiner Fähigkeiten identifiziert die Studie drei für eine solide Haushaltspolitik relevante Charakteristika.

So ist das Haushaltsdefizit signifikant geringer, wenn der Finanzminister über Berufserfahrung im (öffentlichen oder privaten) Finanzbereich verfügt oder wenn er in einer Koalitionsregierung die Unterstützung des Ministerpräsidenten aufgrund der Zugehörigkeit zur gleichen Partei genießt. Das Defizit ist ebenso geringer, wenn der Finanzminister bereits länger amtiert. Für die Ausbildung des Finanzministers kann jedoch wie bereits bei den bayerischen Bürgermeistern kein signifikanter Einfluss auf die öffentlichen Finanzen nachgewiesen werden. Weder das erreichte Bildungsniveau noch die Fachrichtung beeinflussen das Haushaltsdefizit in den Ländern. Auch für diejenigen Charakteristika, die potentiell für die fiskalpolitischen Präferenzen relevant sein könnten, findet die Studie keine signifikanten Effekte – weder für das Alter oder das Geschlecht des Finanzministers noch für Finanzminister mit Kindern.

Finanzminister und Staatsverschuldung in den EU-15-Staaten

Die dritte empirische Studie in Kapitel 5 betrachtet die Entwicklung der Schuldenquote auf nationalstaatlicher Ebene in Europa. Konkret wird dabei analysiert, welchen Einfluss die individuellen Charakteristika des nationalen Finanz- oder Haushaltsministers auf die Veränderung des Verhältnisses von Verschuldung der Zentralregierung zum nationalen Bruttoinlandsprodukt haben. Der neue und selbst erhobenen Datensatz umfasst diejenigen 15 europäischen Staaten, die bereits vor der Erweiterungsrunde 2004 Mitglied der Europäischen Union waren, und beinhaltet Informationen zu insgesamt 167 Ministern, die zwischen 1970 und 2010 den zentralstaatlichen Haushalt verantwortet haben.[5] Bei der empirischen Auswertung kommen dynamische Panelschätzer zum Einsatz.

Auch hier werden insbesondere diejenigen individuellen Charakteristika betrachtet, die für die fiskalpolitischen Präferenzen und die Durchsetzungsfähigkeit des Finanzministers relevant sind. Bei den Charakteristika, die seine Fähigkeit zur Durchsetzung einer soliden Haushaltspolitik betreffen, unterscheidet die Studie zwischen politischer Erfahrung und politischer Unterstützung, der Ausbildung sowie der Berufserfahrung. Im Zusammenhang mit seinen fiskalpolitischen Präferenzen werden das Alter und die Zugehörigkeit zu einer linken Partei betrachtet, aber ebenso das Vorhandensein von Kindern einbezogen. Mit dieser Studie werden erstmalig sowohl die Ausbildung als auch die Berufserfahrung außerhalb der Politik der für den Haushalt zuständigen Minister in Europa betrachtet.

Die Studie zeigt, dass die Fähigkeit des Finanzministers zu einer stabilitätsorientierten Haushaltspolitik von der Unterstützung durch den Regierungschef abhängt. So ist die Veränderung der Schuldenquote geringer, wenn der Finanzminister in einer Koalitionsregierung der Partei des Regierungschefs angehört. Dagegen findet die Studie keine Evidenz, dass andere Charakteristika wie die Ausbildung[6], die Berufserfahrung oder auch die politische Erfahrung des Finanzministers die Schuldenquote beeinflussen. Ebenso lassen sich keine Effekte für die Charakteristika mit Bezug zu den Präferenzen des Ministers finden. Weder seine politische Orientierung, sein Alter noch das Vorhandensein von Kindern beeinflussen die relative Verschuldung der Zentralregierung im Vergleich zur Wirtschaftsleistung.

---

5 In den meisten europäischen Staaten verantwortet der Finanzminister alle Bereiche der öffentlichen Finanzen wie die Finanzmarktregulierung, die Haushaltspolitik, die Steuerpolitik sowie die Verwaltung des öffentlichen Vermögens. In einigen wenigen Ländern, wie Belgien, Frankreich, Italien sowie Luxemburg, wurden diese Politikbereiche von mehreren Ministern verantwortet. In der Studie wurde in diesem Fall das tatsächlich für den Haushalt verantwortliche Kabinettsmitglied und nicht das als 'Finanzminister' bezeichnete Kabinettsmitglied betrachtet.

6 Lediglich für Finanzminister, die eines der so genannten MINT-Fächer (Mathematik, Informatik, Naturwissenschaft, Technik bzw. eine Ingenieurwissenschaft) studiert haben, lässt sich ein statistisch signifikant höherer Anstieg der Schuldenquote nachweisen. Dieser Effekt beruht jedoch nur auf sehr wenigen Beobachtungen aus drei europäischen Staaten, die nicht unbedingt für eine stabilitätsorientierte Haushaltspolitik bekannt sind, und lässt sich daher kaum verallgemeinern.

Zusammenfassung der Ergebnisse

Die erste Studie für die bayerischen Kommunen (Kapitel 3) identifiziert eine deutliche Diskrepanz zwischen der Bedeutung, die die Wähler der Qualifikation der Politiker – im Sinne von Erfahrung im Amt und Ausbildungsniveau – zumessen, und dem tatsächlichen Einfluss der Qualifikation auf die Kommunalfinanzen. Auch die beiden Untersuchungen für die Finanzminister in den westdeutschen Bundesländern (Kapitel 4) und den EU-15-Staaten (Kapitel 5) können nur für einzelne persönliche Charakteristika der Minister einen Einfluss auf die öffentlichen Haushalte nachweisen.

Beiden Untersuchungen zufolge wirken sich bestimmte Eigenschaften, wie das Alter, die Parteizugehörigkeit oder das Vorhandensein von Kindern, die für die fiskalischen Präferenzen des Finanzministers relevant sein könnten, nicht auf die Staatsfinanzen aus. Soweit die Analyse möglich ist, kann auch für das Geschlecht des Finanzministers kein Effekt nachgewiesen werden (Kapitel 4).

Im Großen und Ganzen lässt sich ebenso kein Einfluss der Ausbildung der politischen Entscheidungsträger auf die Finanzpolitik feststellen. Für die bayerischen Kommunen deuten die Ergebnisse jedoch darauf hin, dass wiedergewählte Bürgermeister die kommunale Verschuldung reduzieren (Kapitel 3). Ebenso zeigt sich, dass Landesfinanzminister mit ausgeprägter Amtserfahrung – aufgrund einer langen Amtszeit – signifikant weniger neue Schulden aufnehmen (Kapitel 4).

Anscheinend beeinflusst teilweise auch die Berufserfahrung die öffentlichen Finanzen. So wird für die westdeutschen Bundesländer gezeigt, dass Finanzminister mit Berufserfahrung im Finanzbereich niedrigere Defizite realisieren. Für die bayerischen Kommunen dagegen wurde nachgewiesen, dass die Hebesätze der kommunalen Steuern nach der Wahl eines Landwirts zum Bürgermeister erhöht werden. Den Studien für die westdeutschen Bundesländer und die EU-15-Staaten zufolge führt auch die Unterstützung des Finanzministers durch den Regierungschef (gleiche Parteizugehörigkeit) zu einer solideren Haushaltspolitik in einer Koalitionsregierung.

Insgesamt zeigen die drei Studien, dass die individuellen Charakteristika von Politikern die öffentlichen Finanzen teilweise signifikant beeinflussen. Abhängig von der betrachteten Regierungsebene erweisen sich mit der Berufs- bzw. der politischen Erfahrung sowie der Unterstützung durch den Regierungschef insgesamt drei individuelle Charakteristika als relevant.

Implikationen für die Politik

Die empirischen Studien betrachten insbesondere die Entwicklung der öffentlichen Verschuldung bzw. des Haushaltsdefizits. Obwohl geringe Haushaltsdefizite als Indikator für die finanzpolitische Nachhaltigkeit der Regierungspolitik betrachtet werden können, erfasst diese Kennziffer nicht den Wohlstand oder die Lebensqualität in einem Land, einer Region oder einer Gemeinde.[7]

Darüber hinaus implizieren Haushaltsdefizite nicht notwendigerweise gesamtgesellschaftliche Wohlfahrtsverluste. Vielmehr kann die Defizitfinanzierung sogar wohlfahrtserhöhend sein, wenn dadurch die Besteuerung im Zeitverlauf geglättet oder bestimme effizienzsteigernde Ausgabenprojekte ermöglicht werden.[8]

Nichtsdestoweniger verdeutlicht die europäische Staatsschuldenkrise, wie wichtig solide und nachhaltige öffentliche Finanzen sind, um die langfristige Handlungsfähigkeit der Regierung und das Wohlergehen der Bevölkerung auch in der Zukunft zu gewährleisten.

Da sich das optimale, d. h. die Wohlfahrt maximierende, Niveau für das Haushaltsdefizit in der realen Welt nur schwer bestimmen lässt, kann die hier vorgenommene empirische Analyse zur Relevanz der persönlichen Charakteristika für die Haushaltspolitik allein auf die tatsächlich realisierten Haushaltszahlen zurückgreifen.

Die vorliegenden empirischen Untersuchungen zeigen, dass auch die persönlichen Charakteristika fiskalpolitischer Entscheidungsträger für eine solide Finanzpolitik bedeutsam sein können und diese dementsprechend bei der Besetzung von politischen Führungsämtern berücksichtigt werden sollten. Den Ergebnissen der empirischen Studien zufolge steigt die öffentliche Verschuldung weniger stark, wenn die politischen Entscheidungsträger Berufserfahrung im (öffentlichen oder privaten) Finanzbereich erworben haben (Studie zu den Landesfinanzministern) oder für längere Zeit im Amt bleiben (Landesfinanzminister und Bürgermeister). Der Schuldenanstieg lässt sich ebenso verringern, wenn der Finanzminister und der Ministerpräsident einer Koalitionsregierung der gleichen Partei angehören (Landes- und europäische Finanzminister). Im Rahmen von Koalitionsverhandlungen sollten designierte Ministerpräsidenten dementsprechend das Finanzministerium für ihre Partei beanspruchen.

Abschließende Bemerkungen

Über die oben genannten Implikationen für die Haushaltspolitik hinaus wurde im Verlauf der Arbeit für zwei weitere Bereiche Handlungsbedarf festgestellt. Der erste Bereich ist die Gleichstellung der Geschlechter in politischen Führungsämtern. Die empirischen Studien zeigen für alle drei betrachteten Regierungsebenen, dass von einer Gleichstellung kaum die Rede sein kann. So stellt die Studie zu den bayerischen Kommunalfinanzen fest, dass von den Kandidaten für das Amt des Bürgermeisters seit 1950 lediglich 3 Prozent Frauen waren. Bei den gewählten Bürgermeistern lag der Frauenanteil noch niedriger. Unter den 110 Finanzministern in den westdeutschen Bundesländern seit 1960 finden sich lediglich sieben Frauen (fünf Prozent der Beobachtungen).

7 Vgl. die Diskussion verschiedener Indikatoren zur Wohlstandsmessung bei Jochimsen (2012).

8 Vgl. die Diskussion zur Steuer- und Ausgabenpolitik bei Corneo (2009a,b).

Auf europäischer Ebene sind es mit sieben von 167 Ministern relativ gesehen sogar noch weniger (zwei Prozent der Beobachtungen). Aufgrund dieser geringen Zahl an Beobachtungen sind auch keine validen ökonometrischen Auswertungen zu möglichen Effekten des Geschlechts der europäischen Finanzminister bzw. bayerischen Bürgermeister möglich.

Sofern dieser geringe Frauenanteil in finanzpolitischen Führungspositionen auf mangelndes Vertrauen in deren Durchsetzungsfähigkeit bei der Umsetzung einer soliden Haushaltspolitik zurückgeht, wird diese Befürchtung jedoch durch die Studie für die deutschen Bundesländer widerlegt. Die Studie zeigt, dass weibliche Finanzminister keine höheren – aber auch keine niedrigeren – Haushaltsdefizite zu verantworten haben als männliche Finanzminister. Dementsprechend sollten auch Barrieren, die den Aufstieg von Frauen in finanzpolitische Führungspositionen bisher verhindert haben, beseitigt werden, um künftig eine Gleichstellung der Geschlechter in diesen Führungspositionen zu erreichen.

Der zweite Aspekt betrifft die generelle Transparenz über politische Entscheidungsträger und deren persönlichen Hintergrund. In Deutschland zielte die öffentliche Diskussion bisher insbesondere auf die Veröffentlichung der Nebentätigkeiten von Mitgliedern des Deutschen Bundestages und die Offenlegung möglicher Interessenskonflikte ab. Jedoch zeigt die Studie in Kapitel 3, dass Wähler bei ihrer Wahlentscheidung den individuellen Charakteristika der zur Wahl stehenden Politikern ein hohes Gewicht beimessen. Eine höhere Transparenz über deren jeweiligen Hintergrund würde den Wählern somit eine besser informierte Wahlentscheidung ermöglichen. Die Erhebung der biographischen Informationen der im Rahmen dieser Arbeit betrachteten politischen Entscheidungsträger gestaltete sich – selbst für noch aktive Politiker – zum Teil äußerst schwierig und zeitaufwendig. Daher sollten nicht nur Nebentätigkeiten der Abgeordneten veröffentlicht werden, sondern die Transparenz über die Qualifikation von Politikern insgesamt erhöht werden, in dem ebenso auch Angaben zur Ausbildung und Berufserfahrung von Politikern in einer standardisierten und objektiven Form verfügbar gemacht werden. Dies würde zum einen eine weitergehende Erforschung der Relevanz dieser persönlichen Charakteristika ermöglichen und es den Wählern zum anderen erlauben, ihrer Wahlentscheidung eine breitere Informationsbasis zugrunde zu legen.